Red Hangover

KRISTEN GHODSEE

Red Hangover

LEGACIES OF TWENTIETH-CENTURY COMMUNISM

Duke University Press / Durham and London / 2017

Printed in the United States of America on acid-free paper ∞
Text designed by Courtney Leigh Baker
Typeset in Minion Pro and DIN by Copperline Books

Library of Congress Cataloging-in-Publication Data
Names: Ghodsee, Kristen Rogheh, [date] author.
Title: Red hangover : legacies of twentieth-century
communism / Kristen Ghodsee.
Description: Durham : Duke University Press, 2017. |
Includes bibliographical references and index.
Identifiers: LCCN 2017016455 (print) |
LCCN 2017019342 (ebook)
ISBN 9780822372417 (ebook)
ISBN 9780822369349 (hardcover : alk. paper)
ISBN 9780822369493 (pbk. : alk. paper)
Subjects: LCSH: Europe, Eastern—History—1989– |
Europe, Eastern—History—1989—Fiction. |
Post-communism. | Post-communism—Fiction.
Classification: LCC DJK51 (ebook) | LCC DJK51 .G495 2017
(print) | DDC 947.0009/051—dc23
LC record available at https://lccn.loc.gov/2017016455

Cover art: The grave of Rosa Luxemburg in
Zentralfriedhof Friedrichsfelde in Berlin, January 2016.
Photo by Kristen R. Ghodsee.

Para mi abuelita, Cristina Lugo

HANGOVER (NOUN)   1   A thing or person remaining or left over; a remainder or survival, an after-effect.

2   The unpleasant after-effects of (esp. alcoholic) dissipation.

Oxford English Dictionary

CONTENTS

Two pairs of earrings, four bracelets, and a mixtape inspired me to write this book. I was in the Stadtmuseum in the German city of Jena, peering into the various display cases of an exhibit called *Freundschaft! Mythos und Realität im Alltag der DDR* (Friendship! Myth and reality in everyday life in the GDR [German Democratic Republic]). The exhibit ruminated on the official and unofficial uses of the word "friendship" in the context of communist East Germany between 1949 and 1989. In one case, the museum's curators displayed the personal items of a teenage girl who had gone to a Freie Deutsche Jugend (Free German Youth) summer camp in 1985. There, accompanying some photos and a letter she sent home to her parents, sat a white cassette tape, some plastic bracelets, and two pairs of oversized, cheap earrings, the kind once fashionable in the mid-1980s when every girl's hair was two stories too high.

Back in 1985, I spent several weeks of my summer at a camp in the Cuyamaca Mountains one hour east of San Diego. When I left home, I remember packing several pairs of the same horrible earrings, some plastic bangles, and a stack of mixtapes with my favorite songs recorded off the local Top 40 radio station. Standing in Jena thirty years later, I experienced one of those moments of radical empathy, and tried to imagine what my life would have been like if I'd gone to summer camp in communist East Germany rather than in capitalist California. This girl and I might have shared the same passion for similar material objects, but we would have been ideological enemies, surviving our adolescences on different sides of the Iron Curtain.

From the placard on the display case, I understood that this girl was born in 1971, one year after me. Somewhere out there, this girl was now a woman about my age, and I longed to talk to her, to ask her what she remembered

FIGURE PRELUDE.1. A billboard for the *Freundschaft* exhibit in Jena.

FIGURE PRELUDE.2. Items from the East German *Freie Deutsche Jugend* (Free German Youth).

about that summer of 1985, and how things had worked out for her since. This German girl would have been eighteen when the Berlin Wall fell, and nineteen when her country ceased to exist. She would have just graduated from secondary school, and probably listened to Madonna and Fine Young Cannibals as I did: "Express Yourself," "Like a Prayer," and "She Drives Me Crazy." But where I had the luxury of geopolitical continuity in my personal life, this East German faced a young adulthood of dramatic social and economic upheaval.

When I left the museum, I wandered through the cobblestone alleyways leading off the main market square. I saw posters for two upcoming demonstrations in Jena. The right-wing, anti-immigrant political party Alternative for Germany (AfD) would organize a rally and a march in the *Marktplatz* while Germany's left-wing party, Die Linke (The Left), in a coalition with other centrist and leftist parties, would organize a counterdemonstration in front of the church. The counterprotesters had plastered the small city with posters saying "FCK AFD" and "refugees welcome," and I guessed that the center/left demonstrators would outnumber their right-wing counterparts.

But after the November 2015 terrorist attacks in Paris, and the spate of sexual assaults on women in Cologne on New Year's Eve, many Germans feared for their future. The political appeal of the far right increased across the country, but particularly in the former states of the now-defunct Deutsche Demokratische Republik. In the eastern city of Dresden, "concerned citizens" formed a group called PEGIDA, which stood for Patriotische Europäer gegen die Islamisierung des Abendlandes (Patriotic Europeans against the Islamicization of the Occident).[1] Many ordinary men and women frustrated with their governments' open-door asylum policies supported PEGIDA. On January 11, 2016, as LEGIDA (the Leipzig branch of PEGIDA) celebrated its one-year anniversary, about two hundred masked neo-Nazis marched through the immigrant-friendly neighborhood of Connewitz, smashing cars and windows with axes and baseball bats.[2] One month later, in the sleepy village of Clausnitz, a few kilometers from the Czech border, an angry mob of Germans tried to prevent a bus full of refugees from reaching a shelter.[3] Men and women in the crowd shouted "Wir sind das Volk!" (We are the people), a slogan used by anticommunist protestors in 1989. Twenty-five years ago, this chant reminded the leaders of the GDR that democracy meant rule by the people. Two days after the incident in Clausnitz, a hotel destined to house Muslim refugees caught fire in the Saxon town of Bautzen.[4] Onlookers cheered as the roof burned. Federal politicians condemned the growth of right-wing xenophobia in the former states of the GDR as ever more eastern

FIGURE PRELUDE.3. "Together against Fascism," a poster for the anti-AfD rally in Jena.

Germans felt their voices ignored. As I walked through the streets of Jena back to my university apartment, I wondered about that girl in the museum and the woman she had become. If she still lived in town, which rally would she be attending? With which side would she sympathize, and why?

The year 2017 marks the one hundredth anniversary of the Russian Revolution and the creation of the world's first socialist state. Much of the twentieth century was defined by the presence of this Soviet superpower and its challenge to the political economy of greed and exploitation that underpinned the capitalist system. Built on ideals of self-determinism and social egalitarianism, the Soviet Union became a symbolic beacon of hope not only to people struggling against European imperialism and continued colonial domination, but also to Western workers locked in labor conflicts with avaricious employers. Even after the cruel brutalities of Stalinism and the economic deficiencies of "really existing socialism"[5] became clear, leftists continued to imagine alternative pathways to pure communism, the supposed highest stage of human history. When Eastern Bloc communism collapsed between 1989 and 1991, the whole project seemed consigned to the dustbin of history. The entire decade of the 1990s was one big ideological gloat-fest for the Cold War's winners. Ding dong, the Reds are dead.

The end of the Cold War created an unprecedented opportunity to create a more stable, peaceful, and equitable world, for the Western countries to show moral strength and help rebuild the economies of the former Eastern Bloc in the way they once assisted the West Germans and the Japanese after World War II. Instead, the ideological war against communism continued as if the Cold War had never ended. The communist ideal became straitjacketed to the horrors of Stalinism for at least half a century. Of course, none of the twentieth-century experiments with the communist ideal ever came close to achieving communism in the Marxist sense, a future moment when the state would wither away. To be technically correct, the countries of Eastern Europe should be called state socialist countries, in the sense that the nationalized means of production were always controlled by a centralized state serving as a dictatorship of the proletariat. For Karl Marx, this was only a stage on the way to true communism, a necessary stepping-stone to a brighter future. But because they justified their actions in terms of the communist ideal, and because scholars and politicians in the West always referred to these countries as "communist," I use the terms "communist" and "socialist" interchangeably throughout the book.

Since the late 1990s, I've been doing research and writing books about the experiences of ordinary people who lived through the end of the Cold War in Eastern Europe. My work endeavored to capture a recent past, one that would soon fade and be forgotten. But that day in Jena, I felt the past alive in the present and understood that the legacies of the fall of communism infused current European political realities. Why else would East Germans in 2016 resurrect a protest slogan from 1989? Indeed, once I started thinking about it, all of the major crises of the previous year—the Greek debt crisis, the Russian annexation of Crimea, the Syrian civil war, the rise of the Islamic State in Iraq and Syria, and the massive increase in migration to Europe—could be linked back to mistakes made after the collapse of the Eastern Bloc when fantasies about the world historic triumph of free markets and liberal democracy blinded Western leaders to the human costs of regime change. If the communist ideal had become tainted by its association with twentieth-century Eastern European regimes, today the democratic ideal was increasingly sullied by its links to neoliberal capitalism. How much violence and human misery had been justified in the name of promoting democracy or regime change?

By 2016, Europe teetered on the brink of disintegration as popular right-wing leaders in Poland and Hungary declared their countries "illiberal democracies" and flouted European Union quotas for the distribution of refugees fleeing the conflicts born of Western-supported efforts to bring democracy to the Middle East. Even within the so-called consolidated democracies at the heart of Europe, electorates grew increasingly polarized as a xenophobic right whipped up fear and hatred of the Islamic other. At the same time, Great Britain voted for Brexit and nations within the border-free Schengen Area rushed to reestablish passport controls and instituted new limitations on asylum seekers. Terrorist attacks in France and Germany have sent otherwise moderate and tolerant citizens into the arms of growing nationalist parties.

I wrote most of this book between December 2015 and May 2016 while I lived in Jena, working at a research college affiliated with the Friedrich Schiller University. The center hosted a variety of academic fellows (historians, sociologists, literary scholars), all doing research on the history of twentieth-century Eastern Europe. Most of my fellow scholars hailed from the former communist countries: Poland, Hungary, the Czech Republic, Serbia, and Ukraine. As one of only two Americans, I spent those five months immersed in a community of experts on the contemporary history and politics of Eastern Europe. Although I was working on a different book, I couldn't help but be caught up in current events. The ethnographer in me needed to talk to people, to make sense of the deeper histories behind the headlines. When my Czech office mate, who was fourteen in 1989, bemoaned the imposition of new border controls and told me that freedom of travel had been "the best thing about the end of communism," I decided to stop and reflect on the political chaos emerging around me. I might be living in the last days of the European Union, I thought, and I felt compelled to write about that specific moment in time and how it related to the end of the Cold War a quarter of a century earlier. When Timothy Garton Ash, reflecting on the British Brexit vote to leave the European Union, wrote, "It feels almost as bad a day as the day of the fall of the Berlin Wall was good," I felt even more certain that the chickens of 1989 were finally coming home to roost.[6]

All of the essays included in this book come from my own experiences living, working, studying, and traveling in the former socialist countries of

FIGURE PRELUDE.4. East German memorabilia in the *Freundschaft* exhibit.

Eastern Europe that are now members (or aspiring members) of the European Union. Since 1998, I have lived for about three and a half years in Bulgaria and nineteen months in both eastern and western Germany. Back in the summer of 1990, I also spent two months traveling in Yugoslavia, Bulgaria, Romania, Hungary, Czechoslovakia, and the soon-to-disappear GDR. In the last quarter of a century, I have been a frequent visitor to Eastern Europe, doing research, attending seminars, and delivering invited lectures from Belgrade to Warsaw. As I traveled through the region (often by car or train), I witnessed landscapes pockmarked with the remains of communism: abandoned fields, crumbling factories, decrepit high-rise apartment blocks. I became fascinated with the legacies of twentieth-century communism, and the essays in this book emerge from my personal desire to understand the varied politics of Central and Eastern Europe after 1989.

Amid the essays, I have also included four short stories. In two cases, the fictionalized episodes build upon events or circumstances of which I had only secondhand knowledge. I digested these stories and used my imagination and understanding of local cultures to flesh out the details. In a third case, I dabbled in a little speculative science fiction, imagining a future version of myself applying for political asylum in Germany after the election of someone like Donald Trump. I played on the German history of de-Nazification

FIGURE
PRELUDE.5.
A sign on
a lamppost
in Berlin in
August 2016:
"Here a Nazi
could hang."

and postcommunist lustration to ask whether we can hold individuals responsible for inaction in the face of tyranny. When I first drafted the text of this fictitious future interview with German immigration officials, Donald Trump had not yet won the Republican nomination, and most of my early readers thought the story unrealistic. No one would remember Trump, they said, when the book came out, so I created a different character, one young enough to declare himself president for life in my little alternative universe. And finally, I could not resist the opportunity to include a political allegory, a fable exploring the vulnerability of democracy in the style of other politically charged animal fables of the past. Just as the popular stereotype of communism is rarely uncoupled from the state repression of the twentieth-century experience of it, today I fear that the democratic ideal is becoming inseparable from the social chaos neoliberal capitalism has wreaked in its name. My hope is that these essays and stories provoke discussion and debate; if I haven't angered someone out there, I'm not doing my job.

The essays and stories are divided into four thematic sections. Part I, Postsocialist Freedoms, collects together individual essays and stories about the lived realities of postsocialism in the Balkans. Part II, Reuniting the Divided, travels north and examines the politics of German reunification in 1990 and the broader impacts of Western triumphalism on the nations of Eastern Europe and on the shape of the post–Cold War global economy. Part III, Blackwashing History, collects three essays examining the politics of history and

FIGURE PRELUDE.6. "Islam, no thank you." A PEGIDA supporter in Munich in March 2016.

the uses and abuses of public memory where twentieth-century communism is concerned. Finally, part IV, "Democracy Is the Worst Form of Government, Except All Those Other Forms That Have Been Tried from Time to Time" builds on this famous quote from a 1947 speech by Winston Churchill.[7] For over seventy years, democracy has been widely accepted as the lesser of all evils. My final essay focuses specifically on the unhappy marriage of democracy and capitalism and the wholesale rejection of anything having to do with socialism or communism after the end of the Cold War, including its recognition of the fundamental contradictions embedded within capitalism. My core argument is that those desperate to rescue the democratic ideal today insist that democracy must be separated from the disenfranchisement and gross inequities of neoliberal, free-market capitalism. They admit the damage done by reckless deregulation and the rise of oligarchs and plutocrats that undermine the functioning of liberal polities today. But in the same breath, they often insist that all experiments with twentieth-century state socialism in Eastern Europe must be forever linked to the worst crimes of Stalinism. The democratic ideal must be saved at all costs, precisely because the communist ideal inevitably leads to the gulag. Thus, scholars and politicians assert that one ideal political form can be corrupted by economic realities and historical exigencies while denying that another political ideal might have

FIGURE PRELUDE.7. "No *Volk*, No 'Fatherland,' No *Führer*."

suffered the same fate. It is this hypocrisy that prevents critical reengage-
ments with the state socialist past, and which I believe has led to the swing to
the far right in many former state socialist countries, and increasingly among
Western democracies as well. Frustrated voters embrace nationalism as the
only viable defense against the ravages of global capitalism.

As with my previous collection of essays, *Lost in Transition*, I have written
this book specifically for my students and other young people born after the
events of 1989.[8] For many of them, communism might as well be ancient
history, but understanding this relatively recent past provides an essential
foundation for making sense of the limits of our contemporary political
imagination and the various threats posed to the democratic ideal today.
I have by necessity provided only rudimentary background information,
which some of my scholarly colleagues may find lacking in the appropriate
academic nuance. I apologize for what may seem like hurried brushstrokes
to those deeply embroiled in the production and consumption of scholarship
on Central and Eastern Europe. But this book is not for you. I write instead
for nonexperts curious about how the legacies of the Cold War impact European politics today. This does not mean that I am an apologist for twentieth-
century East European communism. Plenty of books have been written about
the often-surrealist hell imposed on the citizens of state socialist regimes, and

I fully recognize the downsides of central planning, travel restrictions, and the ubiquitous presence of the secret police. But here I plead for historical nuance, for a recognition that not everything was black and white and that the continued demonization of everything about the state socialist past has real impacts on the political landscape today.

Finally, I hope that someday that East German girl from the museum, the girl who is now a woman, reads this book and finds in it something to help her make sense of this crazy world we now share. Maybe she has kids about my daughter's age, and maybe she worries, as I worry, about how best to prepare the next generation for a life in which all the old rules seem obsolete. I hope that a better comprehension of our collective past will help us navigate an increasingly perilous future.

PART I. **Postsocialist Freedoms**

1. Fires

According to scientists, the human body, provided sufficient fuel or kindling to ignite it, can burn for seven hours.[1] Of course, the human being usually expires earlier in the process, but not before experiencing the most excruciating agony imaginable. Being consumed by flames is the worst way to die, which perhaps explains why the ever-so-merciful medieval Catholic Church preferred to burn witches and heretics alive. Although faster and less painful suicide options abound, six Bulgarians decided to set themselves on fire during a forty-five-day period in 2013.

The drama started in February when Bulgarians poured out onto the streets of Sofia to protest a massive hike in their winter power bills.[2] The electricity distributors, now foreign-owned monopolies, unilaterally raised prices in the poorest country in the European Union, a nation where pensioners already had to choose among heat, light, medicine, and food. Few could afford all four. The initial antimonopoly demonstrations morphed into massive protests in front of parliament, with citizens demanding the resignation of their prime minister, Boyko Borissov. Exhausted by stagnant salaries and ever-rising utility costs, many Bulgarians believed that a popular social movement could improve their deteriorating realities. One man held up a poster that read, "Salary 270 levs, Heat 300 levs, Electricity 220 levs, Water 120 levs: How much longer?" When the prime minister resigned and called for new elections, a spark of hope shone new light on the political possibilities of democracy. That spark ignited a flame of citizen participation that media observers called the "Bulgarian Spring," a new blooming of civil society that would lift the country out of its long postcommunist quagmire.[3] But not everyone was so optimistic.

On February 18, 2013, Traian Marechkov, a twenty-six-year-old unemployed environmentalist and social activist from the Bulgarian city of Veliko Tarnovo, walked to a crossroads and dumped gasoline on his head.[4] Witnesses at the scene claimed that Marechkov waved off would-be rescuers, allowing his body to be consumed by the flames.[5] According to one Bulgarian newspaper, Marechkov's last words were, "I give my life for the people, my family, and Bulgaria, hoping that politics and the government will improve the standard of living for the people."[6] He died in the hospital two days later.[7]

On February 20, the day Bulgaria lost Marechkov, a thirty-six-year-old photographer and protest leader in the Black Sea coastal city of Varna, Plamen Goranov, mounted the steps of City Hall. He placed a placard on the ground demanding the resignation of Varna's mayor, believed to have close connections with powerful local Mafia interests. According to security camera footage and the testimony of witnesses, Goranov informed the guards that he planned to set himself on fire. He spread a canvas on the ground and proceeded to pour five liters of gasoline over his head. He flicked a lighter and combusted into flames. Goranov died eleven days later on the Bulgarian national holiday that marks the country's independence from five hundred years of Ottoman Turkish domination. Media pundits quickly likened Goranov's self-immolation to that of the Czechoslovak student Jan Palach, who set himself alight to protest the Soviet invasion of his country after the crushing of the Prague Spring in 1968. The *Guardian* and the *New York Times* ran emotional stories about how the sacrifice of Goranov might finally help Bulgaria fix its long-standing problems.[8] Within seventy-two hours, the Varna mayor tendered his resignation.[9]

Self-immolation boasts a long history as a form of political protest. Because self-immolators use an accelerant such as gasoline, the flames begin to consume the flesh much faster than an accidental fire. According to doctors who treat burn victims, the first moments of a burn cause the most agony as the flames devour the top two layers of skin—the epidermis and the dermis—filled with sensitive nerve endings. Only once these outer layers of flesh peel away can the human mind begin to shut out the acute pain. Most self-immolators suffer third-degree burns, which, if they survive, require extensive skin grafts from other parts of their bodies to heal. Once the inferno eats away all of the flesh and begins to expose the bone, the human body, or what is left of it, is beyond repair by even the most advanced medical procedures. In Tibet, some devout monks drink kerosene to ensure that their insides explode, rendering any attempts at emergency care useless.

In 2013, Bulgarians earned an average monthly wage of about 400 euros (520 dollars), a little more than 6,000 dollars per year.[10] According to one Caritas study, 43 percent of the Bulgarian people counted as "severely materially deprived," meaning that they could not afford at least four of the following nine things: (1) their rent or water and electricity bills, (2) adequate heat for their homes in the winter months, (3) unexpected costs such as unforeseen medical bills or necessary medicines to treat illnesses, (4) to eat meat, fish, or a protein equivalent at least once every two days, (5) a week's vacation away from home, (6) a car, (7) a washing machine, (8) a color television, or (9) a telephone or mobile phone.[11] To put this in perspective, the average percentage of the population suffering from severe material deprivation among the twenty-eight members of the European Union was 9.6 percent. Bulgaria ranked last among all member nations. According to the same study, 21 percent of Bulgarians were at risk for poverty and social exclusion, meaning that they survived on only 60 percent of the median national income, which in Bulgaria would be 240 euros or 312 dollars a month in 2013. It was no wonder that people could not afford cars, televisions, or washing machines, which were no cheaper in Bulgaria even though average annual incomes were the lowest in the EU. The young and educated fled the country in droves to seek a better life in the West.

On February 26, six days after Goranov's immolation, a fifty-three-year-old unemployed man named Ventsislav Vasilev stormed into the municipal office in Radevo, demanding work for himself and his family.[12] Vasilev was father to five grown children. His seven-person household lived on sporadic social benefits and odd jobs, barely surviving in the winter months. Eager for work of any kind, Vasilev begged the local authorities to employ him. When they refused, Vasilev set himself ablaze inside of the municipal building.[13] His twenty-two-year-old son Alan later told reporters that he didn't think it was the inflated January 2013 electricity bill that pushed his father over the edge. It was the water bill. Vasilev was being sued for an outstanding invoice of 215 euros. The water company in Stara Zagora had already initiated court proceedings against him.

On March 6, the Bulgarian government declared a national day of mourning for Plamen Goranov, the most famous of the three men. The world's attention turned to the desperate acts of these frustrated Bulgarians in a country with no political tradition of self-immolation. The patriarch of the

Bulgarian Orthodox Church officiated at Plamen Goranov's funeral, claiming a theological exception for suicides where individuals succumb to temporary insanity. In a public statement to his compatriots, Patriarch Neofit begged Bulgarians not to self-immolate, emphasizing that suicide contradicted Orthodox Christian dogma. On March 10, the hospital announced the passing of Ventislav Vasilev, and once the media started to pay attention, they reported an increase in suicides across the country.[14]

Three days after Vasilev's death, I was taking a break from my work in the Central State Archives when fifty-two-year-old Dimitar Dimitrov lingered for a while at the fountain in front of the offices of the Bulgarian presidency before setting himself alight. The guards in front of the presidential palace, apparently trained to deal with fires, rushed toward Dimitrov with extinguishers. I did not see this self-immolation, but I smelled it, not understanding what had happened. I heard the ambulances only moments later, and learned within the hour that paramedics had rushed Dimitrov to the Pirogov Emergency Hospital with burns covering 25 percent of his head and body. The evening news reported his critical condition. In the days that followed, I studied the faces of the men on the Sofia metro, wondering who among them might have a bottle of gasoline tucked away in his coat.

I had already returned to Maine when another man, a forty-year-old unemployed construction worker, self-immolated in the town of Silistra, on March 22. Todor Iovchev borrowed four levs from his girlfriend, filled a plastic bottle with gasoline, and walked to a stadium on the outskirts of town. According to witnesses, Iovchev cried for help and tried to extinguish himself by rolling around on the earth. But he was too late. He later died of organ failure in the Varna Naval Hospital. Bulgarian newspapers reported that the reasons for Iovchev's suicide were poverty, unemployment, and the resultant family problems.

Three days later, Public Radio International asked me to help make sense of the recent spate of Bulgarian political suicides.[15] I explained about the dire economic situation and tried to inspire concern among the educated Americans who listen to a show like *The World*. For a brief moment, I allowed myself to believe that things could change, that maybe these desperate acts might make a difference. But the promised elections occurred in May 2013, and a new minority government was formed. Within months larger numbers of protesters took to the streets of Sofia to agitate for an end to corruption and oligarchy. They demanded the resignation of the new government and called for yet more elections. Once again observers waxed poetic about civil society and the Bulgarian Spring.[16]

Despite the prospect of a better future, five more Bulgarians died from injuries sustained from self-immolations in the remainder of 2013.[17] One of them was a thirty-one-year-old man named Georgi Kostov in Dimitrovgrad, a communist-era city built entirely by volunteer labor brigades in the 1950s. At an hour past midnight on the fifth of June, Kostov rubbed himself down with gasoline and lit himself up at home, in front of his wife, his sister, and his four- and ten-year-old sons. Kostov had taken a loan of 12,000 levs (6,000 euros) to buy his apartment just months before his employer unexpectedly laid him off. Unable to find work, Kostov grew anxious. The compound interest and penalties meant his debts kept mounting, and he fought constantly about money with his wife. After several months of missed payments, threatening letters arrived, growing more aggressive in tone. Kostov feared that he would go to jail or that Mafia thugs would show up to kill him or his family.[18] The stress overwhelmed him.

As Kostov went up in flames, his wife, Donka, rushed to embrace him, hoping to squelch the fire. Instead, it ignited her clothing, and she began to burn as well. Kostov's sister doused the couple with water, trying to extinguish the flames while her young nephews watched, screaming. Neighbors heard the peals of terror and called the police. Emergency crews rushed Kostov to the hospital with burns covering 30 percent of his body; Donka had 10 percent. Bulgarian doctors in Plovdiv performed the necessary surgeries and, in the end, the two little boys lost neither their mother nor father.[19] But the 12,000 lev debt remained, growing larger with each missed payment.

As the world focused its attention on the Sochi Winter Olympics and the subsequent Russian annexation of Crimea, seven more Bulgarians self-immolated in 2014.[20] Lidia Petrova, a thirty-eight-year-old mother of one son, also chose to complete her suicide in front of the offices of the Bulgarian presidency just six days before the twenty-fifth anniversary of the fall of the Berlin Wall.[21] This time the presidential guards reacted too slowly. The Russia Today news website posted a graphic video of this self-immolation on the Internet, where anyone can see exactly how much fuel a human body provides for a fire. I watched this video in horror, shedding tears for Petrova's poor son, who would no doubt someday watch this terrifying clip of his mother's last desperate act.

The year 2014 also saw a private self-immolation. Less than twenty days after Petrova's suicide in Sofia, police discovered the charred body of Desislava Koleva, a twenty-nine-year-old woman in Pernik.[22] Neighbors noticed a bad smell and called the authorities to investigate. Koleva left a suicide note in her journal explaining that she burned herself alive in the garage so as not to damage anyone's property. She wrote that she was exhausted from living in poverty. Neighbors reported that Koleva had recently visited the local emergency room to have a tick removed from her leg. After admitting her for the procedure, medical personnel turned her out on the street when they realized that she didn't have the 10 levs (5 euros) to pay their fee. Friendless and alone, Koleva wanted no spectacle. She just couldn't take it anymore.

Thanks to the attentions of Bulgaria's best burn specialists, Dimitar Dimitrov, the man who set himself alight in front of the president's offices in March 2013, survived. It seems the Bulgarian president took a personal interest in Dimitrov's case, and the world's media rushed to interview him once his recovery was assured. Dimitrov explained that he hoped to draw attention to the plight of ordinary Bulgarians.[23] At fifty-two, Dimitrov had lived half of his life under communism and half of his life under democracy, or the system that Bulgarians called democracy after 1989. Like so many of his compatriots, Dimitrov had believed that democracy would improve the quality of life. The realities of the next twenty-five years frustrated his hopes: "Under Communism, I had to wake up at 5 AM so that I could stand in line to buy milk and bread for my child. Under this government, I was a blacksmith until my workshop went out of business. The job that was feeding my family went away. Then electricity became impossible to afford. Under Communism, we had money, but there was nothing to buy. Now, there is everything to buy but no money."[24]

Dimitrov suffered the slings and arrows of outrageous fortune of Bulgaria's transition for more than two decades before deciding to act. Plamen Goranov's self-immolation in Varna inspired Dimitrov. In his recollection of the hours before he flicked the lighter, Dimitrov describes his desire to do something that might give his daughter a brighter future:

I had decided to do it the day before. The prime minister [Boyko Borissov] had just resigned and new elections were announced, and I was sick of all of it. So I decided to kill myself in front of the president's building. I woke up early and had coffee with my wife. I had made up my mind, but I didn't tell her anything. I was very quiet. After that, I went to the store and got one beer. I drank it with my neighbors. I went to a gas station and pumped out some gas and poured it in an empty bottle of vodka. I got on the train to go downtown, and when I got there, I walked around for a while. It was about 10 AM, and I walked around until 1:30. During that time, I drank another beer alone in an unknown bar. I have one daughter, and I thought about her. It's not that

FIGURE 1.1. The guards in front of the office of the Bulgarian presidency.

she lives so bad, but I want her to have the same life as American girls. I thought it was worth it for her to not have a father if she could have a better life. One can't live in a constant recession."[25]

When a journalist asked Dimitrov why he didn't just shoot himself in front of the presidential palace, the latter replied, "I did not want to simply commit suicide. We had all of these protests—we're still having them—and nothing gets done. Nothing changes. I didn't want anything from the Bulgarian politicians. I was hoping that the world, people like you, would look at our country with a careful eye. When Plamen Goranov committed suicide, he ousted the mayor of Varna with his self-immolation. I wanted to oust the entire system."[26]

In another interview with the BBC, Dimitrov once again insisted that he wanted to make a difference for his country.[27] "I believe I achieved what I set out to achieve," he told reporter Tom Esslemont. "I might have been a fool, but I hope it will change things for the better here." Although the Bulgarian government deleted all of his social media accounts, fearing his influence on other Bulgarians frustrated with the path their country had taken, Dimitrov imagined himself as their spokesperson.[28] "Now I see that, having survived setting myself on fire, I can be the voice of those experiencing what I have experienced. I hope that by telling my story I can make more people aware of the situation here in Bulgaria."[29]

Perhaps Dimitrov was right. Jan Palach's death in Czechoslovakia spurred Western citizens' resistance to Soviet aggression and human rights violations. The self-immolation of Mohamed Bouazizi, a street vendor harassed by the Tunisian government, is largely credited with inspiring the Arab Spring. Bulgaria now boasts the second largest number of political self-immolations in recent years, trailing only Tibet, where more than 130 Buddhist monks set themselves alight between 2009 and 2015 to protest the continued Chinese occupation of their country.

Of course, the Chinese still occupy Tibet. And as of November 2016, Boyko Borissov still served as prime minister of Bulgaria. Dimitrov's country was still the poorest in the EU, and Bulgaria's electricity distribution monopolies were still demanding higher prices. Only one thing was noticeably cheaper: the price of gasoline.

2. Cucumbers

Most Bulgarians think I'm a spy. It doesn't matter that the Cold War is over or that Bulgaria ceased to be a communist country a quarter of a century ago. It's not relevant that this small Balkan nation now belongs to NATO and the European Union, or that two U.S. military bases grace its soil. Why else would I speak Bulgarian? What else explains my encyclopedic knowledge of their culture? My PhD and scholarly books are obviously just part of my cover. I assure you that no government employs me to gather clandestine information, but I did once pretend to be a spy for the sake of science. Well, social science anyway. This life may sound glamorous, but it isn't. As a professor at a small liberal arts college, I spend most of my days writing lectures and grading undergraduate papers.

My career as a CIA agent supposedly began in 1997. I was pursing my doctorate, and my course of study demanded that I move to another country and live there for at least a year. This extended fieldwork allowed me to master a local language and a specific foreign culture. In the decade that followed the collapse of the Berlin Wall, a lot of American PhD students were attracted to the nations of Eastern Europe. When it was time for me to choose my fieldwork site, I selected Bulgaria, at least partially because I'd met a charming

Bulgarian law student. When the U.S. Fulbright Commission awarded me a generous grant, I left Berkeley with two suitcases and a new husband.

In the era before Internet snooping and mass electronic surveillance, governments gathered intelligence by sending trained agents into the field. In the world of international espionage, two kinds of spies collect state secrets: OCs and NOCs. Those with "official cover" (the OCs) work in embassies and consulates. These political officers and trade attachés enjoy the protection of diplomatic immunity if their true purpose in a country is revealed. At worst, the host nation declares the individual a persona non grata and she leaves with no repercussions.

Those operating under nonofficial cover (NOCs) lack the necessary affiliation with a diplomatic mission to qualify for immunity. These NOCs work at great risk; when caught they face severe penalties, often death, for their transgressions. A plausible cover identity proves essential for NOCs, and sometimes governments create fake corporations or nongovernmental organizations to insert these agents into the field. More often, they integrate into existing structures. Bulgarians assumed that I was a NOC. In the immediate post–Cold War era, only this possibility explained my presence in and knowledge of their country. I spent over a decade denying this double identity until one day a jumpy druggie forced me to embrace it.

By 2009, my supposed cover was complete: a professor at a rural New England college that nobody in Eastern Europe had ever heard of. That summer, I lived in a one-bedroom apartment in a Sofia neighborhood east of the city center. During the communist era, diplomatic residences and foreign embassies populated this part of town, and it enjoyed better infrastructure and amenities than other parts of the capital. Before 1989, the government kept the parks and streets near my flat well manicured and clean. With the advent of democracy, however, weeds grew unchecked and garbage bins overflowed. Mean packs of stray dogs colonized the parks. Beer-drinking and drug-injecting teenagers rivaled their feralness. These lost youth, the human fallout of the upheavals of the 1990s, scattered empty bottles and used needles under jungle gyms and swing sets. Children vanished and people stayed indoors.

To travel to the city center, I walked from my flat to the entrance of the underpass in front of the King's Breakfast restaurant next to the old cinema. Across Tsarigradsko Shosse, I caught a minibus in front of the Hotel Pliska. Most of these communal taxis stopped in front of Sofia University, and from there I could walk anywhere I needed to go: the Central State Archives, the National Library, the Helikon bookstore. To walk to the bus stop, I took a shortcut through one of the run-down parks between a cluster of residential blocks, a path I'd used hundreds of times in the past twelve years.

One Tuesday morning in July, I noticed a trash can at the far end of the park. It overflowed with what looked like communist-era archival folders: pale green and worn. The park was empty, so I walked to the trash can and examined the folders, eight of them crammed full of official-looking papers. Beneath the folders lay an assortment of old journals, mostly professional publications about various Bulgarian crops: fifty or so magazines about corn and tobacco, pamphlets about the wine industry, and booklets about mushroom horticulture.

I opened the folder on top and found the personal documents of someone named Andrei Andreev, born November 1924. Mr. Andreev had been an agricultural specialist working in the Ministry of Agriculture and Food Production. I did a quick calculation. Mr. Andreev would be about eighty-five years old, meaning he lived most of his life before 1989. Maybe these documents were important, I thought. I knew that personal archives like these could be invaluable to historians. Maybe they would be useful for my research on everyday life after communism. I thrilled at my luck.

I pulled the folders from the bin and made a stack on the ground. If I piled the journals on top of the folders, I could haul them all home in one trip. I unearthed the pamphlets and arranged them by size, creating a neat pyramid.

A young man appeared. "Hey auntie, what have ya found?"

"Auntie" was a colloquial Bulgarian way of addressing an unknown woman older than oneself. I balked at the "auntie," but turned around.

He examined the journals with interest.

"Some old papers," I said.

"Ya think they're worth something? Ya gonna sell them?"

I used my most auntie-sounding voice. "No. I'm bringing them to the archives."

"You're not Bulgarian," he said. "Where ya from? You gonna sell 'em? You should give 'em to me."

The young man gazed down at the pile. Since the economic changes in 1989, many Bulgarians had been treasure hunting in the trash. All manner of detritus could be found there. People died and apartments got cleaned out every day. Since Bulgaria had nothing like Goodwill or the Salvation Army, everything went into the dumpsters: unwanted clothes, books, housewares, and personal papers. At a nightly market just down from the central Sofia Synagogue, one could sell salvaged loot. At first, the rubbish scavengers were mostly members of Bulgaria's impoverished Roma minority, but after years of economic decline, pensioners and unemployed youth joined their ranks. Pensioners used the money for medicine, young people for drugs.

I squinted at the young man. "No. They're not worth any money. They're just for historical studies."

He snatched a journal off the top of my pile: a *Bulletin of Mycology* from 1971. He turned it over in his hands. "Someone might buy this," he said. "Maybe foreigners."

The young man jittered. His right leg shook. He was thin, and his brown hair hung long and greasy. I wondered if he was going to attack me over some dusty papers from the trash. If he thought they were worth something, he might. I looked around the park. Just the two of us. My heart sped up.

I wasn't sure what to do. My eyes sized up the young man: nineteen or twenty, hung over or strung out—or whatever it is you call it when you've been up really late on drugs the night before and you're unemployed and probably still living in the home of your disapproving parents. I thought about the Bulgarian word for drug addict: *narcoman*. It meant "narco-maniac" in English. Then I got an idea. A wave of adrenaline washed over my better judgment.

I pushed my dark sunglasses up the bridge of my nose and lowered my voice. "Step aside, sir," I said, inflecting my Bulgarian with a heavy American accent. "This isn't what you think."

I wore my long hair down, so I touched my ear and looked up at the tops of the surrounding buildings. "Official business," I said in whispered Bulgarian.

The young man widened his eyes, glancing at the tops of the buildings behind him. He looked back to me, and then down at the pile of old files stacked up on the ground.

I let my eyes look from left to right and then back up to the top of the building across from me. "Classified. Do not interfere."

The young man froze. I knew that many Bulgarians were paranoid about the CIA, and believed that any American who spoke Bulgarian was either a Mormon or a spy. The narcoman stared at me. I kept my face as straight as possible, hoping he would leave. Of course, now he might consider the documents more valuable, giving him a greater incentive to pummel me. My heart beat faster.

The young man turned and looked up at the top of the building behind him. Almost as if on cue, a figure wandered out onto the balcony of one of the apartments on the highest floor. A man lit a cigarette and surveyed the park below. I touched my ear and nodded up at him.

The narcoman looked back at me and followed my gaze. The smoking man appeared to be watching us. I kept my finger pressed behind my ear, and nodded my head again. I wanted these folders for myself. I found them first.

Nothing happened. The young man stood silent, looking back and forth between me and the smoking man on the balcony. For a moment I felt sure he would call my bluff when he exhaled and placed the journal back on my pile.

"*Izvinyavaite*," he said, backing away. He addressed me formally, asking me to excuse him the way he might ask forgiveness from the president. No more "auntie" for me.

"Thank you for your cooperation, sir," I said in English, emphasizing my *r*s like John Wayne.

My surly *r*s unnerved him, and he dashed out of the park. I gathered up the folders and journals and hurried home before someone else challenged my claim. I was late for an appointment in town, so I stumbled back to my apartment, dumped the pile inside the door, and jumped into the first taxi that drove by. I would avoid the park for a while.

Several hours later, I returned to my apartment and prepared a large bowl of cold soup made with yogurt, cucumber, dill, walnuts, and salt. *Tarator* is a perfect summer dish—the crispness of the cucumber complements the creamy coolness of the yogurt. On hot days, I could add a few ice cubes and eat the soup with hunks of fresh peasant bread, washing it all down with crisp Bulgarian white wine mixed with sparkling water.

I transferred the documents from a floor to the low coffee table and hunkered down to examine them. Who was this mysterious Mr. Andreev? How had his papers found their way into that trash can in the park? I laughed at my ruse with the narcoman, wondering what I would do if the documents actually contained Bulgarian state secrets. I opened the first green folder marked "personal dossier" and found a collection of yellowing pages with frayed edges covered with typewritten Cyrillic text. The first document in the folder was titled "autobiography," something like a personal statement for a job. It was dated August 10, 1976.

Autobiography of Andrei Andreev
*A Specialist Working in the Greenhouse Sector to the Crop
Headquarters of the Ministry of Agriculture and Food Production*

I was born on November 7, 1924, in the village of Cherkovna in the Silistra Municipality. I graduated with an academic secondary school education in Silistra City in 1946. I graduated from university in Sofia in 1954. My family consists of: my spouse, Ekaterina Andreeva, born in Sofia on January 11, 1938. She graduated as an agricultural specialist in Sofia in 1960. She works as a planner in the enterprise Balkanstroi. She is not a member of the Communist Party. My son is Ivan Andreev, born in Sofia in 1974.

I come from an average village family. After I finished my higher education, I started work in an agricultural cooperative in the village of Gurmazovo as a district agronomist. In 1953, I went to work in the agricultural cooperative in Golyantsi village in the Sofia Municipality. During the time of the creation of the vegetable belt around Sofia City, I was appointed as a specialist in vegetable production in the agricultural cooperative in the village of Kostinbrod. In 1963, I was appointed as the chief agronomist in the same cooperative. In 1964, I was granted a leave from the cooperative and was sent to a six-month school for the study of the English language. In 1967, I went to work in the greenhouses in Sofia as a Division Head of the First Category. For my hard work, I have earned many moral and material awards, and for my work in the production of greenhouse crops I was awarded a Victory Passport and Gold Badge, and later another Gold Badge of Excellence from the Ministry of Agriculture and Food Production.

I have been actively involved in politics as an agricultural specialist working for twenty-three years, of which thirteen years were spent working with Polish vegetable crop production and ten years were spent in the production of greenhouse vegetables. As a specialist I have worked faithfully, using all of my knowledge and skills to increase agricultural production.

In the same file I discovered a few character references. In 1976, Mr. Andreev applied for a top position in the Ministry of Agriculture and Food Production, a job that required foreign travel. Since most Bulgarians lived under a regime of strict travel restrictions, the Bulgarian authorities would want to ensure that Andreev was not planning to defect to the West. A man named Stoyan Nedelchev, who knew Andreev during World War II, wrote the first letter. Nedelchev vouched that Andreev supported the antifascist resistance movement against Bulgaria's German-allied monarchy. Although Andreev was not an official member of the Communist Party, Nedelchev affirmed that his old schoolmate was an "honest, principled and tenacious" man who could be relied upon to serve the party and the state. Mr. Vasil Spahahiski, who worked with Andreev in a massive complex of greenhouses outside Sofia, wrote a second letter of reference. Spahahiski attested that Andreev was an "excellent specialist" responsible for the successful importation of patented Dutch cucumber seeds, and an "exceptionally diligent worker."

Under communism, Bulgaria was a planned economy, meaning that the state owned and operated a vast majority of the agricultural sector. The Ministry of Agriculture and Food Production coordinated with central planners to feed the Bulgarian population; no private farmers sold produce at prices determined by the fluctuations of supply and demand. The government built huge greenhouses to keep the vegetable supply constant throughout the year, and sold domestically produced vegetables at fixed and subsidized prices. Mr. Andreev oversaw the daily operation of these massive, indoor vegetable farms, and had earned himself a "golden badge of honor" for his work.

I drank some of my tarator and dug deeper into the personal file. Official approval to visit some Polish greenhouses in 1974. Another permission to take a forty-five-day business trip to Mongolia in 1973. A sheaf of approvals for domestic business trips and annual vacations of four weeks each summer, and two weeks around the Christmas holidays. The deed for an apartment bought in 1974, around the time his son was born. A thick stack of memos—Andreev's own notes on how to successfully grow Dutch cucumbers in Bulgarian greenhouses. He specialized in cucumbers.

As I sat there on my sofa, reading the files between spoons full of cold yogurt soup, I felt like a voyeur. I had sometimes stumbled upon personal documents like these in the archives, but they were always scattered across multiple files, sprinkled throughout the boxes by archivists trying to maintain some kind of thematic consistency. Mr. Andreev had been the archivist of his own life, carefully curating his career milestones. Now he was probably dead.

I sat back and looked around my apartment, my ex-husband's place. He always lent it to me and stayed with our daughter at his parents' apartment while I did my research. My ex and I maintained a friendly relationship, but he too thought I was a spy.

"You're working for the CIA. You just don't know it," he told me about a year after our divorce was final and he'd moved back to Bulgaria. At the time, I was having problems getting a long-term residency permit because the government suspected me of being a NOC.

"What are you talking about?" I said. I'd lived with this man for seven years. He was the father of my child.

"As far as I can tell, you aren't directly employed. But you're still working for them. They just haven't told you."

"How can I be working for anybody if I don't know that I'm working for them?"
He shrugged. *"They probably don't want you to know."*

I closed Mr. Andreev's personal dossier, the smallest of the folders that I rescued from the trash can. Seven additional folders bulged with yellowing news-
print pages, mostly official documents from the Ministry of Agriculture and
Food Production. I thumbed through Andreev's handwritten ledgers recording
production inputs (fertilizers, pesticides, herbicides) and outputs (tomatoes,
cucumbers, corn) over various years. Andreev kept impeccable records.

I put the large green folders aside and turned my attention to Andreev's
collection of professional journals. I found a Russian publication about bee-
keeping from September 1963, and a Bulgarian magazine called *Plant Protection* from March of that same year. I spent an hour examining three issues of
the *Botanical Journal of the Soviet Academy of Sciences* from July, August, and
October 1963, as well as a small booklet of instructions for cultivating mush-
rooms from 1965. Handwritten marginalia surrounded the text, perhaps the
notes of a young Andreev—an architect of Bulgaria's green revolution.

Before communism, Bulgaria's peasants manually tilled the land on small,
private plots. After 1944, the government nationalized land and collectivized
agriculture.[1] Although central planning could produce spectacular inefficien-
cies with regard to consumer goods, the new cooperative farms increased
domestic production. Tractor brigades crisscrossed the country from co-op
to co-op mechanizing the labor-intensive work of land clearing, plowing, and
harvesting. Agronomists introduced new seed varieties and chemical fertilizers. Science ruled the day, and experts like Mr. Andreev studied and implemented the latest discoveries.

Between 1944 and 1989, Bulgaria's central planners surveyed demographic
changes, projected population growth, and calculated the demand for food
based on assumptions about what and how much people ate. Each crop had
its own plan to meet the anticipated domestic demand with perhaps some
extra production for export. The traditional Bulgarian diet contains many
vegetables; tomatoes, onions, peppers, and cucumbers form the foundation
of many popular dishes. Central planners determined the yearly need for
cucumbers, and Mr. Andreev figured out how to fulfill the quota.

Meeting the targets meant acquiring all of the necessary inputs and using
those inputs to produce the desired output. In a centrally planned economy,
procuring seeds, fertilizers, and other agricultural supplies could require
Byzantine machinations, but from what I read in his file, Andreev always met
his quotas. Tens of thousands of cucumbers grown each year. From the long
handwritten columns of figures, I knew that these were the original ledgers,

not mimeographed copies. Andreev would have been sixty-five years old in 1989, well past retirement age. Was he still working in the ministry when communism collapsed? Why had he kept these records?

Perhaps Mr. Andreev retired in 1984 when he was sixty years old, the official retirement age for men in Bulgaria. On that last day of work, I imagined him cleaning out his office in the ministry. He must have boxed everything up, these mementos of a forty-year career, and brought them home. Perhaps he couldn't bring himself to throw them away. For over a quarter of a century, they sat in some box in a basement or under a bed. Perhaps Andreev took them out once in a while to reflect on his life's work. Or maybe he never looked at them again.

Surveying the folders, I felt despondent. I guessed that Mr. Andreev had recently passed away. His wife, Ekaterina, or his son, Ivan, or maybe even a grandchild sorted through his remaining possessions. I imagined his grandchild finding a box of old files and journals.

"Dad, what should I do with these?"

Ivan, now about thirty-five, would inspect the folders: ledgers of greenhouse cucumber crop yields from 1981, approvals for business trips taken in the 1970s, and letters of recommendation for a job in a people's republic that no longer existed.

"Toss 'em," Ivan might have said.

I thought about my own daughter. What was she doing? Was she already asleep, or was her dad letting her stay up late and eat junk food in front of the television? Did he ever say things about me? Would she grow up thinking that I was a spy?

I turned back to Mr. Andreev's papers, and discovered a booklet—in Polish, Russian, and English—with a list of every gas station in Poland from 1968. The pamphlet contained information about the working hours of each station and the types of fuel available: leaded, unleaded, and kerosene. I thumbed through a summer 1970 timetable for Jugoslovenski Aerotransport, the long-defunct national airline of a now-defunct country. The timetable listed the schedules for flights between Yugoslavia and other countries that were no longer on the political map: Czechoslovakia, the German Democratic Republic, and the Union of Soviet Socialist Republics. On July 7, 1970, there was a 14:42 plane from Belgrade to Leningrad, the Soviet city now called Saint Petersburg.

I examined a road map of Bulgaria from 1975, its wide creases signaling that it had been folded and refolded many times by its former owner. Mr. Andreev had perhaps used this map for the business trips he took around

Bulgaria, visiting cooperative farms and greenhouses full of peppers and onions and tomatoes and cucumbers. Maybe this map once guided him to the seaside with Ekaterina and Ivan for their summer holidays. On its cover, a big yellow psychedelic sun rose up above a highway, the colors vibrant and joyful, so contrary to my imagination of the drab gray life of communism.

From between the pages of a corn journal, I extracted a copy of a 1975 youth magazine about science and technology. On the back page I saw a half-completed Cyrillic crossword puzzle. I also came across two copies of the publication "One Week in Sofia," a listing of all cultural and educational activities in the Bulgarian capital. The first issue contained entries for the week of February 14–20, 1977: new books and LPs, cinema times, art exhibitions, activities at the Soviet-Bulgarian friendship center, and a TV guide. At 17:50 on Valentine's Day 1977, Mr. Andreev might have watched a show called *Atlas: Budapest*. At 21:55, he could have been cozied up on his sofa watching a program called *Yesterday, Today, and Tomorrow*, his arm draped around Ekaterina's shoulder after little Ivan had gone to bed. On Saturday, February 19, 1977, he had the chance to view the fourth episode of an animated serial of *The Count of Monte Cristo*, broadcast at 16:40.

The second issue of "One Week in Sofia" covered the period from February 28 to March 6, 1977. This week included March 1, a popular folk holiday when Bulgarians exchange talismans made of red and white string to celebrate the impending arrival of spring, and March 3, a national holiday marking Bulgaria's independence from the Ottoman Empire in 1878. Officials in the Bulgarian Ministry of Culture filled this week with events: plays, concerts, museum exhibitions, and a parade.

To my surprise, the TV schedule for March 3 was similar to that of other weekdays. There was a children's program at 9:35 and an exercise program at 10:30. The news came on at 17:30 and the national "Good Night, Children" song was broadcast as usual at 19:50. Andreev's son would have been three in 1977, and like most Bulgarian children he probably listened to that song each evening before bedtime: "I am Suncho, coming from the woods, to say 'Good night,' children. Many stars are shining outside. It is time to sleep, time to sleep."

I wondered what Mr. Andreev had done with his paid holiday on March 3, 1977. Did he stay home and spend the day with his family? Did he take Ivan to the children's theater? Or did he drive little Ivan out to see the cucumbers growing in those big greenhouses around Sofia? Did Andreev tell his son about that year's cucumber crop and suggest that little Ivan could also grow up to be an agronomist if he studied hard and did well in school?

I put the booklet down and surveyed the folders and journals spread out on the table and floor around me. Mr. Andreev, a man born in 1924, spent his life trying to improve the agricultural productivity of Bulgaria. He labored every day at a job he enjoyed, had a family, and maybe went to concerts and galleries on the weekends. He traveled on business trips abroad and took holidays at the seaside. I closed my eyes and pictured Andreev receiving his golden badge of excellence. I wondered how many Bulgarians knew that their tarator soups and Shopska salads were populated with cucumbers grown in greenhouses from seeds imported from capitalist Holland by Mr. Andreev. For thirty years he kept Bulgarians in cucumbers, but not a single vegetable ever bore his signature.

Those millions of unattributed cucumbers forced me to consider my own life. The days and weeks and months and years seemed to be slipping by. I worked hard, running from here to there, trying to do research and write and teach and grade and be a good mother to my daughter and a good mentor for my students. There were conferences, and congresses, and seminars, and research trips abroad. There were books, articles, book reviews, manuscript reviews, reports, syllabi, grant applications, and letters of recommendation to write. I could keep on top of most of it, but sometimes I felt beaten down. I turned out words like Andreev once produced cucumbers.

I considered Mr. Andreev's files. Nothing from after 1989. What happened to him after communism collapsed? Had he lost his life savings—like so many other Bulgarians of his generation—when the whole banking system imploded in 1996? How had he survived the hyperinflation that destroyed the value of his pension? After working and paying into the system for forty years, did he have to accept money from Ivan to afford the basic necessities? The new Bulgarian government privatized the old state greenhouses to foreign investors who shut them down and then sold the valuable land beneath them. What did Mr. Andreev think when the new democrats broke up the collective farms and sold their tractors for scrap metal? After years of being self-sufficient in food production, Bulgaria now imported shrink-wrapped cucumbers from Turkey and Israel.

I wished I could speak to Mr. Andreev. I had so many questions. In all the time I worked with official documents in the Central State Archives, I'd never seen a half-completed crossword puzzle. Hours had passed since I first delved into his files. I stared at that crossword puzzle, counting the lines he had drawn through the clues. Maybe I could write a book about Mr. Andreev. Maybe I could really save him from the trash can. But I knew I'd deceived that teenager for nothing. Even in the most rarefied ivory towers, the stories of people like Andreev garnered scant attention. What meaning could I salvage from these discarded remnants of a communist-era agronomist whose greatest accomplishment was the successful importation of Dutch cucumber seeds?

I stood up and walked to the refrigerator, refilling my bowl with more tarator. I faced a dilemma. What should I do with all this paper now? I thought I might bring the files to the Central State Archives. But I realized that no archivist would be interested in the personal documents of some random specialist in the Ministry of Agriculture and Food Production. Or worse somehow, they would keep the official ledgers and crop reports and toss the rest: the road map, the letters of recommendation, and the autobiography. Mr. Andreev's life consigned to the dustbin of history once again.

I couldn't bring myself to throw them away. At the end of the summer, I packed them in my suitcase and relocated the files to Brunswick, Maine. Together with my photocopies from the archives, I transferred the papers from my suitcase to a corner of my office where they sat untouched for the entire fall semester. Sometime in December, I gathered Mr. Andreev's files and journals and crammed them into two milk crates, shoving them on a high shelf above my file cabinets. They sat undisturbed for years.

In 2014, my nonofficial cover got a new boost. The college promoted me to full professor and granted me a two-year research leave to work on a fifth book. A replacement professor would be moving into my office, and she needed storage space. I had four tall filing cabinets—each four drawers high and four feet deep. They were stuffed with paper: field notes, scholarly articles, newspaper clippings, teaching evaluations, old phone bills, official correspondence, and other flotsam dating back to my time in graduate school in California: a stolen menu from the Spats bar where I used to meet the Bulgarian law student, movie ticket stubs, tax returns from when I lived below the official poverty line. I opened the first drawer and looked inside. I had labeled some folders—most possessed blank tabs. I had thousands of pages of paper.

Someday I will retire. On the day I give up my office, I'll have to decide what to do with all of this paper. Back in 1984, Mr. Andreev faced a similar decision. If I couldn't bring myself to throw his papers away, I knew I would keep my own. These files would be transferred to boxes and taken home, stored down in the basement or up in the attic to gather dust for the duration of my waning years.

When I die, my daughter will probably have to deal with those boxes. But because I'm a published author and an academic, some library might want them, right? The American Anthropological Association's code of ethics demands that all ethnographers keep their field notes. This is what we all imagine—that future generations of scholars might deem our papers worthy of preservation. Someday, a graduate student might use my old field notes and journals as raw data for her dissertation.

This aspiring PhD student will work her way through my files. Between some old teaching evaluations and notes for unwritten fellowship proposals, she will discover the folders from Mr. Andreev, a collection of communist-era documents from an official Bulgarian ministry. Maybe this will be the evidence she needs to prove that I really was a CIA NOC. Why else would I have these personal files from 1970s Bulgaria? These weren't just crop reports; they were encrypted military secrets, perhaps coordinates for a clandestine underground nuclear weapons manufacturing facility.

The dissertating PhD student will suggest that Mr. Andreev was not an agronomist. He was an undercover agent involved in agricultural espionage. When she convinces the Bulgarian government to release Andreev's secret service dossier and they confirm his true employment, a web of mystery and suspicion will descend over my entire academic career. My books will be reread for information about my secret missions.

Because Andreev and I were Cold War spooks, readers will devour our biographies. Expert cryptographers might scrutinize our half-finished cross-word puzzles. My grocery lists will be scanned and digitally stored in the British Museum. Perhaps a novelist will be inspired to write a cloak-and-dagger thriller about a young American woman who is initiated into an international society by a retired Bulgarian intelligence agent posing as a cucumber expert. The phallic symbolism is irresistible. Neo-Freudians will celebrate. They'll make a movie. There'll be a plastic actionbot of the actress who plays me. My grandchildren will brag in middle school. . . .

"PROFESSOR GHODSEE?" A STUDENT pokes her head into my office.

"Hmm?"

"I know you've got class right now, but I just wanted to turn in my paper because I have a job interview this afternoon and can't come."

Oh shit. I take her paper and remember that I have thirty-four more of these coming in today. I grab my lecture notes: three pages, about eight hundred words. I check the time on my mobile phone. Two minutes past the hour. It takes seven minutes to get to my lecture hall, and only if I run. Damn. I'm late for class. Again.

3. Pieces

(FICTION)

"We've never met, but I'm your auntie," Rumiana said, smiling at the child while the orphanage director fidgeted behind her desk.

The boy stared at Rumiana, licking the powder off the yellow-cheese-flavored pretzel sticks. A generic brand in a clear plastic package, the pretzels cost Rumiana only thirty *stotinki* at the railway station on her way out of town, but the boy cherished them. The hungry hollow of his cheeks accented his large, brown eyes.

"Your mother and I had the same father, just different mothers," Rumiana said. "Your grandfather had a lot of children and we didn't all know each other."

The boy said nothing. His eyes traveled from Rumiana's clean black leather pumps, up past her twenty-denier stockings, and noted her crisp business suit, her manicured fingernails, and the gold ring she wore on the third finger of her right hand. Rumiana continued to smile, hoping to make the boy feel at ease.

"We have no information about Pesho's parents," the director said, glancing at the boy. "Left on the steps outside the orphanage when he was only a few months old. Colic. Screamed day and night."

Rumiana straightened and turned toward the middle-aged director, who had dark pouches sagging beneath her eyes. Rumiana guessed the woman had worked in orphanages since the communist era. The job once paid a good salary with decent benefits, but everything changed after 1989.

"It took us forever to track the boy down," Rumiana said in perfect, grammatical Bulgarian. "My half-sister apparently got pregnant when she was very young, and didn't want to look after the boy. She was dying when she found me a few months ago. She told me she'd left him here in 1994. Very hard times back then, you know."

The director nodded, remembering the early 1990s with an internal cringe. Chaos once reigned as savvy Bulgarian entrepreneurs earned millions running illegal weapons to the Serbs during the Bosnian War. With their ill-gotten riches, they established private syndicates to pillage the remains of Bulgaria's socialist economy. Gangland rivalries and soaring murder rates transformed the little communist nation into an emerging democracy of the Wild Wild East.

Rumiana turned back to the boy. At ten, his golden skin stretched taut over his protruding collarbone. He savored each pretzel stick, taking tiny bites with his remaining front teeth. Rumiana saw little intelligence or curiosity in his eyes, and wondered if he could read or write.

"I'm sorry to say that your mother is dead," Rumiana said to Pesho. "I don't think she ever knew who your father was, but she asked me to come and get you and take care of you. Would you like to come home and live with me?"

The boy showed no reaction to the death of the mother he never knew. But his eyes brightened when Rumiana used the word "home." She rose from her seat to put her arm on the boy's shoulder. He flinched, and then seemed embarrassed for flinching. He took her hand, and nodded up at her, clutching the pretzels against his chest. Rumiana gazed out the window.

Most Bulgarian orphanages were built in the countryside since fresh air and rural living supposedly benefited the wards. Buses shuttled them to and from the local schools where they attempted to mix with other children their own age. But many of the orphans in Bulgaria were Roma children, an ethnic minority pejoratively called Gypsies by those who disdained them. Most teachers ignored them. The other pupils shunned them. Parentless and hated by the ethnic majority, the orphans stuck together until they grew old enough to run away and make a living for themselves in the cities.

"I'm going to need some proof of a relationship," the orphanage director said, her voice soft. "I can't just let you take him."

Rumiana sat back down. "Ma'am," she said, using the formal form of address. "My half-sister got pregnant when she was fourteen and the boy was probably born in a camp with a Gypsy midwife. There's no birth certificate or record of Pesho's existence. He's lived ten years without anyone in the world to love him, but now he has a chance for a better life. I am educated and will see to it that he gets a good education."

The director narrowed her eyes. "You seem nice, Miss, but I've been doing this job for a long time and I know how *you* people are. You dump them when they're babies so the state will take care of them. Then someone comes to fetch them when they're old enough to start stealing or whoring or begging on the street." The director pointed to Pesho. "This one will probably be a thief, no? Too dumb for anything else."

Rumiana inhaled. A racist, she thought. Another racist. Oh well, those are the easiest to deal with. They don't really care about the children. "I have some documents here. They will suffice to prove my interests are genuine."

Rumiana reached into her Italian leather handbag and pulled out a plain white envelope. She placed it on the desk and slid it across to the director, who picked it up and peered inside: twenty 50-lev banknotes. One thousand levs—about three months of the director's salary. Rumiana folded her hands in her lap.

The director sighed. She hesitated for a full two minutes, saying nothing as she searched Rumiana's face. Pesho continued to munch on his pretzel sticks, gazing down at his feet. Rumiana studied the director, feeling her inner struggle, and for a moment Rumiana feared she would refuse. It would be only her second refusal, Rumiana thought, because a thousand levs could buy a lot in the countryside. Some directors accepted the bribe straightaway, as compensation for their now abysmal salaries. Others rationalized the money as compensation for the tax funds spent on caring for the Roma children. Rumiana imagined that some directors put the money into their orphanage's operating fund. One less mouth to feed meant more food for the other children, less work for the staff, and one less hassle when the child ran away.

After the Romanian adoption scandal of the early 1990s, when orphanages sold babies to Western buyers, the postcommunist government in neighboring Bulgaria passed a strict law that rendered it nearly impossible to find foreign parents for abandoned children. During the communist era, the state relished its custody of Roma children, seeing it as an opportunity to modernize the next generation and integrate them into mainstream society. But discrimination against the Roma remained, and after 1989 new nationalisms increased local hatred of the Roma at the same moment when the orphanages lost their funding and the planned economy fell to pieces.

The director sighed again, clenching her jaw.

Rumiana sat unmoving, trying to project kindness and responsibility. She had no Roma ancestry, but her dark complexion ensured that most Bulgarians believed she did. At twenty-six years old, she wasn't old enough to be one of the "good Gypsies" the communists had saved, but she knew how to play the part. She also used her looks. Healthy reddish-brown hair brushed the tops of her shoulders, and two chorus lines of thick lashes framed her dark brown eyes. Her mouth was full, her skin smooth and unblemished. People equated beauty with goodness.

"I'll need a copy of your *lichna carta*," the director said.

Rumiana grinned, reaching into her purse for the fake personal identity card she carried when she did these jobs. "No problem at all."

Within the hour Rumiana drove south toward the Greek-Bulgarian border with Pesho feasting on an array of candy and potato chips in the passenger seat beside her. After gorging himself, he slept, and Rumiana increased her speed so she would have time to check into her hotel and freshen up before the meeting. Pesho needed a shower badly, and she hoped she might have time to get him a haircut and buy him some new clothes.

At the appointed hour, Rumiana brought a transformed Pesho to a new café on the central square. She scanned the tables. Her contact had not yet arrived.

"Sit down," she told Pesho. "You can order whatever you like before your uncles get here. You have Greek uncles, did you know that?"

Pesho smiled. "Anything I want?"

"Of course, darling."

"Even meat?"

"As much as you want."

Rumiana spotted the Greeks crossing the square, and she waved. "Here they come."

The transaction followed the same pattern as usual. She explained to the child that she had some business to see to and would leave him in the care of his uncles, who would pay the bill. She always explained this as the child's orders arrived at the table, usually five or six different dishes. The food would distract him. She stood and walked to the middle of the square. One of the uncles followed.

"The envelope is waiting for you at the hotel," he said.

She nodded.

"Any trouble?"

"Not really," Rumiana said. "But it wasn't as easy as it usually is."

"I'll put a few more documents in next time," the uncle said. He had once told Rumiana that his name was Arber.

"How many more do I have to bring?" Rumiana said. "I should be close to paying it all off."

Arber nodded. "Yes, I've spoken with my associates and you've done very well. Five more and your debts will be cleared."

"Five more? I thought I was closer than that."

Arber raised his eyebrows. "Interest, you know. It accumulates."

Rumiana closed her eyes. She regretted her naïveté, but she had loved her father too much to make a rational decision about money. A year earlier, her father had fallen ill. He was only sixty-four, but he'd long retired from the factory, which now stood crumbling on the outskirts of town. He required an operation, but the public hospital wouldn't admit him. He had paid into the National Health Service his entire life, but things were different now, and hospital administrators deployed red tape to avoid performing expensive surgeries for the elderly. As her father's condition worsened, Rumiana borrowed the money for the medicine, the surgery, the bribes, and then more medicine. Since the banks refused to lend, she turned to unofficial lenders.

Her parents, her maternal aunt and uncle, and Rumiana all shared one two-bedroom flat. They scraped by on meager pensions and set their hopes on Rumiana getting a real job. Rumiana had graduated with top marks from a special French-language secondary school, but the Bulgarian economy choked hopes of a normal life. Most young people left for Sofia or tried to sneak into Western Europe, seeking black market work in Italy or Germany. Many girls from Rumiana's hometown of Rousse signed up with employment agencies promising jobs abroad, but her family forbade it. "You don't know what you're signing up for," her mother would say. "If you don't have money to pay for travel, they take your passport, and then you're a slave. It's too dangerous."

As her friends and classmates left, Rumiana spent four years working in her aunt's *banitsa* shop, baking and selling breakfast pastries for two hundred levs a month, dreaming that one day she might find some better job. For six glorious months, she worked in the Rousse branch of a new bank, but it soon closed for lack of depositors. After the financial collapses of the 1990s, Bulgarians preferred to keep their money in the Bank of Mattress.

When her father died, Rumiana's family found themselves over five thousand levs in debt to some not-so-nice men. If they sold their flat they could pay the debt but would have nowhere to live. Rumiana searched for a job, any legitimate job that would get her out of the bakery, but no one hired her. Each month the debt ballooned, and three men beat Rumiana's uncle as he delivered the flour to the bakery one morning, breaking his nose, three ribs, and an arm.

"You're a pretty girl," the local boss whispered to Rumiana across the counter a week later. Krassen had been a minor officer with the secret police before 1989. Now he led one of the Rousse syndicates. "You could come work for me. I can always make use of a pretty girl."

"No," Rumiana said, setting her jaw. "I won't do that. If you have other work, then yes, maybe. But I won't do that."

"Why so shy?" Krassen said, leering.

She met his stare with defiant eyes. "Dimitrina was my classmate."

Krassen's face tightened, understanding her reference. Rousse boasted only a small population, and far fewer than six degrees separated most people in the city. Krassen and Rumiana's father were born in the same year. They grew up in the same Young Pioneers troop in the 1960s, back when Krassen still aspired to give his life to serve the greater good and the Bulgarian Communist Party. Krassen nodded, taking a banitsa pastry and a bottle of thick brown *boza*. He walked out without paying.

Rumiana pushed the air from her lungs and hung her head.

Dimitrina Dandelova had been the star pupil at the French gymnasium, a beautiful young woman with many friends. Boys worshipped and teachers fawned. When Dimitrina started straightening her wavy hair, curls disappeared from the collective head of every girl in the school. Rumiana admired her too, making note of everything she wore, the books she read, and her dreams for the future.

Dimitrina started dating one of the men in Krassen's syndicate, a handsome young athlete chosen from a young age for Olympic training in wrestling. The wrestler paid for breast implants, and Dimi won a modeling contract. A few print ads, one television commercial, then off to Milan for runway work. She moved to Sofia, recorded a *chalga* album, and left the wrestler for a richer man. Drinking happened, and then drugs, and then god knows what else before Dimi returned to Rousse to make some quick cash. For a hefty sum, high school dreams could come true.

Dimi stumbled into the banitsa shop some months later, frail and twitchy.

"Rumi," she said. "You're Rumi from school."

"Hi, Dimi."

Dimi scratched her nose. "You sell banitsa? All that education to sell banitsa? What a shitty country. What happened to this country?"

Rumiana shrugged. "Bad times, I guess."

Dimi straightened. "I need someone to talk to. We went to school together. Can I talk to you? I need to talk to someone I know, someone who knew me before. You know, just talking."

Rumiana met Dimi at a little café in front of the railway station, where she sat alone with tears streaking her gaunt face. Dimi told Rumiana how she had borrowed money to go to Milan for the modeling work but it hadn't panned out and she met this man whom she loved, and she thought he loved her, but he was just using her and he forced her to do things with his friends and then she needed money and he wouldn't help her and she couldn't find any work and she took another loan to go to Paris where an agency specialized in models from Eastern Europe and they took her passport to make sure she wouldn't run off and there was a hotel where all the models lived but there were so many girls and not enough work and they couldn't leave because they couldn't travel without documents and it's awful because she hadn't known and she feels so stupid for not realizing what was happening. Through Dimi's sobs and hiccups, Rumiana understood that Dimi somehow made it back to Rousse with the help of her wrestler ex-boyfriend still smarting from her betrayal. He forced her to work nights and it wasn't that bad really until one of the drunk johns beat her and sodomized her with a *rakia* bottle and tore her perineum, creating a rectovaginal fistula that required surgery. The feces passed through, creating horrible smells and infections that made it impossible for her to work.

"I have no money, and he won't help me," Dimi said. "He just laughs at me and tells me that it's my fault for leaving him."

The Rousse police found Dimitrina dead in front of the French gymnasium two days later, mutilated by some twisted or vengeful john. The authorities arrested the wrestler, but he walked free fourteen hours later. The case remained unsolved.

Rumiana recalled these events as she stood in the center of Sandanski, staring at the Greek man she called Arber after delivering the boy Pesho. She refused to become a whore, but she needed to pay her family's debt. "I want it in writing," Rumiana said. "Only five more children."

Arber smiled. A written document meant nothing in Bulgaria, and Rumiana knew it. "Don't worry," Arber said. "We only need five more. There won't be any others after that. You've done well."

Rumiana drove back to Rousse, regretting the last six months of her life. Three weeks after their meeting in the bakery, Krassen had set up the initial contact. The man who called himself Arber came to Rousse to interview Rumiana. He told her they needed a Bulgarian woman who looked like a Roma to collect children from the orphanages, explaining that the Bulgarian adoption laws hindered their ability to find homes with willing Western families. The Greeks could transfer them to Western European institutions where they would have a higher chance of adoption.

"They'll have a better life in the West," Arber had told her.

Rumiana hesitated. They wanted her to help traffic children out of Bulgaria. For what purpose, she could only guess. But she knew Bulgarians hated the Roma, and many of the kids in Bulgaria's orphanages ended up on the streets of Sofia or Plovdiv anyway. The streets of Rome or Barcelona had to be better; everything was better in Western Europe.

Still, she shook her head. "I've never done anything like this before."

Arber looked at his watch. "I'll settle your debt with Krassen immediately if you agree to work with us."

"For how long?"

"Temporarily," Arber said. "But no more than a year."

Within the week, Arber bought Rumiana a Fiat Punto and paid to have three elegant suits tailored in dark blue, pink, and gray. He bought her black shoes to match the sleek Italian handbag he pulled out of the trunk of his Mercedes Kompressor. He gave her two envelopes.

"The first one is for you, to cover your expenses. Hotels, gas, food, whatever you need. Manicure your nails and keep your hair conservative. You must make a good impression."

Rumiana nodded.

"The second envelope is for the director of the orphanage. Here is your first assignment. Call this phone number, and you will get the exact instructions."

Rumiana almost bungled the first job. Her nerves failed when the director asked to see her fake lichna carta, but otherwise the orphanage director seemed delighted to get rid of the defiant twelve-year-old girl, and the girl seemed overjoyed to be getting away from the orphanage. Rumiana bought the girl ten ice creams between Sliven and Sandanski. Every time they passed a gas station the girl begged for another flavor.

On her second job, she secured the release of an autistic seven-year-old boy within an hour of her arrival. The boy eyed Rumiana, perhaps thinking that she looked nothing like a relative, but he, too, seemed thrilled to escape the orphanage. He said little to her on the eight-hour drive to Sandanski, and only asked for a few Mura chocolate bars when they stopped for gas in Plovdiv. Next, she "liberated" a sickly ten-year-old boy named Assen, a thirteen-year-old deaf boy named Ivan, and an eleven-year-old girl with a cleft lip. In all three cases, the orphanage directors almost shoved them into Rumiana's car.

For each job, Arber had given her the name of the child, its age, and a plausible story about how Rumiana was related to it. Once she had custody of the child, she drove directly to Sandanski, staying in a different hotel and meeting in a different restaurant. She always ensured the children bathed and used her own money to pay for haircuts and new clothing before she presented them to the uncles. Rumiana only encountered a problem near Stara Zagora when she walked into the director's office and noticed portraits of Vladimir Lenin and Todor Zhivkov on the walls. Arber had warned Rumiana to watch for pictures of the former communist dictator.

"Those old communists cling to outmoded ideas," Arber said.

Rumiana did everything as scripted, but the director refused to surrender the child, believing that life in the orphanage was better than life among the "lazy and corrupting influence" of Roma families. She nearly chased Rumiana out of her office.

Rumiana called Arber to report her failure, fearing his reaction.

"That's my fault," he said. "We should have done a better job of choosing the child. Keep the director's documents for yourself. I'll arrange another job right away."

"Can you put the money toward my debt? I want to be done with this," Rumiana said.

"Don't worry," Arber said. "Only a few more."

Rumiana wanted to refuse the money, but her family had so many bills.

AFTER DELIVERING PESHO, Arber sent Rumiana to southeastern Bulgaria for a child who chatted with Rumiana all the way from Kurdjali to Sandanski. She was thirteen years old and spoke in rapid Bulgarian like any ordinary teenager.

"My parents were killed in a car crash last year," Elza told Rumiana. "I told the director that one of my relatives would come for me soon. I knew they wouldn't just leave me there."

"You were raised by your parents?" Rumiana said.

"Uh-huh. And I went to school and had friends. Real friends, not like the dummies in the orphanage. My best friend is Aisha, and we both like a boy named Mehdi." Elza studied Rumiana. "How are we related again?"

"I'm a distant cousin of your father," Rumiana said, keeping her eyes on the road. The director had let Elza go with no hesitation, even before Rumiana offered her the envelope with the "documents."

"I like Aziz," Elza said. "He's my favorite singer, and Desislava, too. Do you like Aziz?"

"Some songs," Rumiana said. "I don't listen to much music."

"Oh, I love music," Elza said. "I can play the guitar and the piccolo, and I can sing and dance. I'm a very good dancer."

Rumiana fidgeted. "Would you like to listen to the radio? You could find a station you like."

Elza smiled and dove at the radio controls. Rumiana felt relieved when the girl found a pop-folk station and began to sing along. Elza knew the lyrics to each song, and her voice was rich and melodious.

As Rumiana listened to the child harmonizing with the radio, guilt produced nausea mixed with fear. I have no choice, Rumiana told herself. I have no other way to pay. If it wasn't me, they would just find someone else. They always manage to find someone else.

When they met Arber in Sandanski, he seemed especially pleased with Elza, pinching her lightly on the cheek.

"I didn't even use the documents," Rumiana said.

"Good, keep them for yourself," he said. "You should relax for the next month or so. We need to find some more places for the children before we relocate anymore."

"I don't want the money. I want my debts paid."

"You agreed to four more."

"But . . ."

"It doesn't matter. Everything will be paid soon. Just wait for the next job."

Before Rumiana drove back to Rousse, she returned to her hotel and took a second shower, letting the hot water flow over her body for twenty minutes, staring at the transparent whirlpools as they slipped down the drain. The road to Rousse was long, and Rumiana would spend the next seven hours in her own company. She didn't want to feel dirty.

As soon as she got home, Rumiana returned to work in the bakery, waking up at 4:00 AM with her aunt to start the banitsa. Rumiana's mother never recovered from the death of her husband and spent her days in the shared flat watching Turkish and Colombian soap operas dubbed into Bulgarian. She smoked three packs of Victory cigarettes a day, and Rumiana came home each evening to heaping ashtrays full of yellowed butts. Her uncle's arm healed, but her aunt remained fearful.

"Things okay with you?" Rumiana's uncle said.

"Yes," Rumiana said. "Fine."

Her uncle examined her clothes and seemed satisfied that she wasn't showing too much skin. He touched his arm. "No trouble?"

"No, Uncle. Everything's fine."

"I want you to take care of yourself."

Rumiana nodded and rested her gaze on a photo of her father by the television set.

Rumiana's uncle lingered in the doorway watching her. "I'm sorry."

"For what?"

"I'm sorry I can't," her uncle said, refusing to meet her eyes. "I can't help you. Like I should."

After twenty-six days, Arber called Rumiana, arranged the delivery of an envelope, and sent her back to the orphanage where she'd freed the cleft-lipped girl, the first time she returned to the same place twice. Rumiana drove to Botevgrad and presented herself as the aunt of a girl named Svetozara. The orphanage director recognized Rumiana immediately and gestured toward a pretty child no older than six.

"I think there must be a mistake," Rumiana said. "My niece is at least twelve."

"No, this is the one they want. I know about the situation," the director said, staring at Rumiana's sleek suit and the fake gold wedding ring.

Rumiana inhaled. "I'm afraid I don't understand. My late sister said her child was born over ten years ago."

The director smiled. "You don't have to pretend. I know very well what's happening here, and I know the younger ones are worth more. I expect that you will have more documents for me than usual."

Rumiana flinched at the word "documents." She reached into her handbag and grasped the envelope Arber prepared for this job. It felt thicker.

"Perhaps I'm mistaken," Rumiana said. "But I am quite sure that my half-sister said her daughter was older than this one."

The director shook her head. "No, this is the one they want."

The director stood and walked to the child seated with her arms crossed tightly over a one-eyed stuffed bear. She wore a threadbare dress, but had a head of shining brown hair. The director grabbed the child's arm from under the bear, and showed Rumiana a stump.

"You see what her parents did? I've been working here for fifteen years, and I can't count how many of those filthy Gypsy children come to us after they've had an 'accident.' Missing arms and missing legs. Makes them better for begging." The director sneered. "They should sterilize every last one of you."

Rumiana heard the gravelly hatred in the director's voice and handed over the envelope. "I think these documents should suffice."

The director took the envelope and inspected its contents. "I know they get more for the young ones. Especially the girls."

"The child has a better chance of finding parents who will love her in the West," Rumiana said.

The director laughed. "Is that what they told you?"

Rumiana swallowed.

"It won't be parents who are loving her in the West," the director said, slipping the envelope into her desk drawer.

Rumiana drove toward the Greek-Bulgarian border with a tempest tossing around her insides.

"Will you be my mommy now?" Svetozara said in a quiet voice.

Rumiana studied the child tucked into the passenger seat, hiding her half arm under the stuffed bear. "No, sweetie. We're going to find you a better mommy in Italy or Spain."

"Will she be as beautiful as you are?"

Rumiana blinked back a tear. "Much more beautiful."

The child soon fell asleep, sucking her one remaining thumb. Rumiana tried not to stare, but her eyes kept drifting right. She thought of her friend Dimi and the pieces of her once beautiful body scattered across the sidewalk, and swore she would never have children in Bulgaria.

Rumiana stopped to take a late lunch at the Happy restaurant along the motorway. The girl devoured a hamburger and a plate of fries sprinkled with feta cheese. She squealed when Rumiana ordered an ice cream sundae.

"Very delicious," the girl said.

"You've never had ice cream before?"

The child shook her head.

When they arrived in Sandanski, Rumiana checked into a new hotel and gave the girl a bath. Svetozara giggled and played with the shampoo bubbles. Rumiana bought a new dress and a new stuffed bear, but Svetozara refused to surrender her old one. When they walked through the center of town, Svetozara reached up and held Rumiana's hand.

Rumiana found the appointed restaurant and sat down to wait for the uncles. The girl ordered four different desserts without having any supper. Arber came with his usual colleague and a new man who wore a dark blue business suit. He spoke neither Bulgarian nor Greek.

Arber spoke softly to Svetozara and gave her a new Barbie doll in a box. Svetozara squealed with pleasure as she opened it. The child barely noticed when Rumiana took her leave and Arber followed her.

"Who's he?" Rumiana said. "I've never seen him before."

"An Albanian associate of mine," Arber said. "We require his assistance in this case."

Rumiana trembled. "You'll find her a good family?"

Arber studied Rumiana, and placed a hand on her shoulder. "I promise she won't end up on the streets."

"Are you sure?" Rumiana said, glancing back at the girl. "She's so young."

Arber gave Rumiana a large envelope. "This was a difficult job, and you did well. I'm thinking that we should amend our agreement. After this, we only need one more."

"Only one?"

"Only one, and your debts are forgiven."

"You're sure?"

"Absolutely."

Rumiana scratched the nape of her neck. "I don't want to go back to that place."

"This was a special case. It won't happen again."

"Okay," Rumiana said, rubbing the space between her eyebrows. "Only one more. You're sure?"

"You have my word. You'll do the final job next week."

Rumiana left Sandanski and returned to Rousse that evening. In the large envelope she found two smaller envelopes: one marked "documents" and one marked "Rumiana." She had two thousand levs in cash, more than the debt she stilled owed Arber. Or at least she thought so; the compound interest proved impossible to keep track of.

A week passed and she heard nothing. After another week, Arber never called. Rumiana waited a month before she dared to ring Arber on the mobile number he provided her. She got an error message saying the number didn't exist. Rumiana let three days go by and called once more. The same message repeated. Rumiana waited another week before surmising that Arber might be gone. Maybe dead? She had spent a little more than half of her own money, but still had the envelope full of documents.

On a Tuesday morning, Rumiana's aunt asked her to deliver a tray of banitsa to a kiosk at the railway station. Rumiana took the same route she did the morning they found Dimi's body. Someone had scrubbed the pavement, but Rumiana still recalled the blood. She had arrived on the scene just moments after the police. She hurried passed her old secondary school, shuddering with the memory. The mess of severed flesh would haunt her forever.

At the railway station, Rumiana delivered the pastries and stopped at a kiosk to buy her uncle a newspaper. On the front page, a headline caught her attention: "Organ Traffic Ring 'Used Bulgarian Kids.'" She read:

Bulgarian children have been used as part of an international illegal ring for smuggling organs.

According to Greek media, the international network for trade with child organs spans over Greece, Italy and Albania. However, Bulgarian kids might have also become a target of the smugglers, a Thessaloniki lawyer said.

The abhorrent scheme was reportedly described in a secret Greek report from Tirana. It is said to single out names of doctors, diplomats, even former ministers of Greece, Italy and Albania.

The center of the "organ" mafia was believed to be in Yannitsa, northern Greece, where rich Greeks and Italians used to pay tens of thousands euro for the child organs.

Reports suggest that the organs' transfer across border was made possible in the diplomatic luggage, as it is exempt from customs checking. Albanian Prosecutors' Office denies Greek press accusations of Albanian clinics involved in human organs trafficking abroad.[1]

Rumiana stumbled away from the kiosk and collapsed on a bench. Her insides churned; she gagged and swallowed. She pressed her hand to her forehead. The autistic child, the deaf boy, and the girl with the cleft lip: how many were there? Pesho, and Elza, and little Svetozara. "I guarantee she will not end up on the streets," Arber had told her. Rumiana felt a small fissure opening between her stomach and her lungs, filling her chest with bile.

Rumiana rushed to the toilet, guts contracting with the violent need to vomit. She stood bent over the bowl until she felt her stomach empty. She leaned against the wall of the stall, staring at the floor. She left only after someone tapped on the door.

Dazed, Rumiana returned to the kiosk to buy the paper and read the article a second time, sitting alone amid the bustle of the station. The article mentioned a secret report and the Greek media and Albanian clinics. It said nothing about Bulgarian orphanages, said nothing about where the children came from.

Rumiana pressed her face into her hands and thought about Arber. Had Arber been arrested? She had called his number twice. The directors knew her face. She could go to the police, but if she betrayed men like Arber, they might kill her family. They were capable of anything.

Panicked, she ran to the ticket counter. "When is the next coach to Bucharest?"

"About an hour from platform five."

"Is there space available?"

"Yes."

"One ticket please."

"One way or return?"

"One way."

Only a bridge over the Danube separated Romania from Rousse, and Rumiana decided she needed to leave the country. She didn't want to go to prison, even if she deserved to.

Rumiana jumped in a taxi and returned to her family's apartment. She packed her three suits, her black shoes, and her handbag. She grabbed her passport and what remained of Arber's money. She left her car keys and five hundred levs stuffed in the butter cookie tin where her uncle kept his savings. She wrote a short note: "The debt is paid, but I have to leave Bulgaria. If anyone comes looking for me, say I've gone to the West. I'm sorry." Her aunt and mother had grown accustomed to her frequent absences, so she left without a farewell. She shut the door to their collective apartment as her mother half-dozed in front of the old cathode ray tube television, watched over by the photograph of Rumiana's father. Rumiana had about nine hundred levs. If that wasn't enough, she would use her passport as collateral. The Romanians must have employment agencies, too.

Rumiana hailed a cab back to the central station and rushed out toward the platform, keeping her face hidden.

A teenage girl shoved a hand under Rumiana's chin, imploring in Romani.

"I'm not a Gypsy," Rumiana said, waving the young woman out of her way.

The Roma girl switched to Bulgarian. "Please, auntie. Please help me, auntie. I beg you. I'm hungry and my baby needs milk." Rumiana looked up, and guessed the girl was no more than sixteen. She used the generic endearment "auntie" to show respect for Rumiana's twenty-six years.

"I'm in a hurry," Rumiana said.

The girl thrust a swaddled child forward toward Rumiana. The baby slept while the teenager implored, "Please, auntie, please, a few stotinki, please. Just some stotinki. Anything can help."

Rumiana stopped, transfixed. Eyes closed, dark lashes resting on the smooth skin of its cheeks, the baby breathed through parted lips.

"A few stotinki, please. Some food, please. I beg you. Please, auntie."

Without thinking, Rumiana brought out her wallet, and removed a fifty-lev note.

The girl's eyes widened. She clutched her infant to her chest.

Rumiana exhaled and stared down, trying not to look at the girl or the baby. She held out the banknote and felt the Roma girl take it from her hand.

"For the child," Rumiana said. "For the child."

4. Belgrade, 2015

(FICTION)

"It's what your father would have wanted, Jovan."

"I don't care. I'll not see him buried under a star."

"We have to respect his wishes," Adriana said, brushing a piece of lint from her black dress and studying her son. He was a large, strong man now, but Adriana still saw the frail baby boy she brought home from the hospital in 1973.

"He was born a Serbian Orthodox Christian," Jovan said. "He should be buried under a cross."

"But he chose to be a communist. All of his comrades are buried under stars."

"Why should we immortalize his membership in that stupid party?"

Adriana sighed. Dragan, her husband of fifty-two years, was gone, and she had no desire to fill the yawning chasm in her life with bickering about headstones. "The party was your father's life," she said. "Your grandparents were peasants, and your father owed his education and his entire career to the party. He was grateful to be born under the red star."

Jovan huffed. "He doesn't need to spend eternity under one."

Jovan leaned his elbows onto his parents' kitchen table, gazing at the stool where his father used to sit: reading his newspapers, sorting the post, or

FIGURE 4.1. Downtown Belgrade in June 2015.

scribbling thoughts into his notebooks, ideas on how to improve that country now fractured in pieces. At this same table, Jovan had read his conscription notice six months after the Bosnian War began.

"Perhaps you don't understand what the star means," Adriana said, fixing her eyes on her son's tired face. The first time she saw him in that uniform, she had cried. All mothers hate war, but Adriana had only one child, and she prayed that God would keep him safe.

"It means he was ashamed to be a Serb," Jovan said, avoiding his mother's gaze.

In the hills around Sarajevo, Jovan had watched his best friend fall—limbs blown off by a stray mortar shell. So many good Serbian boys cut down by Croats and Bosnians, so many orphaned Kalashnikovs. Jovan survived by shooting first and shooting fast, frightened or enraged or numb, always wondering why. In a bombed cathedral in Banja Luka, Jovan found a voice that soothed, that forgave and loved, and he surrendered to faith. "Mysterious ways" became a reasonable explanation for ethnic cleansing.

"No, Jovan. It means he was proud to be a Yugoslav," Adriana said, recalling her husband's fury at the stupidity of a war between people who shared a country for forty years.

After the Dayton Accords ended the hostilities, Jovan returned home. Adriana made sure he ate enough meat, kept his clothes clean and pressed, and

FIGURE 4.2. A tombstone for a communist with a star instead of a religious symbol.

bought him the soccer magazines he'd read as a teenager, but Jovan was different. She convinced him to study at the University of Belgrade until NATO forces bombed their city in 1999. While Jovan sang Serbian Orthodox hymns in the local cathedral, Dragan organized work brigades to clear the rubble, directing itinerant parties of pensioners with brooms and dustpans to tidy the blasted pavements. In those years, Adriana accompanied her son to light candles in the neighborhood church and marched with her husband at political rallies, suffering in silence as she watched the two men in her life grow apart.

She reached her hand across the table. "I know it's hard for you to understand, but he'd never agree to be buried under a cross. You can't do this to him."

Jovan stared at his mother's outstretched hand, considering the deep lines and brown spots on the thin, almost translucent skin. "But I'm a Christian, and he was a Christian, too. I love him, and want him to be remembered for what he was."

Adriana sighed. "Your father was an atheist, Jovan. He didn't believe in the soul."

Jovan clenched his teeth, remembering his father's stubborn, mocking eyes. "Yes, he was an atheist, so why should he care? This is important for us, for my family. He'll never know one way or the other."

"I'll know." Adriana said, looking at the empty stool. She was an Orthodox

FIGURE 4.3. A husband and wife buried together under a star.

Christian like her son, and she believed that the spirits of the departed lingered for forty days after the death of the body. Dragan was still with them.

Adriana shook her head. "I couldn't live with myself if we went against his wishes."

Jovan pounded his fist on the table. "But you'll be dead soon, too. And I'm the one who'll have to go to the grave and see that star for the rest of my life."

Adriana inhaled, eyes wide.

Jovan closed his eyes and drooped his head. He heard the hum of the refrigerator and the creaking footsteps of the upstairs neighbor. The clock ticked.

"Yes," Adriana said, her voice low. "I will be dead soon."

"I'm sorry, I didn't mean to . . ."

"Your father never wanted to save his soul," Adriana said. "He wanted to leave this world a better place than he found it. He wasn't waiting for some reward in the next life. That's what it meant to him to be buried under a star."

Adriana paused, noticing new wrinkles around her son's mouth. "I think you'll have to bury me under a star, too."

Jovan slapped his hands to his temples. "Never."

"Yes. You will bury me under a star."

Jovan pushed himself away from the table. "Please don't say that."

Adriana looked at her hands. "It is my last wish. You cannot refuse."

"But, Mama, you weren't even a communist!"

Adriana stood, smoothing the wrinkles from her dress, lifting her chin, and speaking to the empty space above the vacant stool. "His fight was always my fight, even when I didn't want it to be."

"Mother, please . . ."

Adriana turned to her grown son, touching her finger to the small gold cross she wore on the chain around her neck. She spoke loudly enough so the spirit would hear her. "Your father will be buried under a star, son. And you will bury me next to him, under my own star. Then the light from our two stars can shine on each other in the next world. Just like they did in this one."

PART II

Reuniting the Divided

5. #Mauerfall25

Give the Germans any excuse to block traffic and drink on the streets, and they will organize a festival. Most Americans know about Oktoberfest in Munich, but the German calendar brims with opportunities for outdoor inebriation. For the year and a half that I lived in Waldkirch and Jena, not a month went by when the local authorities didn't block traffic in the center of town to create a weekend pedestrian zone. Whether it's Christmas markets, Carnival, or local city fairs, people flock like pigeons to breadcrumbs when there is beer and bratwurst on the boulevard.

And so it was that on November 8, 2014, I flew from Prague to Frankfurt and boarded an Intercity Express bullet train to Berlin, a city preparing to mark the twenty-fifth anniversary of the fall of the Wall that once divided it.[1]

FOR THIS SPECIAL EVENT, the city's charismatic mayor and a variety of corporate sponsors transformed Germany's capital into a spectacle of lights, kitsch, and nationalist sentimentality, promising a jubilant *Bürgerfest*. Even as Russian separatists increased violent attacks in nearby Ukraine, and an eighty-three-year-old Mikhail Gorbachev warned of a looming new cold war,

FIGURE 5.1.
A poster for
the festival to
celebrate the
twenty-fifth
anniversary of
the Mauerfall.

tens of thousands of Germans and international tourists flooded the streets of the Mitte district to enjoy the public party planned to commemorate the historic Mauerfall (literally: Wall fall).

Two and a half decades earlier, I had watched the news of the opening of the Wall in a coach station in Barcelona. But back in 1989, I was a poor nineteen-year-old on my way to London to find work for the winter.[2] Although I made it to Berlin just six months later, I always regretted not traveling there in those first days of mid-November when the whole world seemed to change overnight. I'd only been a bus ride away. So in 2014, I was determined to be on the streets beneath the Brandenburg Gate to experience the festivities firsthand. Armed with my Canon 70D and two zoom lenses, I took

FIGURE 5.2. The Lichtgrenze in front of the Reichstag.

a humble room in the Motel One near the Hauptbahnhof and set out to document the event in pictures and video.

The weather cooperated—November 9 was a cool but clear autumn day. I set my alarm to wake up before dawn, and together with a swarm of other amateur and professional photographers snapped images of the amazing Lichtgrenze (light border) erected throughout the city.[3] For fifteen kilometers, a single line of large, illuminated white balloons recalled the original path of the Berlin Wall, what the Germans call "die Mauer," which stood for twenty-eight years between 1961 and 1989. Built by the East German regime to prevent the defection of its citizens to the West, the Wall became an iconic symbol of the Cold War conflict that defined the geopolitical landscape of the second half of the twentieth century.

In those early morning hours, the illuminated balloons reflected in the calm waters of the Spree River behind the Reichstag. Their muted glow felt ghostly in the darkness, creating the phantom presence of the structure amputated from the heart of the city. I followed the Lichtgrenze toward the Brandenburg Gate, watching the sky turn from dark to light purple and then to salmon and pink. Crews of workmen tested the artificial lights on the main stage where a succession of A-list performers would entertain the revelers, including the German-pop darling Clueso and the veteran English rocker Peter Gabriel.

According to the program, the culmination of the Bürgerfest would be a "Ballonaktion." At the appointed hour a handful of dignitaries would mount the main stage, including Gorbachev and Lech Wałęsa of Poland, while Daniel Barenboim conducted the Staatskapelle Berlin and the State Opera Chorus in a glorious performance of the fourth movement of Beethoven's Ninth Symphony. One by one, Berliners would release the balloons (all biodegradable, we were assured) into the skies above their now united city, sending messages of congratulation and hope up toward the heavens.

At dawn on Sunday, November 9, however, only the photographers, the workmen, and the occasional jogger populated the streets. I made my way back to the hotel to grab a few extra hours of sleep before the festivities commenced. But I first downloaded my photos and edited a short video that I posted to Tumblr and YouTube using the hashtags suggested by the event's organizers: #Mauerfall25, #FalloftheWall25, and #FOTW25.[4] My photos would be online before America woke up. Not that many would care; most of my Tumblr followers were born after 1989.

So why did I, a Puerto Rican–Persian American without a drop of German heritage, go through so much effort to attend this event? Other than the obvious allures of street festivals and public drinking, I wanted to experience this commemoration because I believed that many things wrong with Europe in 2014 could be traced back to the early 1990s and the way the Western countries mishandled the end of the Cold War. The last twenty-five years of world history—the triumph of unfettered free market capitalism, the American obsession with democracy promotion and regime change, as well as the steady growth of worldwide wealth inequality—resulted from the greedy and self-aggrandizing stance of Western political and economic elites after the collapse of communism. From the conflict in Ukraine to the Syrian civil war, from the Great Recession to the Eurozone crisis, many of the seeds of our current discontents were planted in the early 1990s and watered with years of arrogance, stubbornness, and neglect.[5] Because democracy and capitalism won, Western leaders rushed headlong into the future, championing the moral superiority of private property and free markets as they scrambled among themselves for economic and political dominance over the former Warsaw Pact countries. They ignored the social costs of their policies, and the deep, simmering resentments they produced among the ordinary people whose lives were upended in the name of freedom. By 2014, public faith in the desirability of liberal democracy was waning. Frustrated electorates began searching for new leaders hoping to usurp the power of established political parties and economic elites.

FIGURE 5.3. The Lichtgrenze Fan Shop.

By 11:00 AM, the streets already heaved with revelers. Police cordoned off much of the center of Berlin, from the Brandenburg Gate to Checkpoint Charlie. I couldn't walk fifty meters without stumbling into another kiosk selling draft pilsner, grilled sausages, or fried potatoes. Portable toilets proliferated around the main stage on Elbertstraße and all the way down the long boulevard of Straße des 17 Juni to the Sieggesäule, the triumphal column topped by Berlin's famous winged angel, Goldelese. People milled around the main stage as a young German folksinger encouraged them to like his Facebook page and tweet his photo to #Mauerfall25. A souvenir stand across the stage sold hats, T-shirts, bags, buttons, and little illuminated toy balls commemorating the Lichtgrenze and the twenty-fifth anniversary celebration. I bought a book called *Mauergeschichten* (Wall stories), containing information in German and English about the history of the Wall as well as a list of the private-sector sponsors of the Lichtgrenze, including Facebook, Air Berlin, Duracell, and Finanzgruppe. People crowded into the shop, so I ducked out and wandered down Elbertstraße in the direction of Potsdamer Platz.

On my left I passed the haunting Holocaust memorial. Somber rows of smooth concrete blocks reminded me that November 9 was also the anniversary of Kristallnacht, the massive and coordinated pogrom against Third Reich Jews in 1938. Indeed, Germans officially mark their reunification on October 3 rather than November 9 because politicians don't want Reuni-

FIGURE 5.4. Berliners and tourists stroll along the Lichtgrenze.

fication Day to compete with the memory of Kristallnacht. But no one on the streets in 2014 seemed to mind this unfortunate coincidence. Families strolled by the Holocaust memorial without a second glance, rushing off to see the remaining portions of the Berlin Wall still standing at various points around the city.

More beer and bratwurst stands crowded the streets around Potsdamer Platz. Large video screens showed films about the history of the Wall, emphasizing the brutal nature of the East German regime and those who lost their lives trying to escape. I also watched video footage of the October 1989 protests in Leipzig where tens of thousands of GDR citizens took to the streets to tell their leaders, "Wir sind das Volk!" Before 1989, the Berlin Wall had bisected Potsdamer Platz; most of the buildings there had been bombed during World War II, and the area was largely left in ruins. The Potsdamer Platz U-bahn station remained closed for four decades, and the S-bahn became one of Berlin's famous ghost stations through which West Berlin trains passed but never stopped. After German reunification, Potsdamer Platz became the site of major redevelopment and home to one of Berlin's massive new shopping malls.

Just one day before, at an official ceremony to commemorate the Mauerfall, Mikhail Gorbachev, the last Soviet premier, accused the West of giving in to "triumphalism" after the end of the Cold War.[6] He would know. Whether he intended to or not, Gorbachev presided over the peaceful dissolution of the Eastern Bloc. By 1989, the centrally planned economies of Eastern Europe were stagnant, and citizens from Gdansk to Plovdiv demanded greater liberties. Gorbachev initiated the twin policies of glasnost (openness) and perestroika (economic restructuring) to try to reform the communist world from within. But Gorbachev oversaw only limited reforms before the whole state socialist project and seventy years of Soviet history came crashing down around him.[7]

Gorbachev's 2014 accusation of triumphalism derived from his outrage over the American response to hostilities in Ukraine. After the Russian government's annexation of Crimea, the U.S. State Department slapped sanctions on individual Russians and hoped to arm pro-Ukrainian activists, a move that threatened to escalate the conflict and destabilize Europe. Gorbachev linked the causes of the Ukrainian mess to American duplicity in the negotiations over the reunification of Germany back in 1990. Gorbachev insisted that U.S. politicians had agreed not to expand the North Atlantic Treaty Alliance (NATO) eastward if the Soviet Union allowed East Germany (an original signatory to the 1955 Warsaw mutual defense treaty) to become a NATO member once it reunified with West Germany.[8]

Indeed, Gorbachev had been a long-standing critic of NATO's eastward expansion, a sentiment echoed by Russian president Vladimir Putin in 2014. Gorbachev believed that the United States violated the spirit of the 1990 negotiations. At the time, he insisted that no NATO troops or weapons of mass destruction would be stationed on the territory of the former GDR, conditions that the Americans accepted. Of course, no one imagined that the Soviet Union would cease to exist by the end of 1991 or that the Warsaw Pact would evaporate, so there was no explicit discussion of NATO expansion into Eastern Europe. But as NATO grew to include Poland, Hungary, the Czech Republic, Bulgaria, Romania, Slovakia, Slovenia, Albania, Croatia, and even the former Soviet republics of Estonia, Latvia, and Lithuania, Gorbachev insisted that the Americans sought to isolate Russia in contravention to the cooperative nature with which they had agreed to the reunification of Germany. The creation of permanent American military bases in Eastern Europe angered the Russians even further. For their part, American politicians and diplomats deny that they gave any such assurances.[9] Nothing was ever put down in writing, they claim, and so they have violated no agreements. In a classic case of "he said, he said," the facts of the negotiations prove difficult to establish, although a 2009 investigation by the German national news magazine, *Der Spiegel*, found that Russian grievances were justified.[10]

When Ukraine declared its independence from the Soviet Union in 1991, it had a large ethnic Russian population, which dominated certain regions of the country, particularly along its long land border with Russia. During the first two post-Soviet decades, Ukrainian politicians sent various signals about the possibility of NATO membership, but it was only after the Euromaidan protests of 2013–2014 that a new pro-Western government tried to forge closer ties with the European Union and distance itself from Russia. In March 2014, Russia annexed the Ukrainian territory of Crimea after a local referendum, and pro-Russian separatists (with Russian support) wreaked political chaos in eastern Ukraine. By November 9, only seven months had passed since the Crimean referendum. Anti-Russian sentiment had reached a fever pitch when Gorbachev attended the Mauerfall commemoration, and it was in this context that he lashed out about Western triumphalism.

I thought about Gorbachev and his warning of a new cold war as I escaped the orgy of consumption on Potsdamer Platz and walked down to see the Hansa Tonstudio at Köthener Straße 38. Here the Irish rock band U2 recorded their album *Achtung Baby* in 1990 and 1991, just as the two Berlins were being reunited. Between 1974 and 1989, the studio, also called "Hansa by the Wall," sat no more than thirty meters from die Mauer, in the shadow of an East German watchtower. British rocker David Bowie recorded his famous *Berlin Trilogy* here, including the title track of his 1977 *"Heroes"* album, one of the few songs about the Wall to become a global hit. In a November 1977 interview, Bowie explained that "'Heroes'" was an ironic song about two West Berliners trying to mask the guilt of an illicit affair by meeting on a bench below Eastern German border guards, making a political statement out of their otherwise clandestine passion.[11]

> I can remember, standing by the Wall
> And the guns, shot above our heads
> And we kissed, as though nothing could fall
> And the shame, was on the other side
> Oh we can beat them, forever and ever
> Then we can be heroes, just for one day.

The key thing about Bowie's "Heroes" is that the title of both the album and the song always appear in quotes. He never intended to use the word "heroes" literally, but instead wanted to interrogate the whole concept of heroism, a subtlety lost on many Germans who consider "Heroes" a protest song against the Wall. From the front of Hansa Studio I could see the balloon Lichtgrenze, but in the no man's land that had once separated the studio from the Wall, there stood a row of massive red brick buildings filled with private offices and flats for those who could afford to purchase real estate in what was now the center of Berlin, the restored capital of reunified Germany.

I strolled back to Potsdamer Platz where tourists posed for photos in front of a large, graffiti-covered panel of the old Wall, and I heard a young mother explaining to her child, "This is part of the wall that used to divide Berlin. One side colorful, the other gray. That's how Berlin used to be. One side colorful, one side gray."

"Why?"

"Berlin was in two countries back then, divided by a big wall."

The child stared at his mother. "Why?"

"Bad people."

"What kind of bad people?"

"Communists," said the mother, huffing.

The boy paused, staring up at the wall. "What's a communist?"

The mother sighed. "A bad person. Do you want French fries?"

My legs started to tire, so I took some photos of people taking photos, and sat down to watch the film clips and peruse the pages of my Lichtgrenze program. In the introduction, I read, "When East Berliners forced the opening of the Berlin Wall in the autumn of 1989, the event marked the dawn of a new era. . . . The fall of the Berlin Wall is an enduring, global symbol of hope for a more peaceful world and for overcoming injustice and dictatorships."[12]

Ah yes, overcoming injustice and dictatorships, I thought. After decades of supporting anticommunist military brutes in Asia, Africa, and Latin America, the end of the Cold War ushered in a newfound American zeal for democratic governance. The United States had become very adept at overcoming injustice and toppling dictatorships, starting of course with the war in Afghanistan to unseat the Taliban and followed shortly thereafter by the Iraq War to depose Saddam Hussein, whose stockpile of weapons of mass destruction was curiously never found by occupying U.S. forces. Then the Americans supported the toppling of leaders in Tunisia, Egypt, Libya, and Yemen, and encouraged civil unrest in Syria, unrest that eventually became a brutal civil war. By November 2014, refugees and migrants from these countries poured into Europe, fleeing the ongoing political and economic turmoil of their homelands.

In almost every Arab country where liberal democracy replaced dictatorship, various extremists groups rose to power, sparking internal conflicts and political chaos. Perhaps the best known in 2014 was what the Americans called Islamic State or ISIS, a lovely gaggle of militants keen on restoring the

FIGURE 5.5.
A family in
front of a
remnant of the
Berlin Wall.

caliphate, blowing up antiquities, and beheading journalists. The promise of human rights and popular sovereignty failed to secure peaceful transitions. The Berlin Wall may have fallen, but twenty-five years later new walls and fences were being erected around the borders of Europe to keep out the dislocated victims of the West's failed democratization efforts across the Middle East and North Africa. By 2014, "democracy" was becoming a dirty word, an ideal used to justify American military interventions and the promotion of U.S. economic interests abroad.

Once again, the contours of current political crises could be linked back to the triumphalism and unlearned lessons of 1989. The uncritical belief in the universal applicability of liberal democracy linked to free market economics provides one example. Too often Western politicians promoted democracy for democracy's sake because it considered the democratization of Eastern Europe after 1989 an unqualified success. They failed to acknowledge the psychological costs of political and economic transitions, even if those transitions were from unsavory dictatorships. The ideological insistence on the superiority of multiparty elections and liberalized economies—despite the complications of local context and the destabilizing effects of rapid change— ignores the fact that the sudden imposition of democracy and free markets can produce more internal conflict, violence, and oppression than the authoritarian regimes democracy seeks to replace.

The jubilation on the streets around me masked the ongoing conflicts between East and West over the terms of the reunification. Although most former East Germans considered themselves economically better off in 2014 than before 1989, there existed much bitterness about the handling of the reunification process, with one East German politician likening reunification to the Nazi German annexation of Austria in March 1938 (the Anschluss). Even within the pages of the official Lichtgrenze program, Seigbert Schefke, a journalist and cameraman who documented protest movements in September and October 1989, admitted, "At those initial demonstrations people called for a better socialism, a better GDR," a sentiment still echoed by many disgruntled former GDR citizens in 2014.[13] Indeed, few East Germans imagined accepting the West German constitution wholesale, or that forty years of their history would be wiped out in eleven months.[14]

The Wall fell in November 1989, and the GDR had its first free elections in March 1990, which functioned as a plebiscite on German reunification rather than an exercise in choosing new leaders for a country that might soon cease to exist.[15] The Christian Democratic Union won a clear mandate and moved forward at lightning speed. I was in the GDR when the East adopted West German currency on July 1, 1990. Because tourists with East Marks weren't allowed to exchange money for West Marks, I spent the night of June 30 buying drinks for jubilant German strangers in a bar on Alexanderplatz. When we all woke up the next day to nurse our hangovers, the leadership of the Federal Republic of Germany and GDR began official reunification negotiations. At this point, the Western powers and the Soviet leadership debated the status of the GDR in NATO, and, if we believe Gorbachev and the journalists at *Der Spiegel*, the Russians walked away thinking that NATO would expand no further east. The two Germanies signed the official reunification treaty on July 31, with an effective date of October 3, 1990, after which the maps of central Europe would have to be redrawn.

As early as July 1, 1990, however, the first inklings of the unequal terms of reunification revealed themselves. According to the fine print, East Germans could exchange their first four thousand Ostmarks worth of savings for western Deutsche Marks at a one-to-one ratio. But after these first four thousand, the exchange rate reduced to two-to-one. This halved the savings of those frugal enough to have money socked away for the future, primarily the middle aged and elderly who had worked most of their lives under the old system, and who would have the most difficulties adjusting to the new one. In 2015, Lothar de Maizière, the last GDR prime minister, recalled, "I always said there was a 10/10 generation—10 years too long in East Germany to really make a fresh start, and 10 years too young to retire. And that is tragic, because they were the people who for 40 years effectively carried East Germany. And then they were told we don't need you anymore."[16]

East German state-owned industries also required privatization to conform with the free market economy of the West. The reunification treaty transferred GDR assets to an institution called the Treuhand, which organized open auctions. The highest bidders proved to be West German companies keen to expand markets for their own goods in the east. Although many GDR industries teetered on the brink of bankruptcy, some factories were still profitable and employed thousands of GDR workers. But the Treuhand (which unfortunately shared the same name as the institution that handled Nazi-seized Jewish assets in the 1930s) cared little for the welfare of ordinary men and women laboring in East German enterprises. "Overnight, we were bolted onto the toughest economy in the world," said de Maizière. "We were spared the wait, unlike the Poles or Czechs, but it was an unbelievable shock for the East German economy. Unemployment was four times what it was in the West. The East Germans emigrated from their country without having left it."[17]

None of this was acknowledged in the twenty-fifth anniversary celebrations. The program of the Lichtgrenze focused on the crimes of the regime and on the 138 men and women who died at the Wall during its twenty-eight-year existence. The event organizers erected small crosses near the balloon installation to commemorate those who lost their lives at the concrete barrier between East and West.[18] The website of the Berlin Wall Memorial also included as victims the "unknown numbers of people [who] suffered and died from distress and despair in their personal lives as a consequence of the Berlin Wall being built."[19]

But I saw nothing to commemorate the millions of East Germans victimized by the sudden upheavals and dislocations of the reunification process.

In 1998, researchers confirmed increased mortality rates for East Germans in 1989 and 1990, and attributed these excess deaths to the "drastic social, political, and economic changes that took place during the transition from the socialist to the market economy.[20]

The German authors of the study found the rise in deaths from alcoholism, heart and circulatory problems, and suicide causally related to the reunification process, mostly among middle-aged men. Thousands lost their lives prematurely from the "psycho-social stress" associated with the transition, but unlike David Bowie's two West German "heroes" near Hansa Studio, these East Germans made little spectacle of their anxieties, quietly drinking themselves into oblivion. One might say that they "suffered and died from distress and despair in their personal lives as a consequence of the Berlin Wall" falling down.

In 2010, one of the leading German Democratic Socialists, Matthais Platzeck, bemoaned the ill effects of reunification in an interview with Reuters:

> There was an "*Anschluss* mentality" at the unification negotiations. There is a lot that went wrong in those talks. We tried to explain [to West German negotiation partners] that when a society takes on a new form with a small group joining a larger group, it's important to include some elements or symbols from the smaller group for the sake of harmony. That way the smaller group won't feel like they've been overwhelmed and run over. But there was nothing of the smaller group [East Germany] left in united Germany. . . . It was like "*Look, children. We'll take you in, we'll pay for it all, but forget your demands. . . .*"
>
> It would have been easily achievable to save a few symbols, a few structures—there are some aspects of the way East Germany handled medical care that are coming back now as good ideas 20 years after they were discarded, some aspects of education like the 12-year school system or pre-school care from a very young age. All these things were thrown out of the unification talks because of ideological reasons. Just taking over one of these things would have been enough. But there was nothing. The rule was: what's from the west is good what's from the east is bad.
>
> Today, 20 years later, all the surveys in the east show that 50 percent of the people don't feel like they're part of united Germany—in their minds and their hearts. Everyone in the west is baffled by that. They ask: "*Why don't you feel like you're part of one country after all the money we spent for you?*" My answer to them is always: "*Just imagine you're*

FIGURE 5.6. "Yesterday = SED Victims, Today = Merkel Victims."

from a society that completely disappears and there's nothing left." You would also feel to a certain extent homeless. Some people got back on their feet but many never did.[21]

From the video displays I watched on Potsdamer Platz, no one would get the sense that East Germans were anything but grateful. The film clips emphasized the stories of those who once longed for freedom and consumerism. As I watched the happy German family narrative unfold on the big screens, I recalled the writings of East Germans like Daniela Dahn and Jana Hensel, controversial voices speaking on behalf of those citizens who preferred a reformed but still independent GDR back in 1990.[22] As seventy-five-year-old East German Joachim Grosskreutz recalled, "What happened was more a takeover than a reunification. . . . When the wall fell, we had a chance. My expectations were dashed very quickly, and very deeply."[23]

With these contradictions nagging at me, I wandered to Checkpoint Charlie, the old Wall crossing controlled by the United States. There I found a plethora of T-shirts and postcards of a U.S. Army sign warning, "You are now leaving the American Sector" in four languages. I could buy Russian hats, communist badges, and small replicas of the Trabant. Hordes of people crowded around to take snapshots with more Wall remnants, and to watch even more films about the many failures of the GDR. It's not that I questioned the accuracy of the films; I accepted the many detestable aspects of the GDR: the travel restrictions, the consumer shortages, and the ubiquitous presence of the Stasi (the secret police). But the narrative was so one-sided, so single-minded in its message that democracy had solved all problems. It seemed that the only East German lives that mattered were those lost trying to escape through the Wall, the "heroes" of 1989.

The crowds thickened. More people poured onto the streets swilling beer as they strolled past the stylized slow-motion videos of an East German May Day parade. I checked the time on my phone. The main event at the stage under the Brandenburg Gate would not begin for at least another hour or two. I decided to return to my hotel to download some photos and take a rest. I also wanted to read the press coverage and social media posts about the Mauerfall Bürgerfest. Had anyone else questioned the political motivations behind the event? Was I alone in thinking that the projection of the happily reunified Germany ignored the persistence of resentment and anger in the East?

It was thus by accident that I stumbled into the official counterprotest in front of the Reichstag. In a fenced-off area before the imposing structure of the German parliament, a conglomeration of anarchists, communists, democratic socialists, social democrats, feminists, pacifists, and Greens assembled to protest the public commemoration of the triumph of capitalism. Among them milled hundreds of police in full riot gear, with black body armor, Plexiglas shields, and helmets worthy of a moon landing. Despite the heavy presence of the Polizei, young men and women waved red communist and black anarchist flags, and a rapper named Fortune inveighed against the racial and economic equalities in modern Germany. A middle-aged man held up a placard that read, "Yesterday: Victims of SED [the old GDR communists], Today: Victims of Merkel [the current German chancellor]." Various speakers took to the podium to rail against the Transatlantic Trade and Investment Partnership (TTIP) and the international intrigues of the American National Security Agency (NSA). Others complained about the pervasive presence of *video überwacht* or closed-circuit television in Germany, which recorded more footage of ordinary Germans than the Stasi. A young man challenged the rights of banks and credit card companies to collect private information, and named Facebook and Google as tools of American corporate imperialism. A woman wearing a headscarf complained that German prosperity depended on the exploitation of guest workers. A small group protested the rise of fascism in Ukraine.

I stayed at the counterprotest taking photos until the hour grew too late for me to return to the hotel. As I walked back toward the main celebration at

FIGURE 5.7. German police in riot gear in front of the Reichstag.

FIGURE 5.8. Young communists at the November 9 counterdemonstration.

the Brandenburg Gate, surrounded by hordes of drunken partiers, I considered the promises of democracy and free markets after 1989. Just one Monday earlier, Branko Milanovic, an economist at the City University of New York, took stock of the outcomes for all of the postcommunist states and found the landscape depressing. In his blog post "For Whom the Wall Fell," Milanovic asserted that for 80 million people in Tajikistan, Kyrgyzstan, Moldova, Ukraine, Georgia, Bosnia, and Serbia (roughly one-fifth of the total population in all of the independent postcommunist countries), the basic standard of living (when measured by real GDP per capita) was still below its level in 1990.[24] Milanovic explained that these were "countries with at least three to four wasted generations. At current rates of growth, it might take them some 50 or 60 years—longer than they were under communism!—to go back to the income levels they had at the fall of communism."[25]

Above these utter failures at transition, Milanovic named three other groups of countries: "the mild failures," "the mild successes," and "the real successes" as measured by growth rates. But upon closer inspection, Milanovic found few real successes if one discounted the influence of oil and other natural resources, and if success required a stable and consolidated liberal democratic political system. Milanovic wrote:

> Most people's expectations on November 9, 1989 were that the newly-brought capitalism will result in a convergence with the rest of Europe, moderate increase in inequality, and consolidated democracy. They are fulfilled most likely in only one country (Poland), and at the very most in another, rather small, two. Their total populations are 42 million, or some 10% of all former Communist countries. Thus, 1 out of 10 people living in "transition" countries could be said to have "transitions" to the capitalism that was promised by the ideologues who waxed about the triumph of liberal democracy and free markets. . . . So, what is the balance-sheet of transition? Only three to at most five or six countries could be said to be on the road to becoming a part of the rich and (relatively) stable capitalist world. Many are falling behind, and some are so far behind that they cannot aspire to go back to the point where they were when the Wall fell for several decades.[26]

Commenting on Milanovic's findings, *New York Times* columnist David Brooks opined, "Twenty-five years after the fall of the Berlin Wall, the biggest surprise is how badly most of the post-communist nations have done since."[27]

Economic figures are one thing, but what do they mean when applied to ordinary men and women across the postcommunist world? If we look outside of Germany to the social costs of the transition in Eastern Europe, the economic upheaval caused at least a million early deaths.[28] In a 2009 article in the premier British medical journal, the *Lancet*, David Stuckler, Lawrence King, and Martin McKee published an examination of the change in mortality rates of working-age men between 1989 and 2002 in the countries of the former Soviet Union and Eastern Europe.[29] By examining the effects of mass privatization (which they defined as the transfer of 25 percent or more of previously state-owned assets to private hands within twenty-four months), and controlling for other factors to isolate the specific effects of so-called shock therapy, the authors found a statistically significant link between privatization, male unemployment, and premature death, similar to that found in Eastern Germany in 1989 and 1990. Russia provided the direst example, with male life expectancy falling by more than seven years between 1985 and 2002. While Soviet men lived to an average of sixty-seven years, their Russian counterparts barely survived to sixty.

In the case of Germany, the reunification and the massive transfer of funds from West Germany obscured the picture of the true impacts of transition in the former GDR. Although unemployment remained higher and wages were lower in the East, young people could flee a bleak economy for better opportunities in the wealthy Western states.[30] But the post-1989 malaise in Berlin and many former Eastern cities and towns was still palpable in 2014, especially as the federal government moved to house refugees in villages depopulated after the dismantling of the GDR's industrial base. The unilateral nature of the reunification, the callous privatization process, and Western perception of ungrateful *Ossis* (East Germans) explain part of the lingering resentment. As Lothar de Maizière explained in 2015, "I visited a lawyer friend in Prague three years ago and asked why people there seemed more content than those in Berlin. Two things, he said: We are comparing with earlier, while you still compare with the West. And we are changing, while you were changed."[31]

Back in Berlin, the hour grew later, and I reentered the festive fray about halfway between the Brandenburg Gate and the Sieggesäule, determined to wend my way up to the front. By ducking and wiggling through the throng, I secured a spot just ten meters from the stage. Above the sea of heads, I planned to take videos and snap photos of the pop stars and politicians there to commemorate the Mauerfall.

The first part of the show featured a set by the crooner Clueso, the object of adulation for millions of German teenagers and young adults. Born in the East German town of Erfurt in 1980, Clueso (a.k.a. Thomas Hübner) was

FIGURE 5.9. The light show at the Brandenburg Gate.

only nine years old when the Wall fell, and his songs were upbeat and energetic, setting a festive tone. At 18:00, unaccompanied drummers pounded out a percussive soundtrack to projected images of GDR soldiers patrolling the old Wall as large white screens slid in to form a backdrop for the stage: simple and dramatic. People cheered when the MC appeared, a German actor who reminded me of an aged Robert Downey Jr. He chatted with the crowd, eliciting laughter and trying to keep the mood light despite the solemnity of the previous videos. He introduced three former GDR citizens, all of whom had been persecuted by the regime for political activity. My favorite was the singer-songwriter Karl Wolf Biermann—a funny-looking guy with a ridiculous mustache—who talked about singing protest songs in the GDR before he was expelled in 1976. He sang his famous tune, "Ermutigung," much to the pleasure of the crowd.

The ordinary citizens were followed by more musical acts: a punk singer named Silly and the Fantastischen Vier, a German Beastie Boys knockoff that worked the crowd up into an old-school hip-hop frenzy. A grandfatherly Peter Gabriel took the stage and sang a moving verse from "Heroes," absent any sense of David Bowie's original irony. Clueso played another song, and eventually the German Robert Downey Jr. introduced the mayor of Berlin, Klaus Wowereit, who launched into a long speech. None of the Germans in

TWEETS 7,460 · FOLLOWING 388 · FOLLOWERS 70.3K · LIKES 8,650 · LISTS 4 · Follow

GermanForeignOffice ✓
@GermanyDiplo

News from the German Foreign Office -
Follow us in German as well
@AuswaertigesAmt

📍 Berlin
🔗 diplo.de/EN
📹 34.4K Vine Loops
📅 Joined January 2012

Tweets | Tweets & replies | Photos & videos

GermanForeignOffice @GermanyDiplo · 3h
Good-bye, David Bowie. You are now among #Heroes. Thank you for helping to bring down the #wall.
youtu.be/YYjBQKIOb-w #RIPDavidBowie

↩ ⇄ 3.6K ♥ 3.6K ••• View media

FIGURE 5.10. A tweet from the German Foreign Ministry on the day of Bowie's death. Notice the fireworks above the Brandenburg Gate and that they have omitted the quotation marks around "Heroes."

the crowd seemed particularly moved by his lecture, and I guessed their beer buzzes were wearing off. The temperature fell.

Finally, the visiting dignitaries appeared. Poland's Lech Wałęsa and Mikhail Gorbachev raised cheers from the crowd. Various German politicians, children, and citizens of Berlin joined them on stage, each holding one of the illuminated balloons. When Wowereit gave the signal, they simultaneously released their balloons at the first notes of Beethoven's "Ode to Joy." Video images of the balloons drifting up filled the screens behind the orchestra and choir. One by one, the citizens along the Lichtgrenze released their balloons as the orchestra played. Back at the main stage, fireworks lit up the sky, and lights flashed and blinked and glowed. Wałęsa seemed to be enjoying himself, but Gorbachev's face remained stoic. The pyrotechnics kept pace with the crescendo of the Ninth, and the word "FREEDOM" eventually sparkled upon the Brandenburg Gate as choral voices rose up in triumphant glory. People whooped and cheered as the MC returned to introduce another musical act. The crowd around me loosened. Those who had waited for the balloon release wandered off, perhaps in search of toilets or more beer. I decided to call it a night; I'd been out on the streets for over seven hours.

From the main stage I walked toward the Reichstag hoping to exit the event on Elbertstraße so I wouldn't have to walk through the park alone in the dark. The scene I encountered was tense, with police holding back an angry crowd. An older German woman shouted at a policeman. He insisted that she had to enter the event from the middle of Straße des 17 Juni, far from the main stage where the next performance was about to start. Another policeman pointed me toward a line of about forty people trying to exit the Bürgerfest. Two large security guards managed a narrow gap in the metal barrier, allowing people to leave one at a time. The shouting woman pointed to those of us leaving, and demanded that she and the others waiting should be let in. The police refused, trying to wave them away.

"We are Berliners," the woman said, and at that moment four young men stormed the metal fence, jumping over and dashing for the main stage. In the melee that ensued, the police rushed after these youths, tackling them to the ground and pushing them back toward the barrier. The crowd grew angrier. Most of them were middle aged or older, and those in front pushed at the metal barrier. One policeman spoke into a phone, clearly nervous. Another tried to explain about security and safety.

Once the guards let me out, I was curious to see how many people had gathered on the eastern side of the Brandenburg Gate. But everything was blocked; Pariser Platz was inaccessible. I asked a policeman how I could get to Unter den Linden, and he directed me to walk down toward the Spree until I found a passable street. I walked several blocks out of the way until I could make my way around to Pariser Platz, but the plaza was deserted save for me and a few other confused people trying to find their way to the event. Guards patrolled the area to ensure that no one could pass. Even though Johann Gottfried Schadow's famous sculpture *Quadriga*—a horse-drawn chariot bearing the victorious goddess Athena holding a staff adorned with the Prussian eagle and an iron cross enclosed in a wreath of laurels—looked eastward toward the television tower at Alexanderplatz, and the whole purpose of the Bürgerfest was to commemorate the reunification of the two Germanies, the Mauerfall organizers had sealed the crossing at the Brandenburg Gate. Tall metal fences surrounded the famous Berlin landmark, creating an impermeable barrier. Only now, it wasn't the East German border guards keeping people in. It was German police and private security keeping people out.

I'm sure David Bowie would have seen the irony.

6. The Enemy of My Enemy

On January 10, 2016, over ten thousand people took to a different set of streets in Berlin, red flags waving in an early Sunday morning winter's breeze. Shouted chants and old partisan songs beat out a rhythm for my footsteps. I could see my breath when I exhaled, but the rain forecast for the afternoon held off until the demonstration ended, as if the skies urged participation. I dashed in and out of the crowd, snapping photos and taking videos with my Canon, perched on that thin line between participation and observation. But I felt included, there in the thick of it, soaking up the anachronistic fantasy that feet on the streets could effect political change.

I tried to suspend cynicism for the day, and admired the political variety of lefties marching in the cold: social democrats, democratic socialists, socialists, communists, Marxist-Leninists, Trotskyists, anarcho-syndicalists, anarchists, pacifists, feminists, Greens, and a motley assortment of unaffiliated individuals who otherwise despised fascism, neocolonialism, and market fundamentalism. Dutifully following their police escort, tight bands of demonstrators carried placards and held aloft banners with slogans in both German and English. "Another world is possible: Make Capitalism History." "Wir Wollen Frieden—We Want Peace." "'Regime Change' Politik = Staats-Terrorismus." "Nationale Souveränität Syriens respektieren." "Rebellion Is Justified."

FIGURE 6.1. "Stop Wars! Strike back at the Empire you must!"

Surveying the crowd, I saw peace signs, red stars, hammers and sickles, rainbow banners, raised fists, and the old GDR flag. In addition to the representatives from the local chapters of the major German left political parties and civic organizations, activists from Austria, Denmark, the Netherlands, and Poland had joined the parade. A small band of members of the Chilean Communist Party shouted slogans in Spanish. Above the heads of the demonstrators, I saw representations of Marx, Engels, Lenin, Che Guevara, and Yoda. But more than anyone else, I saw the semblances of Karl Liebknecht and Rosa Luxemburg, the two German socialist martyrs whose memories we gathered to honor.

The Liebknecht-Luxemburg Demonstration (L-L Demo) is the world's largest annual funerary demonstration, and the largest political rally of the German left.[1] Two parallel events occur on the second Sunday of each January: the commemoration at the cemetery where Karl Liebknecht and Rosa Luxemburg are buried along with other fallen socialist and communist comrades, and the annual march from Frankfurter Gate to the graves at Friedrichsfelde.[2] Organizers plan these events on the Sunday closest to the anniversary of the murders of Liebknecht and Luxemburg on January 15, 1919. The year 2016 marked ninety-seven years since their deaths, and the activists had assembled on January 10.[3]

FIGURE 6.2. Funeral for Liebknecht and Luxemburg in 1919.

Karl Liebknecht (1871–1919) was a member of parliament from the German Social Democratic Party (SPD) in the years before World War I. When the Great War broke out in 1914, Liebknecht opposed the hostilities and was the only SPD MP in the Reichstag to vote against a further extension of war credits to the kaiser.[4] Rosa Luxemburg was a Polish-Jewish communist who believed that all wars were ultimately wars of imperialism.[5] She was often in prison for her pacifism and her dangerous revolutionary and antinationalist ideas. Luxemburg argued that workers in different nations should not fight against each other in World War I, but rather should join forces and overthrow the economic elites that caused the war in the first place.[6] Luxemburg wrote tomes about how best to achieve socialism in Germany, criticizing both Vladimir Lenin's notion of the dictatorship of the proletariat and the embrace of bourgeois democracy by the SPD.[7]

I had traveled from Jena to Berlin to attend this L-L Demo, to experience the political culture of the German left for myself. Although I was American, and most of the protesters were hostile to NATO and what they called "United States imperialism," I didn't worry. There once existed a real American left, too, and Germans well remembered the Abraham Lincoln Brigades of the Spanish Civil War and cherished the folk songs of Yanks like Woody Guthrie and Pete Seeger. I was too young to have marched against Vietnam, but I had

FIGURE 6.3. "Our Crisis Advisers," a poster of the German Communist Party.

UNSERE KRISENBERATER

DKP

protested the Iraq war and agreed with the basic idea of putting people before profits. I felt no qualms about being counted among this multitude, at least until I turned around and my eyes fell on the wide red banner held aloft by members of the Turkish Communist Party. There, beside the faces of Marx, Engels, and Lenin, was none other than my ideological archnemesis. Instinctively, I flinched. Just a glimpse of his visage ruined my mood.

Goddamn Stalin follows me everywhere. Usually I mean this metaphorically, in that the crimes of Joseph Stalin cast a long shadow over my scholarly research on everyday life in Eastern Europe. When I try to complicate stereotypes about communism, people accuse me of being an apologist for Stalinism. When I write about maternity clinics or the social welfare policies of pre-1989 Bulgaria, hostile colleagues verbally assault me with claims that I ignore Stalin's purges, the gulag, or the famine in Ukraine. It doesn't matter that I'm talking about Bulgaria in the 1970s and they are talking about the Soviet Union in the 1930s; to them socialism equals Stalinism. And it doesn't matter that Stalin ruled the USSR for only roughly twenty-five of the Soviet Union's seventy-year history. Conflating everything left of Bill Clinton with Joseph Stalin proves a most effective strategy for discrediting all criticisms of, and suggested alternatives to, the ravages of unfettered free markets and global capitalism.

Although most German leftists hated Stalin and everything he represented, his face loomed on the banner behind me. He was literally following me. When the Turkish communists started shouting his name, I moved off to the side of the parade and allowed them to march past. I had personally penned many pages condemning the paranoid dictator for co-opting and deforming the ideals of European communism in the 1930s and 1940s, and the last thing I wanted was to have my photograph taken beneath his image. This was a man responsible for the arbitrary purges in the 1930s, ordering assassinations of perceived political rivals within his own party, many of whom fought by his side during the revolution. He sent multitudes to labor camps in Siberia to be worked to death through a brutal regime of forced labor. Stalin's rapid collectivization of agriculture caused millions to die in a horrific famine, and his secret police considered everyone a potential enemy of the state. Stalin betrayed many fellow communists fleeing from right-wing regimes in Finland, Bulgaria, Germany, and other countries in Eastern Europe who sought refuge in the Soviet Union and ended up in the gulag when Stalin decided they were all fascist spies. It was Stalin who reversed most of the initial progress on women's rights, outlawing abortion and insisting on traditional, nuclear families, which reinscribed anachronistic gender roles. And on top of all this, Joseph Stalin hated Rosa Luxemburg and the democratic socialism for which she stood. Without a doubt, the mainstream German media would focus their cameras on this one banner of Stalin to discredit the voices and opinions of the thousands of other Germans out on the streets. Infuriating. What the hell was the Turkish Communist Party thinking?

I fumed silently as I rejoined the parade a few hundred meters behind the Turks. But after I got away, I realized that in a march celebrating Luxemburg's famous quote, "Freiheit ist immer Freiheit der Andersdenkenden" (Freedom is always the freedom of those who think differently), the German organizers of the L-L Demo could hardly censor the members of the Turkish Communist Party. The whole idea of freedom of speech would be undermined. Turks formed a large ethnic minority in Germany, and silencing their opinions would smack of racism. I later learned that the German organizers openly disapproved of the Turkish banner, but allowed them to march anyway. In response, cemetery officials agreed to the addition of a memorial plaque to the victims of Stalinism near the graves of Liebknecht and Luxemburg in 2006.[8] Some Turks and Marxist-Leninists were outraged by the plaque, and their continued hero worship of Stalin caused deep fissures in the German left, rendering it as crippled and vulnerable as it was back in 1919 when Liebknecht and Luxemburg were murdered in the first place.

Although few leftists disagree with Karl Marx's basic diagnosis of the problems of capitalism, there have always been fierce debates over how to realize the German philosopher's vision in practice. The history of the political left in almost every country is one of internecine struggles, and left-left violence between rival Marxist factions often proves bloodier and more twisted than direct confrontations with right-wing, conservative forces. Although they managed a brief Popular Front during the Spanish Civil War, anarchists and communists and socialists decimated each other both during and after the conflict, thanks, at least in large part, to Comrade Stalin in Moscow.

For the one day of the L-L Demo, members of Germany's different leftist parties managed to share the streets, but when elections came, they fractured. In the 2013 federal elections, for instance, Angela Merkel's Christian Democratic Union (CDU) won 37.2 percent of the vote, while the SPD won 29.4 percent and the Democratic Socialists (Die Linke—The Left) won 8.2 percent for a combined total of 37.6 percent.[9] If we include the Greens, who won 7.3 percent of the vote, it is rather remarkable that Angela Merkel became chancellor, given that her party won only 37 percent when the SPD, the Greens, and Die Linke had 45 percent combined. How did the conservative CDU maintain its power? In coalition with the SPD, of course—the very same leftist party that once persecuted Liebknecht and Luxemburg.[10] And this was actually the second time in less than a decade that the SPD had formed a grand coalition with the conservatives. Social Democrat politicians refused to share power with Die Linke, the successor party to the old East German Socialist Unity Party (SED).[11]

So why the hell can't the left get its act together and what does this have to do with Stalin? Everything. As I marched through the streets of Berlin with my camera, I snapped photos of the faces of the people around me; men and women, students, young parents with their children, the middle aged, and the elderly all shared the pavement. Germans and foreigners mixed indiscriminately, shouting for an end to all wars and the welcoming of refugees. Others admonished us to support the international brigades now fighting against the Islamic State in Rojava (western Kurdistan), where Kurdish anarcho-feminists had set up an independent society based on the principles of direct democracy, environmental sustainability, and full gender equality. A band of jubilant students sang "Bella ciao!" I marveled at the energy and passion of the young people, in whose hands the future of Europe lay. They could achieve so much. If only they could overcome the weighty historical baggage of the leftist fratricide inspired by the mustachioed Georgian.

When Karl Marx and Friedrich Engels published *The Communist Manifesto* in 1848, there was indeed a specter haunting Europe. Workers' uprisings shook the entire continent, most famously in the Paris Commune, but also in Prussia, the largest and most powerful predecessor state of modern Germany. Monarchs crushed these revolts, but demands for democratic representation, as well as communist and socialist ideas of a more equitable distribution of political and economic power, lived on. Today, the German SPD traces its origins back to the 1860s and to the political activism of men like August Bebel and Wilhelm Liebknecht, Karl Liebknecht's father.[12]

By 1912, the SPD became the most popular party in Germany.[13] Both Rosa Luxemburg and Karl Liebknecht were members of the early SPD, which embraced radical antinationalist, anticapitalist, and anti-imperialist politics. But when World War I broke out, SPD politicians voted in favor of extending loans to the kaiser, contradicting their own internationalist pretensions. The end of World War I saw Germany defeated. The kaiser abdicated and the Weimar Republic, Germany's first democracy, was formed with SPD at the helm. Disgusted by the duplicity of their former colleagues, Liebknecht and Luxemburg founded the German Communist Party (Kommunistische Partei Deutschlands, KPD) in the hope that a system of workers' councils would replace the so-called bourgeois democracy of the Social Democrats. When a workers' uprising began on the streets of Berlin in January 1919, Liebknecht, Luxemburg, and other German communists supported it. In an effort to maintain political stability, SPD leaders ordered members of German paramilitary units (the Freikorps) to crush the uprising. Liebknecht and Luxemburg were arrested and summarily executed, their bodies buried in a paupers' cemetery in an area reserved for criminals.

During the turbulent years of the Weimar Republic, the German economy at first looked like it would recover from the war, but many structural faults challenged the young democracy. The victorious Allies demanded crippling reparations, which caused hyperinflation and growing poverty. Unemployment devastated the middle class. Meanwhile, the Red Army had won the Russian Civil War in 1922, and the Soviet Union consolidated the world's first socialist state. At the local level, the KPD forged closer links with the USSR and grew in strength. Now SPD politicians had good reasons to fear a German dictatorship of the proletariat. After the 1929 stock market crash left the world economy in shambles, a workers' revolution looked imminent.

But the threat to Weimar democracy came not only from the far left. Right-wing activists stoked popular fears of Russian/Jewish Bolshevism to justify the need for authoritarian control. Adolf Hitler led a failed putsch attempt in 1923. During his time in prison, Hitler resolved to work within democracy, using the electoral system to gain support for Nazism. Throughout the 1920s, the KPD clashed regularly with the far right, but SPD leaders consistently punished left-wing violence more harshly than right-wing terror. At the same time, Stalin encouraged the German Communists to view the Social Democrats as an equal or greater enemy than the Nazis. The KPD branded the

FIGURE 6.4. The original 1926 memorial for the murdered socialists.

SPD "social fascists" and spent much political energy undermining their rule. With the German left squabbling among itself, the National Socialists grew in influence.[14]

As Germany drifted steadily toward political chaos, the country's economic elites, the military, and the press increasingly threw their support behind Hitler. As with Mussolini in Italy, the Nazis used the specter of Bolshevism to garner support from the rich and powerful who saw fascism as the only antidote to communism. Even in 2016, Germans remember well that Hitler's first victims were the domestic communists who violently opposed his rise to power. As I walked closer to the cemetery where Liebknecht and Luxemburg were buried, I studied the faces of the men and women around me. How many of them, I wondered, had grandparents or great-grandparents who protested against National Socialism in the 1920s and 1930s?

After Lenin's death in 1924, the KPD added his name to the annual procession, and it became known as the Lenin-Liebknecht-Luxemburg demonstration. Lenin's Soviet Union, despite the civil war and its economic problems, provided a beacon of hope for the German Communists who now believed that parliamentary elections would never allow a true workers' government. Economic elites proved too adept at manipulating democracy for their own ends. In 1926, the renowned architect Ludwig Mies van der Rohe inaugurated a special memorial for Liebknecht and Luxemburg called the Revolutionary Memorial to the Murdered Socialists.[15] This consisted of modernist red blocks and bore the symbols of the Soviet Union: the star, the hammer, and the sickle. On the monument was an inscription regarding the fate of the communist revolution: "Ich war. Ich bin. Ich werde sein." (I was. I am. I will be.)

This first monument to the murdered socialists stood for only seven years. After blaming the Reichstag fire on the communists, Hitler whipped up domestic fears of a Bolshevik-style revolution to convince Germany's president to declare martial law. Civil liberties such as freedom of speech and expression, freedom of assembly, freedom of the press, and the right to citizen privacy when communicating by mail or telephone were suspended because of the supposed communist threat. In the name of national security, Hitler pushed through the Enabling Act on March 24, 1933, an amendment to the Weimar Constitution that granted him full dictatorial power over Germany.

As Führer, Hitler banned the Lenin-Liebknecht-Luxemburg Demonstration, razed the monument, and paved over the graves.[16] Before Hitler's ascent to power, Germany had the second largest Communist Party after the Soviet Union. Today, few outside Germany realize that the first concentration camp inmates were German communists, persecuted by the hundreds of thousands. Some fled west, such as the playwright Bertolt Brecht, who led an L-L-L Demonstration in exile in New York. Others sought asylum in the Soviet Union, then under the control of Joseph Stalin, who initially welcomed them, only to purge them during the late 1930s. In this sense, many KPD members were victims of both Hitler and Stalin. But the true scope of Stalin's crimes remained unclear until after his death and Khrushchev's secret speech in February 1956.[17] And during World War II, Western leaders turned a blind eye to Stalin's brutality because they needed him to help them defeat Hitler, a cause for which upward of 25 million Soviet citizens lost their lives.[18] The enemy of my enemy is my friend.

After World War II, the Friedrichsfelde cemetery fell in the Soviet occupation zone, and workers uncovered the graves of Liebknecht and Luxemburg. The first postwar L-L-L Demonstration occurred in 1946, in front of a hastily erected replica of the original Ludwig Mies van der Rohe monument. Exiled German communists returned home to a divided Germany. In the GDR, Stalin forced the old Social Democrats (SPD) to unite with the communists (KPD) to create the Socialist Unity Party, known by the German acronym SED. During the four decades of SED rule, the Lenin-Liebknecht-Luxemburg Demonstration morphed into "the march of the cold feet" since the SED choreographed mass participation.[19] Politburo members led the march, giving speeches in front of the graves of Liebknecht and Luxemburg, and co-opting the revolutionary credentials of those who fell in 1919 to legitimize the political

FIGURE 6.5. The postwar reconstruction of the 1926 memorial destroyed by the Nazis.

FIGURE 6.6.
"The dead
admonish us."

structure of the GDR. The East German secret police, the Stasi, infiltrated East German society through a wide network of informants, and strict travel restrictions prevented East Germans from leaving their country, even for the funerals of parents or relatives in the West. In 1956, when Nikita Khrushchev revealed the crimes of Stalin to the world, and Soviet tanks crushed the Hungarian Uprising, the West German government outlawed the SED. Western leftists turned against the Soviet Union and began to embrace alternative revolutionary figures such as Trotsky and Mao. The term "de-Stalinization" describes the relative liberalization that occurred throughout Eastern Europe after 1956.

To this day, opinions differ on Khrushchev's motivations for his secret speech. Did he truly want to move Soviet communism away from the methods of Stalin, or was he merely using Stalin as a scapegoat? For those who worshiped Stalin, the man who led the Soviet Union to victory during what Russians still call the Great Patriotic War, Khrushchev's betrayal proved unforgivable, and when he fell from power, he became a persona non grata in his own country.[20] Stalin's defenders see him as the champion of communism, the only man willing to challenge capitalism, economically develop the Soviet Union, and defeat Hitler at any cost. They argue that during the years of Stalin's rule, the Soviet economy caught up with that of the West. Stalin also mobilized immense resources to beat the Germans, and without him, many of his admirers claim, the Nazis would have won World War II. Given the immense challenges he faced, and the legions of enemies openly or secretly conspiring against him, the members of the Turkish Communist Party marching under Stalin's banner would argue that he persevered because he knew how to do what needed to be done.

The majority of Germans on the left, even the far left, would disagree. They see Stalin as a brutal dictator, obsessed with power. Even Lenin had grave reservations about leaving the Soviet Union in Stalin's hands. For many, Stalin took the ideals of communism and twisted them to persecute his political enemies and secure his rule. He reversed many of the liberal laws passed under Lenin and collectivized agriculture at the cost of millions of lives. Stalin, and the leaders he supported in Eastern Europe, murdered, exiled, or imprisoned legions of fellow communists, including many who fought with the Red Army or with partisan forces in Eastern Europe. As twentieth-century communist economies in Eastern Europe stagnated, and populations demanded reform, the faults of what was called "really existing socialism" (as opposed to the ideal of communism) accreted to Stalin, and those, like Erich Honecker in East Germany, who remained committed to hard-line Stalinist positions and resisted reforms.

FIGURE 6.7. The March of the Cold Feet, a 1978 L-L Demo.

More than half a century after her death, Rosa Luxemburg continued to influence the imagination of the German left, especially her writings critical of the Russian Revolution and Bolshevism. In 1988, a group of East German dissidents unfurled an unapproved banner at the official L-L-L Demo, quoting the words of Luxemburg herself: "Freedom is always the freedom of those who think differently." This quote is taken from the following paragraph: "Freedom only for the supporters of the government, only for the members of one party—however numerous they may be—is no freedom at all. Freedom is always and exclusively freedom for the one who thinks differently. Not because of any fanatical concept of 'justice' but because all that is instructive, wholesome and purifying in political freedom depends on this essential characteristic, and its effectiveness vanishes when 'freedom' becomes a special privilege."[21]

The Stasi quickly arrested and deported the dissenters, but a handful refused to leave and remained in prison, hoping to bring Gorbachev's glasnost and perestroika to the GDR.[22] Sympathy for the jailed dissidents set off waves of defections and protests across East Germany, events that helped lead to the fall of the Berlin Wall on November 9, 1989.[23] Three major parties contested in the first (and last) free elections in the GDR. The SED supposedly purged itself of its Stalinist elements and became the Party of Democratic Socialism (PDS). The SPD reestablished itself in East Germany for the first time since it was forced to unite with the KPD after World War II. But the CDU and their

Alliance for Germany ran on a platform of reunification with the West, and won the plurality.

After reunification, observers expected that the L-L Demonstrations would fizzle out as the government no longer compelled East Germans to attend. Instead, the demonstrations continue to this day, waxing and waning in size depending on the domestic or international political situation. Masses of Germans opposed both the first and second Gulf Wars at L-L Demonstrations, and the huge turnout at the 1995 demonstration stunned international observers.[24] Over 100,000 people took to the streets in 1999 for the eightieth anniversary of the march.[25] In 2000, Berlin police canceled the demonstration on short notice after they received bomb threats, but five thousand people turned up anyway, and police had to scatter the demonstrators with water cannons.[26] Eighty thousand participated in the demonstration for the ninetieth anniversary in 2009.[27]

In 2016, about twelve thousand people at the L-L Demo opposed the NATO politics of regime change in the Middle East and the increasing tensions with Russia in Ukraine. Many held signs welcoming Syrian and Iraqi refugees and demanding peace, but mostly, the marchers shouted antifascist slogans, aimed, I presumed, at the growing German far right, particularly the new anti-immigrant party Alternative for Germany (AfD). Like Rosa Luxemburg so many decades before them, Germany's left believed that ordinary Germans should unite with the Middle Eastern refugees to challenge the elite economic interests that promoted the politics of regime change in the first place.

After two hours of walking in the cold, my toes felt frozen and my fingers numb. I took hundreds of photos, mostly managing to avoid the Turkish Communist Party and their Stalinist banner. In past years, I'd read that the Turks deliberately trample the carnations placed upon the plaque to the victims of Stalinism. I considered trying to get some photos of them doing this, but hunger got the better of me. After the Lichtenberg U-bahn stop, the march bottlenecked toward the entrance of the cemetery; a street festival–like atmosphere reigned. Vendors sold mulled red wine, bratwurst, and fried *Kartoffelpuffer* with warm applesauce. Others hawked secondhand leftist books, mostly in German, although I did see four volumes of Mao in English. At one bookstall, I bought a copy of the documentary film *Red Army*, about the famous Soviet hockey team. I also purchased a coffee cup to support the German newspaper *Junge Welt*. The mug featured the outline of a white dove with an olive branch in its mouth against a red background, accompanied by the words "Frieden statt NATO" (Peace instead of NATO).

FIGURE 6.8. A dachshund keeps warm in a communist flag.

All of the left political parties and organizations had their own booths, either giving away or selling various branded goods. Die Linke had a large booth near the entrance of the memorial. At their stall, I bought some red gummy hearts and paid twenty euro cents for a packet of tissues that said, "Für rote Nasen!" (For red noses!), a nice pun given the chilly January air. I also picked up a pamphlet containing their political platform:

> DIE LINKE as a socialist party stands for alternatives, for a better fu-
> ture. . . . We pursue a concrete goal: we fight for a society in which
> no child has to grow up poor, in which all men and women can live
> a self-determined life in peace, dignity and social security and can
> democratically shape social relations. To achieve this we need a dif-
> ferent economic and social system: democratic socialism. . . . We are
> not prepared to accept a world in which profit interests determine the
> prospects of millions of men and women and in which exploitation,
> war and imperialism cut whole countries off from hope and the future.
> Where profit rules above all else, there is little space for democracy.[28]

Until the migrant crisis, Die Linke's anti-austerity message appealed to many Germans, and in the state of Thüringen, where I lived, Die Linke even managed to win a plurality of votes in 2014. Their leader in Thüringen, the West

FIGURE 6.9. "For red noses!"

FIGURE 6.10. GDR flags.

German Bodo Ramelow, campaigned with a red bust of Marx on stage with him, and just weeks after the Berlin events celebrating the twenty-fifth anniversary of the fall of the Wall, Germany had its first state ruled by the grandchild party of the old SED.

Did this mean that the old fissures among the German left had been healed? Of course not. Social democrats still disagreed with democratic socialists who also fought with Marxist-Leninists, communists, and anarcho-syndicalists. Among these groups alone there existed such a diverse array of ideas about how to end exploitation and redistribute wealth that they spent more time bickering among themselves than resisting the unbridled capitalism they all despised. The enemy of my enemy is still my enemy.

And then there was the problem of Stalin. Some looked upon his face with horror, while others embraced his legacy, believing that only a strong and uncompromising leader could face down the juggernaut of global capitalism. Some would never join a political movement that valorized his legacy, while others, like the Turkish communists, would never join a movement without him. And the number of Stalinists appeared to be growing. Only one day after the 2016 Liebknecht-Luxemburg march, the *Guardian* newspaper reported the opening of a new cultural center dedicated to Joseph Stalin in Penza, Russia.[29] Georgy Kamnev, the leader of the local Communist Party there, responded to the incredulous questions of the Western journalist by saying, "Why is Stalin gaining relevance? He is the answer to all problems. And he'd resolve today's problems very effectively."[30]

From the Die Linke booth, I also bought two red carnations to place on the graves of Liebknecht and Luxemburg, and made my way into the cemetery. The solemnity of the crowd surrounding the graves moved me. People shuffled forward in an orderly queue to pay their respects to these heroes of the German left. I waited among the throngs until I had my chance to stand before Luxemburg's grave, covered with a mountain of red flowers. A black-and-white photograph of a young Rosa looked up at me. Although she died so long ago, for almost a century Luxemburg still managed to bring together men and women from different nations, races, religions, and varying political commitments, to celebrate the idea that another world is possible.

If only we could agree on how to get there.

7. A Tale of Two Typewriters

When I was a child and lived in the same house for fifteen years, I collected stamps, mostly international stamps from far-off countries I hoped someday to visit. Now that I am middle-aged—visiting those countries and changing my address every three years—I collect typewriters. Typewriters weigh considerably more than stamps, and I often long for the easy portability of my philatelic youth. Typewriters, like kids and dogs and mortgages, weigh you down. But as of April 2016, I owned twenty-three manual typewriters, only one of which originated in the United States.

For the record, I am not a Luddite. New technologies make me giddy, and I couldn't function without my eleven-inch MacBook Air and my noise-canceling headphones. Nor am I (too) paranoid about the National Security Agency reading my field notes. And although I am old enough to have written many early college papers on a typewriter, my first machine was electric. In 1990, I switched to a basic word processor and bought my first laptop (a gray Macintosh PowerBook 145B) as soon as I could afford one. My manual typewriter fetish struck me later in life.

It started innocently enough. Over two decades after I parted ways with correction fluid, my partner surprised me with a vintage Smith-Corona Skyriter as a birthday present. I wrote a few letters on the machine, and then

FIGURE 7.1. My two typewriters.

started typing up my daily to-do lists because I loved the clack of the keys. When I started free writing on the typewriter, my productivity soared. E-mail, social media, and the lures of the World Wide Web couldn't seduce me away from writing. Now I use the machines on a daily basis: to bash out first drafts, to write notes, and to keep my daily journal.

I moved from Maine to the western German state of Baden-Württemberg in August 2014, settling into a small hamlet in the Black Forest, just a stone's throw from the French and Swiss borders. I could lunch in Basel and dine in Strasbourg if the mood suited me, but mostly I commuted between my village of Kollnau and the city of Freiburg. Although marketed as a portable typewriter, my Skyriter took up too much of my fifty-pound suitcase allowance, so I left it behind in the United States. But within six months, I had replaced my Smith-Corona with over a dozen different German QWERTZ models, including two of my favorites—one made in the Federal Republic of Germany and the other made in the German Democratic Republic.

In late August 2014, I found a 1950s, gray, SM3 Olympia at a *Flohmarkt* in the nearby town of Waldkirch. The seller told me the typewriter belonged to her mother, who had once loved it but never used it anymore. I asked for a piece of paper and typed the sentence: "the quick brown fox jumps over the lazy dog." It worked perfectly. I bought it for fifteen euros and promised to take good care of it. I took the machine back to my flat and detached it from its case. Only then did I notice the small metal plate stuck to its back. It read: "Olympia Werke West GMBH—Wilhelmshaven—Made in Germany West-

FIGURE 7.2. The placard on the back of my Olympia.

ern Zone." I knew little about the history of the German typewriter industry at the time, but I imagined that the reference to the Western Zone meant that West Germans had built this particular machine soon after World War II. Since the machine had no other plates on it (stating, for instance, the name of the business where it was used), and someone had penned in her home address on the inside of the case, I guessed the typewriter had spent its whole life as the private property of the seller's mother, a West German housewife who probably used it for family correspondence.

Olympia typewriters were the most popular typewriter in Germany before World War II. After 1945, Olympia Werke made about half of all typewriters in West Germany, no small feat given that they cost much more than other brands. In the United States, collectors refer to them as the Mercedes Benz of typewriters because of their elegant design and durable engineering. This typewriter took center stage in the 1964 Alfred Hitchcock film *Marnie*, as Tippi Hedren tapped out her neurotic episodes on an Olympia. The novelist Paul Auster wrote a book about his relationship with an Olympia in *The Story of My Typewriter*. I thrilled at the idea of owning one of these Teutonic beauties.

FIGURE 7.3. The placard on the back of the Rheinmetall.

But sixteen months later, I found another love (I am a typewriter polyg-
amist). I moved northeast from my little perch in the Black Forest to the
university town of Jena in the heart of Thüringen. On my fourth day in the
city, I found an antique shop with a collection of old typewriters including a
plastic Cyrillic Erika from the 1970s and a rusty Triumph Adler. But the darling that caught my eye was a teal green East German Rheinmetall covered
in at least a decade's worth of dust. I liberated it for thirty euros. When I got
it home, I noticed that it too had a metal plaque on the back, inscribed with
the words "VE Lichtspielbetreib (B)—Gera—Inv. Nr. G 37/72/351." Without
knowing it, I had inherited the typewriter (or one of the typewriters) of the
"people-owned" movie theater in the nearby city of Gera. Unlike my Olympia, produced in postwar capitalist West Germany and privately owned by a
housewife in Baden-Württemberg, my new Rheinmetall was built by men
and women in a *Volkseigener Betrieb* (people-owned enterprise) and used
in a people-owned cinema. Thus, until rather late in its biography, my new
Rheinmetall had never been private property.

By February 2016, all of my other German typewriters had been hand
carried or shipped back to the United States (anyone who came to visit me
had to agree to take a typewriter back with them). But I kept the Olympia

and the Rheinmetall with me in Jena. As I wrote the essays and stories for this book, I used one of these two typewriters every day, probably annoying my upstairs and downstairs neighbors. Back in the Black Forest, my daily typewriter pages had become a habit, and my landlord there (who lived in the apartment above me) once knocked on my door to inquire about the source of the clacking sound. Jörn, a West German from Hamburg in his midforties, evinced surprise when I told him I wrote on a manual typewriter.

"Can you do me a favor?" he asked.

I nodded, bracing myself for a request to cease and desist. "Sure."

"Can you make a recording?"

"Excuse me?"

"When you're typing, can you record some fifteen minutes of the sound?"

I furrowed my brow. "It doesn't bother you?"

Jörn shook his head. "No, I like it. I want to listen to it more."

So I never felt guilty for the year I lived below Jörn, but when I moved into the university guesthouse in Jena, I limited my clacking to the afternoon and early evening, and then only with a towel under the typewriter on the dining room table.

Typewriters have history because there was no planned obsolescence. As long as you don't drop them and do keep them well cleaned, they can work forever. In Germany, the history of typewriters reflects the broader trials and tribulations of German industry. They say the pen is mightier than the sword, but here typewriters and guns actually share a common origin. Indeed, if Germany had won more of the wars it started, my Olympia and Rheinmetall typewriters might have never existed.[1]

Rheinmetall was and remains one of the world's largest arms manufacturers, its fortunes waxing and waning with the prevalence of war. The first Rheinmetall company was founded in 1889 to manufacture weapons and ammunition.[2] By 1890, the original factory in Düsseldorf employed 1,400 workers producing roughly 80,000 bullets a day. But the real breakthrough came with the invention of the "first fieldworthy recoiling cannon, one of the outstanding engineering achievements of the age."[3] In 1901, Rheinmetall bought a munitions and weapons factory in Sömmerda, Thüringen, which specialized in the manufacture of handguns and more precision instruments of death.

At the outbreak of World War I, Rheinmetall was among Germany's biggest arms manufacturers, employing 8,000 workers in early 1914. This workforce expanded to 14,000 in 1915, and by 1918, almost 50,000 Germans worked in Rheinmetall factories, including some 9,000 women (since so many German men were otherwise occupied with using Rheinmetall weapons at the front).

With the cease-fire in November 1918, German production of armaments screeched to a sudden halt. The punitive terms of the Treaty of Versailles banned the German production of large armaments, and Rheinmetall was forced to retool its factories to build industrial goods that didn't kill people. The small gun factory in Sömmerda began to manufacture typewriters and accounting machines in 1920, attempting to compete with Olympia, another typewriter manufacturer based in nearby Erfurt.

The Olympia typewriter company originally started in Berlin in 1901 as a subsidiary of the European General Electric Company (AEG).[4] After a commercial success with its Model 3 Mignon typewriter, AEG bought a small factory in Erfurt in 1923. This factory dated back to 1862 when it served as the Royal Prussian Gun Factory, which, like the Rheinmetall Sömmerda factory, had to adapt its machines to produce civilian goods after the Treaty of Versailles. AEG thus built most of its typewriters on machines that were also once used to make guns. The company started using the brand name Olympia in 1930.[5]

Meanwhile, the Allies allowed Germany to begin limited production of smaller weapons in 1921, and the German Reich acquired a controlling stake in Rheinmetall by 1925, making it a state-owned enterprise. During the 1930s, Rheinmetall started developing new weapons for the Nazi Ministry of War. In contravention of the Treaty of Versailles, Rheinmetall returned to the production of heavy weapons, and the Sömmerda factory abandoned typewriters in favor of guns. After the German invasion of Poland in September 1939, Hitler nationalized all weapons manufacturing facilities and forced other factories, such as Olympia in Erfurt, to begin producing weapons and munitions in support of the German war effort.

Between 1941 and 1944, Rheinmetall engineers, with full Nazi support, developed some twenty new weapons systems for use against the Allied forces.[6] Technological innovation spurred greater demand, and Rheinmetall became the second largest arms manufacturer for the Third Reich. But labor shortages limited Rheinmetall production capacity. In 1944, about a thousand Jewish women were transferred from the nearby Buchenwald concentration camp to do forced labor in the Sömmerda Rheinmetall factory, making bullet casings on the machines that once made typewriter keys.[7]

In 1945, the Allies bombed both Erfurt and Sömmerda, severely damaging the Olympia factory but leaving the Rheinmetall factory unscathed. As Allied troops moved toward the region, the concentration camp prisoners and the forced laborers at Sömmerda began a death march toward Czechoslovakia. On April 11, 1945, American soldiers arriving in Sömmerda found an intact but abandoned factory. A few days later, Soviet soldiers occupied both Er-

FIGURE 7.4. Typewriters in the Erfurt Stadtmuseum.

furt and Sömmerda and the Soviets expropriated both the Rheinmetall and Olympia factories. In Rheinmetall's official corporate history, available on its website in 2016, the company makes no mention of the Jewish forced laborers in its Sömmerda factory during the war, and merely states that after 1945, "assets in the areas occupied by the Red Army are lost. Up to 1950, there is a complete ban on production."[8]

Between 1945 and 1960, there existed two Rheinmetalls, one in West Germany, which, after 1950, resumed arms manufacturing as its core business, eventually developing into Europe's largest supplier of "army technology."[9] The Sömmerda factory was almost immediately reopened by the Soviets in 1945, employing some 1,500 workers to build automotive parts. In 1949, the Soviets transferred ownership to the new government of the GDR, and the Sömmerda factory became the Volkseigener Betrieb Büromaschinenwerk Sömmerda (People-Owned Office Machine Works Sömmerda). Beginning in the early 1950s, workers in the Sömmerda factory returned to making typewriters and other office machines under the Rheinmetall brand, including the green typewriter I bought in Jena in December 2015. By 1957, the Sömmerda factory began experimenting with electronics. In 1960, the factory abandoned the name Rheinmetall and sold its products under a new brand: Supermetall. The enterprise took its first steps into the age of computers in 1962 using the brand name Soemtron, which eventually became a member of the Volkseigener Betrieb (VEB) Kombinat Robotron, a conglomerate of electronics manufacturers that made the GDR's computers and printers.[10] VEB Kombinat Robotron employed tens of thousands of workers in the GDR and existed right up until German reunification, when it was broken up and sold off in parts.[11]

Perhaps my interest in typewriters and typewriter history seems eccentric, but when you start collecting something it's normal to dig up a little background information on your fetish. For instance, I know the actor Tom Hanks harbors his own typewriter obsession, a collection he started in 1978, which has expanded to fill up his office, his home, his storage facility, and the trunk of his car.[12] Hanks loves typing so much that he created an application that simulated the sound of a typewriter for electronic devices: the Hanx Writer.[13] Typewriter collectors band together across Europe and North America, and the German club for old office machine aficionados is the I.F.H.B., the Internationales Forum Historische Bürowelt, which publishes a journal and a newsletter and has over three hundred individual and institutional members.[14] Everything I ever wanted to know about how old typewriters work could be found at the www.antike-schreibmaschinen.de website. My daughter calls it steampunk, but most of the collectors online are less interested in the aesthetics of old office equipment than in preserving an appreciation for the human ingenuity of the past.

But in addition to the joys of being a collector, I swear that my typewriters have made me a better writer. I produce early rough drafts without the distractions of the computer and without the temptation to edit too early in the writing process. I have so far resisted the lures of optical character recognition (OCR) technology, which can produce an electronic text file from a typewritten page. Instead, I use my typewriters for getting ideas on paper, and then retype the prose I want to keep into the computer using my sleek, wireless, and virtually soundless keyboard.

So yes, I know that typewriters are inefficient, that they're noisy, that they're heavy, and that they require ribbons that aren't easy to find. But consider the advantages. Typewriters never crash, never need software updates, don't become obsolete every four years, and require no backing up. Because manual typewriters function without electricity, they're also environmentally friendly. When I type outside, I can work in full sunlight and not have to worry about the glare on my screen. If I spill a drink on the keyboard, nothing terrible happens to my machine. Typewriters never overheat. When something goes wrong with my typewriter, a screwdriver and some machine oil are usually all I need for the repair. When I am sitting on my backside for long hours writing, my typewriter gives my fingers a good workout, so I feel like I'm exercising. My eyes never hurt from staring too long at my typewriter. Perhaps most importantly, when I write on a typewriter, my friends, family, colleagues (and neighbors) can all hear that I'm working, so they're less likely to disturb me. I can misspell words and use bad grammar without my word processing program judging me, and typewriters encourage my writing by providing a celebratory ding when I reach the right margin. It's like a little party every time I finish another line.

Like my Rheinmetall typewriter, my Olympia also dealt with a post–World War II division. As the Soviets marched into Thüringen in 1945, some employees fled westward with Olympia typewriter designs, and built a new Olympia factory in Wilhelmhaven on the North Sea. In the new GDR, the government repaired the original Olympia factory and workers reverted to building typewriters and other office machines. After a protracted legal dispute over the brand name, which had to be settled by the International Court in The Hague, the Wilhelmshaven machines continued to be called Olympia while the East German machines were sold under the name Optima.[15] The West German company renamed itself Olympia Werke, and the East German factory became VEB Optima Büromaschinenwerk, which eventually became a part of the VEB Kombinat Robotron in 1978.[16] Optima continued to produce standard typewriters until the end of the communist era, but from 1961 onward, East German portable typewriters were sold under the brand name Erika, which were ubiquitous in the flea markets and thrift stores of Thüringen in 2016.

But the days of the typewriter (and of the GDR) were numbered. The tale of the demise of the East German typewriter and electronics industry encapsulates the brutal swiftness of the privatization process following the reunification of the two Germanies in 1990. The desire to create a free market economy in the GDR meant that all people-owned enterprises needed to pass from state to private hands. The political merger between East and West Germany occurred on October 3, 1990, when the official Treaty of Unification came into effect and the GDR ceased to be an independent country. The five states of the east acceded to the Federal Republic of Germany, and West German laws replaced those extant in East Germany, a total administrative change effective immediately.

The economic unification of the two countries proved more contentious than the political reunification. East Germans desired democracy, but many had reservations about free market capitalism. On July 1, 1990, the currency union abolished the GDR currency, and the new German leaders pursued a shock therapy course of privatization, transferring all GDR assets (land, factories, forests, mines, etc.) to a holding company called the Treuhandanstalt (Trust agency), or Treuhand for short. As I discussed briefly in chapter 5, the federal government charged the Treuhand with the immediate sale, liquidation, or return to previous owners of all East German assets. It took control of about 13,687 companies responsible for employing 4.1 million East Germans.[17] The fate of VEB Robotron, the parent conglomerate of the typewriter manufacturing factories in Sömmerda and Erfurt, lay with the bureaucrats in the Treuhand.

The politics of privatization differed throughout the former communist region, but the basic transfer of property from public to private hands remained the same everywhere. The colonization of East Germany through the process of privatization differed from that in other postcommunist countries because the GDR alone became part of an already existing capitalist country with a functioning market economy.[18] But no matter where they occurred, post-1989 privatizations were fraught with difficulties, and many ordinary people came to view the process as a form of theft, whereby new economic elites stole the once collectively owned assets of entire nations.

It's essential to remember that, despite their many faults, state socialist regimes prohibited the private ownership of the means of production in order to prevent the exploitation of the working classes. Communist leaders justified bureaucracy, stagnation, and economic inefficiency with egalitarian promises of a classless society. These beliefs structured everyday life in East Germany for four decades, and the sudden and unexpected collapse of state socialism could not instantly erase local ideals, no matter how discredited those ideals had become in practice. Thus, privatization of the people's property required not only the physical transfer of assets from the state to private individuals, but also the ideological justifications to make this radical reconcentration of property acceptable to the local population.

Countries like Poland, Czechoslovakia, and eventually Bulgaria tried to implement privatization programs based on the relatively equitable distribution of shares in the socialist state's assets to the population at large.[19] This form of privatization involved the distribution of investment points to all adult citizens. Each citizen received vouchers that could then be traded for shares in any state enterprise, or handed over to an investment fund that pooled the vouchers, made the investment decisions, and later paid dividends to its shareholders (much like a mutual fund). Although plagued by various forms of internal corruption, these programs allowed the local population to feel like they benefited from the privatization process. Even when corrupted, mass privatization favored old managers and new domestic elites rather than predatory foreign investors with few ties to the local economy. But mass privatization was never an option in the GDR. East Germans watched helplessly as the Treuhand dismantled the industrial base and shuttered the people-owned enterprises to which many had given their lives.

The responsibilities of the Treuhand included the valuing of East German enterprises and finding interested buyers. Some enterprises were outdated or falling apart and required massive capital investment to bring them up to West German standards. Additionally, many enterprises held considerable debts, which the Treuhand assumed only if it deemed the enterprise potentially profitable in the future. Because the East German state guaranteed full employment to its citizens, many enterprises also supported surplus workers, with wages subsidized as a matter of public policy. The rationalization of the workforce (corporate speak for firing people) proved an essential step in preparing enterprises for sale. Finally, the old GDR traded with the Eastern Bloc before 1989, with more than two-thirds of its production going to fellow socialist countries. The currency reunification of 1990 suddenly rendered East German products too expensive for its old trading partners. Markets for East German goods evaporated just as the Treuhand needed to measure their future viability.

In practice, the Treuhand favored large West German corporations, which snapped up the crown jewels of East German industry at bargain prices because they had the best investment plans. In some cases, factories became the workshops of West German companies like Rheinmetall, Krupp, or Siemens. In other cases, West German businesses bought their East German competition and simply shut down production lines to eliminate competition for their own goods. So, for instance, the East Germans once produced Trabant cars, small vehicles with a relatively fuel-inefficient two-stroke engine, which were the most popular car in the GDR and were exported across the Eastern Bloc. Once made by VEB Sachsenring Automobilwerke Zwickau in Zwickau, Saxony, Trabants provided competition to West German car manufacturers. Volkswagen bought the privatized factory in 1991, discontinued production of the Trabant, and retooled the factory to manufacture auto parts for Volkswagen cars. Manfred Bock, the former director for privatization of the Treuhandanstalt, admitted in the fall of 1991, "West German industry has mainly used privatization to broaden its production base and gain access to a new market of 16 million consumers."[20]

At the same time Bock lamented, the Treuhand sold its property in a buyer's market, since expediency forced it to sell enterprises as quickly as pos-

FIGURE 7.5. Old GDR street signs now on display in the Erfurt Stadtmuseum.

sible without being able to wait until better offers came along. Imagine an estate sale where all goods must sell within four hours and where all potential buyers know that anything not sold in these first four hours will be thrown away. Bidders will compete for the most valuable items, but for anything for which there is no competition, the buyer can simply wait until the sale is over and take it home for free (or ensure that it is destroyed). This "Everything must go!" mentality produced devastating social consequences in terms of sudden redundancies and personal upheavals. And although the Treuhand understood these effects and saw clearly the havoc wreaked on the lives of ordinary East Germans, it continued with its program of shock therapy. In 1991, Bock observed, "The present privatization process is also characterized by grave labor difficulties. Although the enterprises of the [Treuhand] presently employ 2.1 million people (after 4 million one year before), some 400,000 will have to be dismissed by the end of 1991. . . . Their official dismissal will mean that unemployment in East Germany could go up to 40 percent by the end of the year."[21]

Firms that could not find buyers were liquidated, with old but still functioning machines sold off as scrap. Old but still functioning workers were treated no better. The Treuhand made millions of men and women redundant overnight, replacing people with machines or outsourcing jobs to countries where labor was cheaper. West Germans complained bitterly about the solidarity taxes necessary to support the newly unemployed, but cared little for the psychological effects of unemployment on a population raised to value work as a right of citizenship. In the heydays of the 1960s, VEB Optima employed 6,900 workers before it was folded into the VEB Robotron conglomerate, which employed 68,000 East Germans across ten different divisions.[22] When the Treuhand gained ownership over VEB Robotron, bureaucrats broke the Kombinat into smaller pieces to make them more attractive for sale. The most valuable bits were sold off to West German companies, but those left unsold faced liquidation.

To make matters worse, East German bidders had little chance in the privatization transactions, largely because they lacked the necessary capital to modernize the enterprises. But even when East Germans secured the capital, the Treuhand questioned whether East German owners possessed the skills necessary to produce viable business plans for future competitiveness in a market economy.[23] If no West German or foreign bidders appeared, the Treuhand considered offers from former enterprise directors. VEB Optima in Erfurt was one enterprise privatized through a management buy-out, but with limited capital and limited markets, the new private company was forced to downsize.[24] By 1992, the factory employed only 250 workers before it went bankrupt. VEB Soemtron fared little better. In 1995, demolition experts destroyed the old factory in one dramatic explosion as former employees looked on.[25]

By August 1994, as it prepared to close its doors, the Treuhand had spent 217 billion dollars in its efforts to restructure the companies, pay down extant debts, and honor labor contracts.[26] The Treuhand raised 46.8 billion dollars through the sale of assets from the acquired companies, but a 170 billion dollar deficit remained to be paid by future German taxpayers (effectively a transfer of East German public wealth to private West German corporations). At the same time, the industrial base of the East was destroyed as West German corporations smashed competition to ensure future market share for their goods and services. Of the 4.1 million jobs supported by the enterprises inherited by the Treuhand, only 1.5 million remained in East Germany by 1994. In the span of four years, 2.6 million men and especially women became surplus labor in the new market economy, their old jobs eliminated, mechanized, or sent abroad. East German women, who had long suffered from the double burden of formal employment and domestic work, were expected to go home and enjoy their new freedom as unremunerated housewives, economically dependent on their husbands for the first time in their lives. While some surplus labor was employed in the GDR's industries (as a matter of public policy), the unemployment that followed the Treuhand clearance sale also resulted from liquidating enterprises that competed with extant West German firms rather than from efficiency gains.

Local memory of these dramatic upheavals lingered even twenty-five years after the events. In Erfurt, I met the daughter of a typewriter engineer who used to work at the VEB Optima factory. Although she was only four and a half years old when the Wall came down, and she said she was happy to live in a reunified Germany, Juliana collected GDR typewriters and insisted that "not everything was so bad at that time." She told me that her parents, who had been opposed to the regime, were still angered by the economic ruin visited upon them in the early 1990s. In Jena, I became acquainted with a young man from one of the rural parts of Thüringen who also bemoaned the fate of his parents, dislocated after the early 1990s. He felt particularly frustrated for his mother, who was well educated and once had a full-time job in a textile factory. Since 1991, she had been employed only sporadically, changing workplaces more than six times, and still unable to find a full-time job. Although he was too young to have worked in a people-owned enterprise, Tobias could recite from memory the exact number of workers once employed at VEBs the Treuhand had liquidated in his region.

Also in Jena, I met a party activist for the Social Democratic Party, a leader of their women's section. She fumed, "My mother is sixty-two and has a working biography of forty-five years, and her pension is going to be a joke. In these twenty-five years since reunification, they haven't managed to fix this." Since Germans face a mandatory retirement age of sixty-five, this activist's mother would be unable to support herself on her state pension. "So many lives were ruined by these changes," the SPD leader told me. "Of course they're angry." Frustration with these negative economic impacts of reunification contributed to the state victory for Die Linke in Thüringen in 2014.[27]

But East German workers weren't the only victims of the changing times.[28] We know from history that "the bourgeoisie cannot exist without constantly revolutionizing the instruments of production."[29] Even the West German workers weren't immune to the whims of global markets and the impacts of technological change. For private corporations labor is just an expense, a line item on a ledger sheet, and profits can be increased by shifting production abroad or by replacing workers with technology. And so it went with the venerable old typewriter, swept away by the generations of computers and versions of Microsoft Word that replaced it, soon to be pushed aside by the tablets and smartphones that become antiquated five minutes after you buy them. After several unsuccessful attempts to diversify its product line,

West German Olympia Werke went bankrupt in 1992. The production of the few remaining Olympia typewriters moved to Mexico where labor cost less. In that year, 3,600 West German employees were turned out of their jobs when the Wilhemshaven factory closed, despite their efforts to create a new technology park in its place, joining their East German counterparts in the swelling ranks of surplus workers in the reunified Germany.[30] Technological obsolescence provided the justification for moving jobs abroad.

In my apartment in Jena, I alternated daily between my Olympia and Rheinmetall typewriters. Although they were both more than half a century old, everything continued to work: the individually spring-loaded keys, the typebars striking against the platens and returning to their nests, and the carriages gliding smoothly to the right when I pushed the return bars to begin a new line. Sometimes I set them side by side, like an old married couple in a retirement home, and anthropomorphized them, imagining their conversation.

"I was built in the free West, by free workers, who enjoyed the benefits of free markets and free elections," the Olympia would say. "My owner was a good mother and a good wife, and I spent many years with her, writing her letters, and keeping her company when the children were off at school."

The Rheinmetall would sneer. "You were a slave, always a piece of private property: first a commodity that produced profit for the corporation exploiting the workers that made you, and then a toy for a bored housewife whose domestic labor was exploited by those that depended on her work but were unwilling to pay for it. I was built in a people-owned factory and used in a people-owned cinema that projected films to working women when they finished their shifts. I was never a commodity. I was a means of production."

"You supported an oppressive state apparatus that limited personal freedoms!"

"You supported a bourgeois order that waged war to increase profits for the rich!"

"Communist!"

"Capitalist swine!"

A silence would follow, and then Olympia would huff, "I can't believe I have to share my new owner with you filthy red garbage."

"I didn't ask to be here," Rheinmetall would say. "I had no choice in the matter. I still work perfectly fine. They retired me against my wishes."

At this, Olympia would simply nod her carriage. "Me, too," she would say, sighing. "Me, too."

PART III. **Blackwashing History**

8. Gross Domestic Orgasms

Do communists have better sex? That is the question posed in a 2006 German documentary film called *Liebte der Osten anders?—Sex im geteilten Deutschland* (Did the East love differently? Sex in divided Germany), a wonderful reflection on how the two contrasting political and economic systems of the twentieth century manifested themselves in the realm of intimacy.[1] Every once in a while I read a book or watch a film that makes me spend the next weeks regretting that I wasn't the person who wrote or directed it. That's how I felt about *Liebte der Osten anders?*, and that is why I (perhaps foolishly) agreed to lead a discussion about it with an audience full of West Germans when I was a fellow at the Freiburg Institute for Advanced Studies (FRIAS) in March 2015. In the spirit of open academic inquiry, I thought it might be possible to publicly explore whether an oppressive political system like that of the GDR could paradoxically lead to greater individual satisfaction in everyday life.

My FRIAS hosts had announced my talk to the whole university and the wider Freiburg scholarly community. The old anatomy classroom filled with my colleagues and a surprising number of younger people, unfamiliar faces, who slid into seats behind the narrow wooden bench desks that ran in long, tiered semicircles around the back arch of the room. The ceiling of the lecture hall was high and the seating was steeply angled; I would deliver my talk from behind a podium in a small round pit below the audience. At exactly thirty minutes past five o'clock, the academic director of FRIAS introduced me, and I started by showing three clips from the film.

The documentary builds on sexological research conducted in the months immediately following the fall of the Berlin Wall. Here were two populations of Germans—more or less similar in all respects save for the four decades they spent under capitalism and communism. The film starts with a scene of animated East Germans flooding into the West clutching televisions and bananas. A cartoon sociologist proceeds to measure "from a strictly scientific point of view, of course, everything having to do with sex in the two Germanies." This animated sociologist stands between two couples: one from the West and one from the East. A blue curtain falls in front of the West Germans and a red curtain falls before the East Germans. When the curtains rise, the West German man sits satisfied atop the West German woman while the positions of the East Germans are reversed. The narrator then reports, "the East German women's orgasm rate was apparently double that of their West German sisters." Sex in the former GDR was "earlier, better, [and] more often" than in the West. The question: why?

The second film clip discusses the differences between women's social position in West versus East Germany after World War II. The devastated postwar economies of both Germanies suffered acute labor shortages and surpluses of women. But whereas the East German government fully incorporated the ladies into the labor force, liberating them from their economic dependence on men, the West German government reinforced the traditional family structure as a way of distancing itself from the supposedly loose morality of the Nazi era.[2] Where East German women got state support for their roles as mothers and workers in the form of expanded nurseries, kindergartens, public laundries, canteens, and generous maternity leaves and child allowances, the government of the Federal Republic of Germany taught West German women to cook and clean and stay at home with their children. According to the filmmakers, the economic emancipation of East German women perhaps resulted in greater control of their bodies and sexuality. They could choose partners out of love and attraction rather than financial necessity.

The final clip investigates the commercialization of sex in Western Germany after the sexual revolution in the late 1960s and 1970s. Prominent German sexologists discuss how sex and sexuality became commodities in the West, something to be bought and sold, or at least manipulated to sell products. In the absence of consumer culture, pornography, or advertising, amorous activities supposedly remained free and natural in the East. Finally, over 90 percent of the East German population participated in the mass culture of nudism that prevailed in the GDR, a totally unsexualized, family activity that the government once tried to suppress but later fully embraced as evidence of the superiority of socialism.[3]

I showed these three snippets of the film hoping to spark a debate about the public memory of Germany's communist past. "Today," I said, "stereotypes about communism in Eastern Europe lead us to believe that everything was bleak and gray. But when I talk to people about ordinary life under communism in Bulgaria, for instance, they tell me that it wasn't always bad, that there were some good things, especially with regard to social stability and women's rights. But when I talk to people in the West, all I hear about is the labor camps and the secret police. I once gave a lecture in Washington, DC, about postcommunist nostalgia in Eastern Europe. When I finished, a West German woman asserted that I couldn't trust the opinions of people from East Europe. She said they suffered permanent psychological damage because they lived under a totalitarian regime."

I caught the eye of a young woman in the second row, another fellow at FRIAS, who had been born in the GDR. I knew from our lunch conversations that her grandparents were fervent communists filled with what the Germans called Ostalgie (nostalgia for the East). She looked wary, warning me with her eyes that it was useless to challenge West German prejudices about communism. I often met resistance to my scholarly research on women's rights before 1989, especially from those invested in the narrative of totalitarianism. Most West Germans embraced the uncritical view that people who lived under communism were either duplicitous collaborators or mindless automatons. It was my mission to try to complicate things.

Of course, sexual satisfaction is a subjective category, one based on men's and women's personal recollections of their experiences. I agree that self-reporting presents methodological challenges. But when a sociological study finds that East German women claim greater sexual satisfaction than their Western peers, and this study is conducted by the same researchers under the same circumstances—asking the same questions about the frequency of sex and how often this intercourse leads to orgasm to a representative sample of both East and West Germans—it seems worth investigating why. There was a fact of the matter: women were either having sex with their partners or they weren't. And despite the vast differences in the political and economic systems of the FRG and the GDR, the basic mechanics of the act remained similar on both sides of the Iron Curtain. Moreover, even if the East German women just imagined that their sex lives were more satisfying, this still tells us something important about their erotic proclivities compared to their Western counterparts. Since love and sex play a large role in the vast majority of adult lives, we might glean important lessons about the intimate effects of capitalism compared to state socialism. As the historian Dagmar Herzog asserted, "Sex can be the site for talking about very many other things besides sex."[4]

"So why would East German women report that they have better and more frequent sex than their Western sisters?" I said to the audience. "The film suggests some possible answers, but leaves this open to interpretation."

Silence filled the lecture hall until a West German FRIAS fellow raised his hand. "Maybe East Germans had nothing better to do."

I smiled and nodded. "Yes, that might account for part of it. For example, there were fewer opportunities for shopping. I read a recent study that found that 55 percent of British women in relationships found shopping more satisfying than sex with their partners."[5]

A few members of the audience laughed.

A middle-aged woman raised her hand. "What about the role of the state? Maybe private lives were more important in East Germany because people lacked freedom in the public sphere."

One great thing about my job is that I get to read a lot of books about everyday life during and after communism in Eastern Europe. Even if I haven't done primary research on a topic, I can reference those who have. I responded to this question by citing the work of the Oxford historian Paul Betts, who agreed that East Germans retreated to the private sphere to avoid an over-intrusive state.[6] Another historian, Josie McLellan, specifically examined sex in the GDR during the Honecker years (1971–1989) in her book *Love in the Time of Communism*. She argued that the East German sexual revolution reflected popular frustrations with state policies. As East Germans grew more pessimistic about their political and economic situation, they embraced nudism and sensual enjoyments as a salve for their existential woes. The regime responded by decriminalizing homosexuality, encouraging premarital coitus, and destigmatizing single motherhood as a way to placate a restless population.[7] The East German communists said, "Sex yes, travel no."[8]

Another hand went up. "What about the role of the church, which was much stronger in West Germany than in the East? Were things different in Poland, where the Catholic Church still played a role under communism?"

In response to this question I discussed the work of Agnieszka Kościańska, a Polish colleague of mine and an anthropologist studying the history of sexology in her country. She examined sex education and the treatment of sexual dysfunctions in Poland before and after communism and found that, despite the influence of the Catholic Church, progressive sex education was widely available in schools and abortion remained legal. Kościańska contrasted the biomedical and physiological understanding of sexuality in the United States with the more holistic view supported by communist sexologists. After 1989, the dominant narrative in scientific circles was that "the backward East had to catch up with the West," but Kościańska's research showed that, in many ways, the East surpassed the West in terms of having a more nuanced understanding of human sexuality.[9] She argued that American researchers William Masters and Virginia Johnson focused exclusively on physical aspects, claiming that good sex was the result of proper stimulation for both men and women, who moved through a four-stage sexual response cycle. This view, based on laboratory experiments, came to dominate the international field of sexology and led to the medicalization of sexuality, ultimately benefiting the U.S. pharmaceutical industry, which developed drugs targeting physiological problems.

In Poland, by contrast, sexologists complemented their medical knowledge with psychology, history, and philosophy. They viewed human sexuality as embedded in the wider context of human interactions. Polish sexologists explored individual desires for love, intimacy, and meaning, and listened carefully to the dreams and frustrations of their patients. The communist government paid salaries and provided research budgets, a stark contrast with the prevalence of private and corporate funding in the West. In her interviews with sexologists, Kościańska explained that they only realized their previous privileges after 1989:

> My interlocutor, a sexologist and psychiatrist of the older generation, recalled in interviews a visit to Poland of a group of North American sexologists in the early 1990s. He told me that the guests had been impressed by the freedom Polish sexologists had under socialism. They envied their colleagues on the other side of the Iron Curtain because they were not dependent on the pharmaceutical industry and could rely on state funding. At the same time, my interlocutor described North American sexology as commercial, which meant restricted to conducting research and training that had market value.[10]

After the fall of communism, market pressures impacted Polish sexologists as much as their North American colleagues, but there remained a sex-positive legacy, which accounted for higher rates of sexual satisfaction even decades after communism ended. According to the studies cited by Kościańska, 75 percent of Polish women were free of sexual dysfunction compared to only 55 percent of American women.[11]

"So despite the conservative gender roles promoted by the Catholic Church and the post-1989 ban on abortion," I said, "Polish women are still having a much better time in bed than women in the West."

Five more hands shot up. A French woman asked if I had rates of female sexual satisfaction for other European countries. I didn't.

My East German colleague raised her hand, and I nodded at her.

"My mother was East German," she said, "and she had to work and take care of the children and the housework, and she was so very busy and very exhausted. Yes, women had rights in the workplace, but men did not help in the home. There was still a lot of inequality between men and women."

"Yes, the notorious double burden." I said. "This often comes up when I talk about women's rights under state socialism. Women did have a lot of responsibilities in the home and in the workplace, and they were not allowed to stay at home and be housewives or to work part time. The state forced everyone to work at a formal job, and not all of these jobs were so great. But socialist countries conducted a lot of surveys, and when women were asked if they would prefer to stay home if their husband's income could support them, the overwhelming majority of women in all communist countries said 'no.' Women wanted to work."

I walked around to the front of the podium and leaned against the table. "But the fascinating thing is that women in the West *could* stay home and be housewives. They weren't trying to combine work and family, but they still reported having less sex with their partners, and less satisfying sex, than women in the East. Doesn't that seem like a contradiction? Western women had more time for themselves—to sleep, to work out, to do yoga, or whatever— but by their own report they had sex less often. If Eastern women were exhausted, apparently their Western counterparts were more so."

I continued by explaining that in my twenty years of research in Bulgaria, people often told me that they had much more time under communism. Sure, they complained about having to wait in line to procure basic goods, and about the soul-crushing bureaucracy involved in procuring a private car or a new apartment, things that could take years without the right connections or a well-placed bribe. Some basic things like tampons or disposable diapers were impossible to buy, and time-saving consumer appliances were in limited supply, increasing the time needed for domestic work. At the same time, they complained to me that life is faster now, that they must run everywhere to get everything done, and that they lead exhausting, multitasking lives with no time for friends or family or lovers. The conundrum for me, however, is that I've seen time budget data from 1969. Back then Bulgarian women reported that they labored for about 14.5 hours a day if you combined their home and work responsibilities, and also included time spent commuting or waiting in line for scarce goods. Despite the sheer number of hours they worked, somehow time moved more slowly. Bulgarians often recall weekends and paid holidays free from modern anxiety and stress.

"So maybe the comparison is not about the actual amount of time spent at home or at work or waiting in line for toilet paper, but about the stress one feels about the passing of time, the anxiety produced by living in a society where time is money. Maybe in the East, time, like sex, wasn't something to be bought or sold."[12]

I paused to gather my thoughts and walked back behind the lectern. "The second part of your comment is something I hear quite often. And it's something I spend a lot of time thinking about in my own research."

My Ossi colleague raised an issue that haunted every talk I gave about women's rights under state socialism. Western feminists always pointed out that the situation of women in the communist countries was never as good as their governments claimed: patriarchy at home remained; there existed a gender division of labor and a gender pay gap; and communist political elites were overwhelmingly male. East European nations encouraged heterosexual relationships and often promoted traditional gender roles to improve falling birthrates. Much of this was true, but not at all times or in all state socialist countries.

And focusing on these negatives deflected attention from the many positives; East European women enjoyed far more rights and privileges compared to Western women, particularly when it came to state supports for finding a work-family balance. Western feminist demands were often for things already granted to women in state socialist countries: formal legal equality enshrined in the constitution, expanded educational and professional opportunities, full incorporation into the labor force, abortion on demand, liberalized divorce laws, the ability to keep one's maiden name, and equal property rights, as well as massive social supports for childbearing and child rearing. All of these changes meant that women gained independence from men and no longer felt compelled to trade their bodies for the economic security that bound Western women to unhappy marriages and sexually incompetent lovers. My colleague Dagmar Herzog recalls a fascinating conversation she had with several East German men in their midforties in 2006: "It was really annoying that East German women had so much sexual self-confidence and economic independence. Money was useless, they complained. The few extra Eastern Marks that a doctor could make in contrast with, say, someone who worked in the theater, did absolutely no good, they explained, in luring or retaining women the way a doctor's salary could and did in the West. 'You had to be interesting.' What pressure. And as one revealed: 'I have much more power now as a man in unified Germany than I ever did in communist days.'"[13] In other words, the economic disadvantages that capitalism creates for women give greater power to men who don't have to "be interesting" if they have money.

The financial and sexual independence of women was not only particular to Eastern Germany. At various points, communists advocated for free love and sexual liberation throughout the Eastern Bloc, starting, of course, with the Soviet Union after the Russian Revolution in 1917.[14] One early Russian women's rights advocate, Alexandra Kollontai, proposed that satisfying one's desire should be like quenching one's thirst—having sexual intercourse should be like drinking a glass of water. For their part, early socialist thinkers believed that monogamous marriage was a tool for the bourgeois enslavement of women, an institution that guaranteed the production of legitimate heirs who could inherit a man's private property. Do away with heritable property and you do away with the need for marriage. Or you can do away with monogamous marriage, and thereby challenge the basis of the economic system responsible for the reproduction of class inequalities. That was the idea anyway.

Beginning in October 1918, the Soviet Union liberalized divorce and abortion laws, decriminalized homosexuality, permitted cohabitation, and ushered in a host of reforms that instigated a red sexual revolution.[15] But without birth control, this early emancipation produced many broken marriages and broken hearts, as well as countless children born out of wedlock. The epidemic of divorces and extramarital affairs created social hardships when Soviet leaders wanted people to concentrate their efforts on growing the economy. Giving Soviet women control over their fertility also led to a precipitous decline in the birthrate, perceived as a threat to their country's military power.[16] By 1936, Stalin reversed most of the liberal laws, ushering in a conservative, pronatalist era that lasted for decades to come.[17]

But the example of the early Soviet experiment with a liberalized family code, as well as the continued importance of socialist theories about women's emancipation, had important impacts on East European nations after World War II. In Czechoslovakia, for instance, the sociologist Kateřina Lišková argues that the idea of women's economic and political equality with men infused all of the early sex manuals available to Czechoslovaks between 1948 and 1968.[18] For the first two decades of state socialism, Czechoslovak sexologists advised the population that satisfying sexual relations and healthy marriages could only result from an equal relationship between male and female partners. The state sponsored publications and television shows to educate the population on the desirability of equitable partnerships well before Western feminists even had a language to critique the myth of the happy housewife.

In Bulgaria, the state women's committee pursued strategies to promote sexual equality within both the workplace and the home. In a 1972 Politburo decision to enhance the status of women and increase the birthrate, the socialist government explicitly called for the reeducation of men so that they would share household responsibilities with their wives.[19] The Bulgarian state-run women's magazine, *The Woman Today*, published articles discussing the important role of fathers and showing images of men changing diapers and boiling laundry. Legal provisions for maternity leave allowed mothers to transfer part of their unused leave to their husbands, and the state encouraged men to take a more active role in parenting as early as 1968. In the end, most efforts to encourage men to help at home proved unsuccessful. Patriarchy remained strong in Bulgarian families, proving that the centralized authority of a communist state was not as all-powerful as many in the West imagine it.

By the time I finished talking, I gauged the crowd and felt their attention fading. I still saw several raised hands, but I made eye contact with the professor who had introduced me. He put up a finger, signaling me to take one more question. I scanned the hall and pointed to an economist that I'd seen around the FRIAS lunchroom.

"What does it matter if people had better sex lives?" he said. "Sex is no substitute for freedom." The word "freedom" hung in the air. For many West Germans, freedom served as the trump card. Freedom of movement, freedom of speech, freedom of choice. Questioning freedom made you an apologist for dictatorship. A room full of eyes turned on me.

I inhaled and left the podium, walking around to address the economist without the protection of the formal lectern. I chose my words with care, deciding to speak not about Germany but about the country that I knew best.

"I am American, and I usually live in the United States." I pressed a hand to my chest. I lowered my voice and spoke in a slow and clear tone to ensure that my words were not misunderstood. "In my country we have freedom of speech, of assembly, of the press, of religion. I have the freedom to buy a gun, or many guns, and I have the freedom to vote in democratic elections at the local, state, and national level. All of these are rights guaranteed to me as part of the social contract."

I paused to think about the message I wanted to convey. "But there are many people in my country who live precarious lives: people who have lost their jobs, or who fear losing them. People who have jobs, who are working full time, but do not make enough money to pay their bills. People living without health insurance or access to basic health care. People who are homeless. Children who are homeless. Men and women who don't know where their next meal is coming from. People who want to work, but who can't find jobs. They are technically free, but is that the most important thing for them?"

I stopped again, gathering my thoughts and examining the faces around the hall. "I suppose everything depends on what you mean by the word 'freedom.' Maybe when you have your basic needs taken care of: when you know that you'll have food to eat and a roof over your head; when you know that you will be taken care of if you get sick and that your children will be able to go to good schools; when you know your body is not something you need to sell to survive; maybe that produces a different kind of freedom. I don't think these two types of freedom need to be mutually exclusive, but in practice it seems to me that our Western societies privilege the first kind of freedom over the second."

I looked up at the economist. He glared down at me, frowning. I straightened up. "I suppose what I find most interesting about the film is the idea that communists did have better sex and that this more satisfying intimacy arose because of their society's commitment to equality, particularly between men and women. I'm not denying that the GDR got a lot of things wrong: the consumer shortages, the travel restrictions, and the Stasi listening in on everyone and compelling people to inform on their family and friends. It's just that too often we allow our stereotypes about communism to blind us to the possibility that there might have been a few good things under that system, even if these were only very personal things like having better romantic relationships."

I scanned the faces in the room once more. "After 1989, maybe the West threw the baby out with the bathwater. Maybe we could have learned a few things from the East. Instead we just discredited everything. I think we might all have very different opinions about what is most important in life: feeling free or feeling secure or feeling loved and respected by our partners. Maybe different people in different circumstances, in different cultures and historical eras, have worldviews that differ from our own."

I rested my eyes on a young student sitting in the third row. She smiled at me. I smiled back. "Even about something as basic as what it means to be free."

9. My Mother and a Clock

I want to begin with a confession, but I fear placing the words on a written page and publishing them in a book. They will haunt me for the rest of my living days and perhaps cast a dark shadow over my memory when I am gone. Some things should be kept private, uttered only in the safe confines of a therapist's office and protected by strict laws of doctor-patient confidentiality. Certain secrets should remain secret. But in the interests of science, I will admit that I like socialist realism.

There. I said it. I've exposed myself to eternal ridicule and incredulity. Perhaps only the art cognoscenti will understand the true magnitude of my aesthetic crime, but I nevertheless shiver in terror at the thought of my intellectual colleagues reading this admission. They will marvel at my poor taste, regarding my lack of disdain for socialist realism as a greater embarrassment than, say, an abiding passion for Barry Manilow or a heartfelt admiration for the literary quality of Danielle Steele romance novels. So in my defense, I will try to explain why, despite its universal derision, I find some socialist realist art and literature appealing. For this, my most heinous cultural faux pas, I blame my mother and a clock.

My descent on this staircase of uncultivated disrepute began in 2000 when I was a Fulbright scholar in Bulgaria doing my dissertation research on women in the tourism industry. My mother, a Nuyorican from Washington Heights, visited me in Sofia for two weeks in the early spring. Bulgaria provided her first experience in a postcommunist country, and she arrived brimming with Cold War stereotypes. Born in 1949 to a Puerto Rican garment worker who left her to be raised by Catholic nuns until she was fourteen years old, my mom only graduated from high school and married my father at eighteen. She spent her whole life working as a secretary for people with college degrees, and she harbored a solid Hispanic working-class sensibility. But socialism and communism counted among the bad words in her limited political lexicon, not because she understood what they meant, but because Cubans and Russians were communists, and every good American knew that Cubans and Russians were our enemies.

On several occasions I attempted to explain the basic ideas behind socialism—collective ownership of the means of production, economic planning, and the more equitable redistribution of accumulated surplus value—but she failed to understand. I tried again with examples from the cooperative movement and other employee-owned enterprises. She thought this sounded like "hippie stuff," and she disliked hippies because "they didn't bathe enough." Finally, I tried to use examples from the Catholic Church, telling her about liberation theology and the priests that advocated for land reform. But she replied that all the priests she knew were Irish who didn't even bother to learn Spanish. In truth, politics held little interest for her. She came to Bulgaria to sightsee.

I have this vivid memory of driving from Sofia to the winter ski resort of Borovets just outside the town of Samokov. The road to Borovets winds through the Rila Mountains, and beside the two-lane highway there stood a massive statue of a construction worker.

My mom put her camera down and pointed. "What's that?"

"It's a monument," I said. "Probably commemorating the workers who built the road."

"A particular worker?"

"No, just all of the workers."

She wrinkled her brow. "Why would they do that?"

"Well," I said, realizing that she would see a lot of these kinds of statues around Bulgaria, "because the socialist countries valorized the labor of ordinary people. The road didn't build itself. A lot of people probably worked for a long time building this road, so the statue is there to remind you that you are driving on a road built by people."

"But who paid for the road?" she said.

"The government did, just like governments do everywhere. But the gov-

FIGURE 9.1.
A socialist
realist sculpture
in porcelain.

ernment pays people to do the work, and without the workers there would be no road."

My mom stared out the window for a few moments. "Is that communism?"

"Sort of," I said, shifting down to third gear to make a sharp turn. "The idea that a country can't function without working people, and that the workers are the most important part of society. The communist countries were trying to create a system where workers were respected, rather than just providing labor for the rich people who employed them."

My mom digested my words, scratching her nose like she did when she balanced her checkbook. "Are secretaries workers?"

"Sure, anybody who works for a living is a worker."

FIGURE 9.2. An East German socialist realist sculpture of Hans and Sophie Scholl.

My mom nodded. She looked back out the window, watching the pine trees as the road twisted through the mountains. Maybe five minutes passed before she spoke. "So why is communism bad?"

"A lot of bad people did bad things with these ideas." I said. "Dictatorships suck, and a lot of innocent people got sent to camps and things. But the ideas themselves aren't so bad."

I drove for another kilometer, shifting up and down between third and fourth gear. "But rich people hate them," I said.

My mom snorted. "Of course, rich people hate them. They don't know anything about hard work. My boss wouldn't be able to function without me, but he never says so. He gets paid the big bucks but I do all the work."

After that drive, I took special care to point out all monuments and statues dedicated to workers and peasants. These included simple representational sculptures of young, optimistic men and women: cooperative workers harvesting grain, miners leaning on their picks. She took photos of them all, snapping her camera at each artistic vestige of Bulgaria's recent past. Although she regretted that we found no bronze or granite renderings of female office workers, my mom later reported that "the communist statues" and the "tasty Shopska salads" were her two most favorite things about Bulgaria.

People like my mom formed the target audience for these works of socialist realism, art created to be relevant and understandable to the lives and experiences of ordinary laborers. The "socialist" part of the term refers to the partisan nature of the art—it should have a clear and simple message supporting the ideological perspectives of socialism. The "realist" part of the term meant that the sculptures, paintings, poems, and works of literature produced under this style should be representational or realistic, preferably depicting scenes and activities from everyday life. Socialist realist artists endeavored to create an art for the masses, a positive, forward-looking art that celebrated ordinary men and women. Critics lambaste it as mere propaganda. They deride it as kitsch because socialist realism caters to the tastes of the poor and uneducated, never indulging in the luxury of art for art's sake, but rather "Art for Marx's Sake."[1] Abstraction plays no role here, and no one requires a special course to understand why something counts as art.

In the twentieth century, the mass appeal of socialist realism proved so powerful that the American secret services went out of their way to counteract it, forever shaping what educated elites considered good art. In the mid-1990s, a former CIA case officer revealed that his agency had worked tirelessly behind the scenes to popularize American modern artists such as Jackson Pollock, Mark Rothko, and Willem de Kooning. "It was recognised that Abstract Expressionism was the kind of art that made Socialist Realism look even more stylised and more rigid and confined than it was," Donald Jameson explained in 1995. "And that relationship was exploited."[2]

Working through the Congress for Cultural Freedom, the CIA sponsored major international exhibitions of American painting and published reviews in influential art magazines, promoting the American aesthetic as part of an ideological strategy to win the Cold War. Unbeknownst to the artists, the CIA served as a secret patron, ensuring that their works came to dominate the art world in Europe. Tom Braden, the first head of the CIA's International Organizations Division, served as the executive secretary of the Museum of Modern Art in 1949. He played an important role in the promotion of nonrepresentational art, recalling:

> We [the CIA] wanted to unite all the people who were writers, who were musicians, who were artists, to demonstrate that the West and the United States was devoted to freedom of expression and to intellectual achievement, without any rigid barriers as to what you must write, and what you must say, and what you must do, and what you must paint, which was what was going on in the Soviet Union. I think it was the most important division that the agency had, and I think that it played an enormous role in the Cold War.[3]

FIGURE 9.3.
A relief of two
women with
doves.

The CIA acted covertly because most of the American public, including my mother, hated modern art. When the U.S. government spent 49,000 taxpayer dollars to buy paintings for an exhibition called *Advancing American Art* in 1946 and 1947, conservative artists and politicians derided the collection, claiming that it was unrepresentative of real American art and a waste of public funds.[4] Then secretary of state George C. Marshall canceled the exhibition and promised that public funds would no longer be used to purchase modern art. From then on, the CIA worked through cultural front organizations to advance American arts and sciences in Western Europe. By contrasting the freedom of American artists compared to their communist counterparts, the United States hoped to win the hearts and minds of West European artists and intellectuals, many of whom identified with socialist politics if they weren't already members of communist parties. The goal of CIA support for nonrepresentational art was to wrest high culture from the left. Writing in the *New Yorker* in 2005, Louis Menand explained:

> Abstract painting was an ideal propaganda tool. It was avant-garde, the product of an advanced civilization. In contrast to Soviet painting, it was neither representational nor didactic. It could be understood as pure painting—art absorbed by its own possibilities, experiments in color and form. Or it could be understood as pure expression—a "school" in which every artist had a unique signature. A Pollock looked nothing like a Rothko, which looked nothing like a Gorky or a Kline. Either way, Abstract Expressionism stood for autonomy: the autonomy of art, freed from its obligation to represent the world, or the freedom of the individual—just the principles that the United States was defending in the worldwide struggle.[5]

Although the story of CIA involvement in the promotion of modern art is now well known, these clandestine battles over what defined great art still inform our modern tastes, including the continuing deprecation of the socialist realist style. This is not to deny the censorious conditions under which much socialist realist art in the Eastern Bloc was produced; artists who did not follow the party line were denied opportunities to create and show their works and had few possibilities of legally emigrating to more liberal artistic communities in the West. The communist states consistently interfered with the private realm of artistic expression, often going so far as to persecute deviant artists who refused to conform, but it was not as if the artistic communities in the West were free from state interference. At least in the late 1940s and 1950s, the surrealist hells of communist censorship were mirrored in the United States during the McCarthy era when many filmmakers and writers were hauled up in front of the House Un-American Activities Committee and blacklisted.

The U.S. government not only intervened in the visual arts but also shaped expectations about what constituted good literature. In a controversial 2014 story on the involvement of the CIA in the founding of the Iowa Writer's Workshop and creative writing programs across the United States, Eric Bennet argued that the development of American fiction was deeply influenced by the desire to distance itself from socialist realism. As with painting and sculpture, there should be no messages in good fiction. Feeling, not thinking, should infuse literary writing. A story should be told for its own sake. In American creative writing programs, rich descriptions of the sensual world ruled supreme, and too many engagements with the realm of philosophy or politics became the hallmarks of bad writing, habits to be beaten out of you before you graduated. Bennet writes, "At Iowa, you were disappointed by the reduced form of intellectual engagement you found there and the narrow definition of what counted as 'literary.' The workshop was like a muffin tin you poured the batter of your dreams into. You entered with something undefined and tantalizingly protean and left with muffins."[6]

With full awareness of the CIA's involvement in defining what counted as good art, I attended the first exhibit of Bulgaria's new Museum of Socialist Art in Sofia in 2012. The curators of this Museum of Socialist Art initially considered opening a Museum of Totalitarian Art, since the art was produced during what many people refer to as the country's totalitarian era: 1944–1989.[7] But controversy swirled around this first choice of name because the artists included in the exhibit rejected the term "totalitarian art," which was a historically inaccurate description of their work. Instead, they embraced the term "socialist realism," situating their work within the global artistic movement that defined much of the early twentieth century, and not only in Eastern Europe. They objected to the retrospective politicization of their art because of the era in which it was produced.[8] It would be like branding all pre-1863 painting and sculpture in the United States as "slavery art."

At the same time, opposition to the museum emerged from artists whose work had been banned or censored during the pre-1989 era. They despised the idea that a museum would celebrate the work of those artists who kowtowed to the previous regime rather than to those who resisted it. These artists, inspired by trends in Western modern art, never followed the aesthetic dictates of socialist realism and therefore lacked the support of the communist government. They believed (perhaps as the CIA wanted them to) that they were artistic dissidents against communism. The heated public debate about the new museum threatened the whole project as Bulgarians chose sides either for or against the socialist realists, many of whom were famous Bulgarian painters and sculptors. In the end, the minister of culture sided with the idea that the artistic movement known as socialist realism unified the artistic production of Bulgaria's so-called totalitarian era, and that aesthetics should be separated from politics, especially when it concerned a potentially lucrative tourist attraction.

The Museum of Socialist Art now sits far outside the center of Sofia, and most visitors to the city have a hard time discovering the location of this curious cultural outpost. Even as late as 2015, Sofia taxi drivers could not find it. Although there is a metro stop nearby, the entrance to the museum is still a good ten-minute walk away with little signage to guide even the most intrepid visitor. The whole complex hides behind a tall, mirrored business tower, and the only clue that you have found it is the large red star that peeks over the gates at the entrance. This star, a symbol of communism, once sat atop the Party House in the center of Sofia, only to be hauled away by helicopter after the fall of the Berlin Wall. It spent much of the 1990s gathering dust in a junk heap before finding a home in the new museum.

Unlike the private DDR Museum in Berlin, the Museum of Socialist Art is a state institution, a branch of the National Art Gallery.[9] It consists of a permanent outdoor sculpture garden, an indoor painting and sculpture gallery for temporary exhibitions, a video screening room, and a small souvenir shop. The sculpture garden preserves the stuff that my mom loved when she visited back in 2000. The statues, busts, and reliefs well represent the style of socialist realism. As pieces of public art, funded by generous government grants, these works once populated the central squares of Bulgaria's towns and cities, only to be torn down after 1989 in the effort to "decommunize" the Bulgarian landscape. Some had been unceremoniously dumped into municipal warehouses, while others fell victim to metal scavengers who stole them and sold them as scrap. In some towns, families of local heroes who had been immortalized in bronze and stone privatized the sculptures to prevent their defacing. State curators for the new museum rescued these relics of the past, hoping to preserve the artistic production of this period of their country's history, if only to open the pockets of foreign tourists.

The two largest pieces in the sculpture garden were a four-meter-tall stone Vladimir Lenin by the Soviet artist Lev Kerbel, and a five-meter bronze rendering of Bulgaria's first communist premier, Georgi Dimitrov. There were a few more heads of Lenin and of Karl Marx, as well as some diminutive busts of Bulgaria's leader for thirty-five years, Todor Zhivkov and his daughter, Lyudmila Zhivkova, who once served as the country's minister for culture. But Zhivkov disliked the Stalinist cult of personality, and the vast majority of sculptures in the permanent collection revered the everyday heroism of the working classes.

These works commemorating nameless peasants, workers, and partisans outnumbered those of great communist leaders. Several wonderful bronzes celebrated ordinary Bulgarians: digger women, milkmaids, and miners. Sculptures of partisan fighters commemorated the bravery of the men and women who took up arms to fight the Nazi-allied Bulgarian monarchy in World War II. One sculpture called *Head of a Worker* exemplified the quiet respect that the socialist realists showed to the common person. The face exuded confidence, determination, and hope. The CIA hated this stuff. It took twenty-two

FIGURE 9.4.
The head of a
worker.

years before the Bulgarian government created a home for sculptures such
as *Head of a Worker*, and it is difficult to know how many like it were lost to
vandalism and pilfering.

The indoor gallery space has hosted a wide variety of exhibitions over the
years, but none compares to the carefully curated splendor of the opening
show back in 2011, which unearthed the pre-1989 gems in the basements of
the National Gallery of Art. These included colorful paintings celebrating
rural Bulgarian life or valorizing industrial workers in factories and mines.
A famous painting of Georgi Dimitrov defending himself before the Nazi
tribunal loomed on one wall, and there were several works celebrating Bulgarian partisans. I especially liked the stone bust of a woman member of the

cooperative farm, or the small statue of a reaper woman. Although created in the style of socialist realism, many of the paintings were beautifully rendered, a testament to the skill and creativity of the artists. Some may have been committed communists willingly embracing the ideals of socialist realism. Others may have compromised with the regime to develop their own talents, working within the popular aesthetic of the time. Quotidian themes dominate: a miner reading a newspaper, joyful women in traditional Bulgarian costume returning from the harvest, peasant men sawing on fiddles.

Detractors of socialist realism always point to state interference in artistic production to discredit its aesthetic value. But states throughout history have supported art that promotes their own goals (or the tastes of their upper classes) while censoring or discrediting that which does not. The CIA's role in supporting modern art has not diminished its appeal. Moreover, when the Cold War ended and the U.S. government no longer needed to weaponize creativity, artists fell to the mercy of markets, in itself a form of censorship for those who do not wish to produce the type of art meeting the aesthetic tastes of those rich enough to buy it. I have spoken with artists, filmmakers, journalists, and writers across the former communist countries. They complain bitterly that their creativity is more constrained today by free markets than it ever was under the socialist state. Even in the United States, critiques of the commodification of art abound.[10] In 2015, legendary *Star Wars* director George Lucas claimed that filmmakers in the Soviet Union had more freedom than those working in Hollywood, who, he asserted, "have to adhere to a very narrow line of commercialism."[11]

I returned to the Museum of Socialist Art about a year or so later to see a new exhibition in the indoor gallery, but this second collection of paintings disappointed beyond measure. A few of the best and most famous paintings from the original show remained, but the curators replaced all the others with gargantuan portraits of Bulgaria's communist leaders, particularly Valko Chervenkov, Stalin's puppet in Bulgaria in the early 1950s. The purpose of this second exhibit seemed clear: to remind both foreign and Bulgarian visitors that communism was a totalitarian system that could only produce terror, labor camps, and dangerous cults of personality around a few revered leaders. Gone were the joyous peasants, valiant workers, and fierce partisans of the first exhibition. In their place, I saw the visual embodiment of Bulgaria's continuing struggle to come to terms with its state socialist past. In truth, perhaps that first exhibition had romanticized the pre-1989 era a bit. By focusing on the ideals and the dreams, and by sharing the artistic vision inspired by those ideals and dreams, the original choice of paintings and sculptures

FIGURE 9.5.
Cubist Marx
and Engels.

glossed over the more brutal sides of the previous regime. But there existed
little subtlety in the message of this second exhibit; curators used works once
criticized for being too political to make a political statement.

I had the same impression when I visited Hungary's Memento Park. Ban-
ished to a remote suburb of Budapest, the park contains representative pieces
of Hungarian communist-era statuary from the capital and caters to tourists hoping for a photo op with a bust of Lenin. The main part of the park,
called Statue Park, is officially named "A Sentence about Tyranny." It feels like
a communist graveyard with monumental headstones. Some of the sculptures are impressive for their sheer size: a colossal worker caught in midstride

as he marches toward the bright future. But much of the collection consists of figures of Marx, Engels, Lenin, Dimitrov, and personalities from Hungary's communist past. The curators also included a preponderance of Soviet war memorials and statues celebrating Soviet-Hungarian friendship. Only a handful of sculptures represented ordinary workers and peasants.

At the gift shop, I could buy a red poster of "The 3 Terrors: Stalin, Mao, Lenin" in the style of the posters for the Three Tenors (Pavarotti, Domingo, and Carreras). They also sold small red cans of "the last breath of communism," featuring the image of Lenin with a yellow hammer and sickle. The poster by the exit gate read, "Forgot something maybe? You cannot take the statues and their atmosphere home but its last touch you can! The last breath of communism saved in a can. Best gift from Memento Park available at the gift shop."

I asked the shop attendant what was in the can.

"Nothing," she said. "Just air."

"Do people actually buy this?"

She shrugged. "All the time."

Across from the main part of the park, stone likenesses of Marx and Engels gazed over a pedestal bearing a replica of Stalin's boots, a symbol of the 1956 Hungarian uprising. On either side of the pedestal sat two double-wide trailers used for educating Hungarian schoolchildren about the horrors of communism. Memento Park had no interest in preserving specimens of Hungarian socialist realism. Like the second exhibition in Sofia's Museum of Socialist Art, the creators of Memento Park crafted the exhibition to reject Hungary's communist past and fleece a few tourists along the way.

I visited Memento Park in October 2014, just two weeks before my planned trip to Berlin for the twenty-fifth anniversary of the fall of the Berlin Wall. The Hungarians showed me the ugly side of socialist realism. Maybe they were right. Maybe the political conditions of its production obliterated its aesthetic qualities. Maybe, at the end of the day, rich and educated consumers of high art possessed better taste than working-class secretaries. Maybe socialist realism shared a category with velvet Elvis portraits or the cloying paintings by Thomas Kinkade.[12] Perhaps there existed genuine aesthetic truths about beauty, and I was simply too deficient to recognize them. Or maybe I just had bad taste, which, like my olive skin and curly hair, I inherited from my mom. For fourteen days, I resolved to swear off socialist realism.

Then I met the clock.

On November 6 and 7, two days before I traveled to Berlin, I delivered a lecture and taught a seminar in the Department of Sociology at the university

FIGURE 9.6. Worker striding toward the revolution.

FIGURE 9.7. An empty can containing the "last breath of communism."

FIGURE 9.8.
The Olomouc
astronomical
clock.

in Olomouc in the Moravian half of the Czech Republic. My hosts put me up
in a little guesthouse, and I had some hours to explore the environs before
meeting them for dinner. Right in the center of Olomouc, on Horní Náměstí,
sits the old town hall. Built into the side of the building is an astronomical
clock, one of only two in the Czech Republic and among the handful of those
left in Europe. Astronomical clocks not only show the date and time but also
track the movements of the sun, moon, and sometimes the planets. In May
1945, retreating Nazis fired upon the Olomouc astronomical clock, originally
built sometime in the late fifteenth or early sixteenth century, leaving little
more than a rubble heap. The clock remained in ruins for the rest of the 1940s
until a local artist decided to rebuild it.

FIGURE 9.9. The Olomouc town hall.

FIGURE 9.10. The blacksmiths that spin on the hour.

FIGURE 9.11.
The mosaic of a
mechanic.

The present clock stands fourteen meters high in an arched recess in the side of the town hall. The clock has six dials, two large and four small, which keep track of the minute, hour, day, month, moon phases, and year, as well as the positions of the sun, earth, and planets in relation to the twelve houses of the zodiac. Around the circumference of the lower of the two larger dials are the names of the 365 saints' days. A delicate mosaic in subtle earth tones provides the backdrop. Just above the dials are two arches from which models of human figures move in a circular progression at midday to the music of the glockenspiel. But unlike other astronomical clocks that venerate the lives of saints and kings, the Olomouc clock valorizes members of the proletariat.

The artist who reconstructed the clock in the 1950s embraced the aesthetic of socialist realism. On one side of the lower dials stands a mosaic mechanic grasping a wrench. On the other side, a scientist in a white lab coat examines the contents of a beaker. On the inside of the framing arch, one can find a harvest scene for each month of the year. Two blacksmiths hammer out each hour on a miniature anvil, and at noon little communists slowly spin to the sound of traditional folk music. The figures include a mother with her child, a young woman clutching a volleyball, a factory worker, a miner, a farmer, and other ordinary men and women with no saintly or aristocratic pretenses. The artist maintained the structure of the clock but completely changed its iconography, signaling a break with the hierarchies of the past.

On first inspection, one might dismiss the Olomouc clock as an ugly reminder of communist kitsch, the aesthetic author Milan Kundera railed against so passionately in his novel about the Prague Spring, *The Unbearable Lightness of Being*.[13] Workers and peasants have no right being on an astronomical clock. The faded figures circling around at noon might seem silly, even sacrilegious. Surely, it is profane to replace the regal procession of saints and kings with a pathetic parade of desk clerks and auto repairmen.

But as I studied the dials of the astronomical clock, I thought about the inevitable passage of time: the minutes, hours, days, months, and years ticking by. I considered the smallness of the little square in the little city of Olomouc, in the little country that was now the Czech Republic. I felt the tininess of the earth compared to the vastness of the heavens represented on the star map. In the face of all this insignificance, of the infinities of time and space, I paused to appreciate those twentieth-century idealists who believed that the tractor drivers and secretaries of this world deserved their own little place in the grandeur of the cosmos.

My mom would have loved it.

10. Venerating Nazis to Vilify Commies

I'm lucky that I'm not a scholar of Ukraine. If I wrote books about Ukraine like the ones I've written about Bulgaria, they would now be illegal. My articles would be illegal, too. In fact, my thoughts and opinions would be illegal. My observations and arguments, based on years of historical and anthropological research, would be illegal. Even asking the kinds of questions I ask, posing the kinds of thought experiments I pose, would be illegal.

When a postcommunist government limits freedom of speech to suppress the historical memory of communism, they either fail to see the point of democracy or they are rewriting its rules. It's like Joseph McCarthy using fear and intimidation to fight against a political regime hated for its use of fear and intimidation. Some might argue that you have to fight fire with fire, but the metaphor fails if what you must preemptively scorch includes human minds. A new government of Ukraine wants its citizens to accept one state-sanctioned truth about their country's past and has criminalized historical questioning.[1]

This official decommunization process began in April 2015 when Ukrainian lawmakers proposed to erase all physical vestiges of their Soviet past. On May 15, President Petro Poroshenko signed a new law calling for the removal of all Soviet-era statues and symbols, and the renaming of towns and villages saddled with names deemed too communist by the government.[2] Across the country, demolition crews dismantled World War II monuments commemorating the Red Army victory over the Nazis, while local authorities endeavored to scrub maps clean of the proper nouns they deemed inappropriate for the new democratic Ukraine.[3]

But the most controversial section of the new statute, "On condemning the communist and National Socialist (Nazi) totalitarian regimes and prohibiting propaganda of their symbols," outlawed public questioning of the "criminal character of the communist totalitarian regime of 1917–1991 in Ukraine."[4] In other words, the Ukrainian state legislated the correct opinion their citizens should have about a recent past through which many of them had lived. Any suggestion in a newspaper or magazine that the era between 1917 and 1991 had some redeeming qualities was unacceptable. The Kharkiv Human Rights Commission in Ukraine reported, "President Poroshenko has signed highly contentious laws one of which effectively criminalizes public expression of views held by many Ukrainians."[5] This included the recognition of the 1.5 million Ukrainians who fought against Hitler as soldiers in the Red Army. In an April 2015 "Open Letter from Scholars and Experts on Ukraine," sixty-nine academics from North America and Europe preemptively condemned the proposed laws, writing, "However noble the intent, the wholesale condemnation of the entire Soviet period as one of occupation of Ukraine will have unjust and incongruous consequences. Anyone calling attention to the development of Ukrainian culture and language in the 1920s could find himself or herself condemned. The same applies to those who regard the Gorbachev period as a progressive period of change to the benefit of Ukrainian civil society, informal groups, and political parties."[6]

Also in April 2015, Dunja Mijatović, the representative on freedom of the media for the Organization for Security and Cooperation in Europe (OSCE), wrote to President Poroshenko to persuade him against adoption of the proposed laws. She stated, "While I fully respect the often sensitive and painful nature of historical debate and its effect on society, broadly and vaguely defined language that restricts individuals from expressing views on past events and people, could easily lead to suppression of political, provocative and critical speech, especially in the media."[7] But Poroshenko ignored the protests. The law allows the government to shut down offending media outlets and carries potential prison sentences of five to ten years.[8]

Even more disturbing was the companion law "On the Legal Status and Honoring of the Memory of the Fighters for the Independence of Ukraine in the 20th Century." This statute criminalized public critiques of certain organizations that fought for Ukrainian independence, including the Organi-

FIGURE 10.1. The author with Angel Wagenstein, a ninety-year-old Jewish filmmaker who fought as a partisan during World War II.

zation of Ukrainian Nationalists (OUN) and the Ukrainian Insurgent Army (UPA).[9] Writing in opposition to the law, historians Christopher Gilley and Per Anders Rudling asserted that both the OUN and the UPA "were demonstrably guilty of mass murder," and that the new laws promoted the valorization of individual Ukrainian fascists.[10] The OUN had split into two divisions by 1940, one led by the more moderate Andriy Melnyk and the other by the more radical Stepan Bandera, who eventually formed the UPA, which carried out the large-scale ethnic cleansing of Poles and Jews. In Volhyn and eastern Galicia, historians estimate that the UPA massacred up to 100,000 Poles, including women and children.[11] In their open letter to President Poroshenko, the sixty-nine concerned North American and European academics insisted that if the proposed laws passed:

> Not only would it be a crime to question the legitimacy of an organization (UPA) that slaughtered tens of thousands of Poles in one of the most heinous acts of ethnic cleansing in the history of Ukraine, but also it would exempt from criticism the OUN, one of the most extreme political groups in Western Ukraine between the wars, and one which collaborated with Nazi Germany at the outset of the Soviet invasion in 1941. It also took part in anti-Jewish pogroms in Ukraine and, in the

case of the Melnyk faction, remained allied with the occupation regime throughout the war.[12]

Despite continued international opposition (and the revelation that the law on honoring the fighters for Ukrainian independence was initiated by the son of a former commander in the UPA), Poroshenko's government proceeded with its plan to eradicate anti-Ukrainian symbols and ideas. On December 17, 2015, a Kiev court upheld the legality of the government's ban on the Ukrainian Communist Party, on the grounds that it promoted separatism. The party (whose flag included a hammer and sickle) refused to comply with the May 15 law outlawing Soviet symbols and the use of the term "communist."[13] The next day, the European Commission for Democracy through Law (the Venice Commission) and the OSCE Office for Democratic Institutions and Human Rights (OSCE/ODIHR) issued a joint opinion stating that the Ukrainian law, "On Condemning the Communist and National Socialist (Nazi) Totalitarian Regimes and Prohibiting the Propagation of their Symbols" (Law No. 317-VIII) did not comply with the legislative standards necessary for a European democracy.[14] The opinion stated, "The law is too broad in scope and introduces sanctions that are disproportionate to the legitimate aim pursued. Any association that does not comply with Law No. 317-VIII may be banned, which is problematic with regard to every individual's freedom of association. This is particularly the case when it comes to political parties, which play a crucial role in ensuring pluralism and the proper functioning of democracy."[15]

The beautiful irony of the Council of Europe and the OSCE opinion is that the inspiration for the Ukrainian laws most likely drifted eastward from the European Union in the first place. For the last eight years, I have watched with increasing interest (and occasional outrage) as EU bureaucrats tried to legislate a revision of European history. Conservative forces within the EU wanted to legitimate the narratives of the two totalitarianisms and the double genocide, two once-fringe perspectives equating communism with Nazism, and promoting the idea that the suffering of East Europeans under Soviet occupation should be treated as equal to that of the Jews during the Holocaust. After 2007, many Europeans (and especially Germans) have embraced this equivalency, unthinkable in the 1980s.

Although these historical debates have roots in the Cold War, a key date for me was June 3, 2008, when a group of right-leaning Eastern European politicians and intellectuals signed the Prague Declaration on European Conscience and Communism in the Czech parliament. The signatories to this declaration proclaimed that the "millions of victims of Communism and their families are entitled to enjoy justice, sympathy, understanding and recognition for their sufferings in the same way as the victims of Nazism have been morally and politically recognized" and that there should be "an all-European understanding . . . that many crimes committed in the name of Communism should be assessed as crimes against humanity . . . in the same way Nazi crimes were assessed by the Nuremberg Tribunal." The signatories addressed their demands to "all peoples of Europe, all European political institutions including national governments, parliaments, the European Parliament, the European Commission, the Council of Europe and other relevant international bodies."[16]

The Prague Declaration contained a list of demands, including compensation for victims. It also called for the establishment of a European "day of remembrance of the victims of both Nazi and Communist totalitarian regimes, in the same way Europe remembers the victims of the Holocaust on January 27th." The Prague Declaration further advocated for the creation of a supranational Institute for European Memory and Conscience as well as increased support for memorials, museums, and national historical institutes charged with investigating the crimes of communism. Finally, the declaration demanded the "adjustment and overhaul of European history textbooks so that children could learn and be warned about Communism and its crimes in the same way as they have been taught to assess the Nazi crimes."[17]

Between 2008 and 2013, and against a backdrop of growing social unrest in response to the global financial crisis and Eurozone instability in Spain and Greece, European leaders instituted many of the recommendations in the Prague Declaration. The European Day of Remembrance for Victims of Stalinism and Nazism was created by the European Parliament in 2008. This new day of remembrance was officially endorsed by the OSCE in the Vilnius Declaration of 2009, a declaration that also instructed the nations of Europe to create a collective policy on "the world financial crisis and the social consequences of that crisis."[18] The Platform of European Memory and Conscience was founded in Prague in 2011, and by 2013 this consortium of nongovernmental organizations and research institutes had forty-three members from thirteen European Union countries as well as in Ukraine, Moldova, Iceland, and Canada.[19] The United States was home to two organizations that were members of the Platform of European Memory and Conscience: the Joint Baltic American National Committee and the Victims of Communism Memorial Foundation.[20] The latter was an organization headed by Lee Edwards, the Heritage Foundation's Distinguished Fellow in Conservative Thought and "a leading historian of American conservatism."[21]

On January 20, 2012, the seventieth anniversary of the 1942 Wannsee Conference that chose the Final Solution, two academics presented the Seventy Years Declaration to the president of the European Parliament. Seventy members of the European Parliament signed this declaration rejecting all "attempts to obfuscate the Holocaust by diminishing its uniqueness and deeming it to be equal, similar or equivalent to Communism as suggested by the 2008 Prague Declaration."[22] The Seventy Years Declaration rejected the idea that European history textbooks should be rewritten to promote the idea of the double genocide—the moral and historical equivalence of the Jewish victims of Nazism and the East European and German victims of Soviet communism.

Because of my research in Eastern Europe, I often wondered why politicians resurrected these historical debates seventy years after the end of World War II and more than twenty years after the collapse of communism. But once I began to examine the broader context for the Prague Declaration, I believed that the Eastern European desire to equate communism and Nazism might stem (at least in part) from a political desire for victimhood status. The idea of the twin totalitarianisms and the double genocide produced a historical narrative wherein post-Soviet and postsocialist nations become martyrs—nation-states sacrificed by the West on the red altar of Soviet imperialism. In countries such as Ukraine, where local populations and Nazi-allied governments or militia groups participated in the systematic murder of domestic Jews, the concept of the double genocide also mitigated their culpability by questioning the uniqueness of the Holocaust.[23]

In addition to this desire for historical exculpation, however, I also believe that the rewriting of history to equate Nazism and communism must be viewed in the context of the rightward drift in Eastern Europe, and the emergence of illiberal democracies in countries like Poland and Hungary. In the face of growing economic instability, massive migrant inflows, and anti-austerity protests on the peripheries of Europe, the two totalitarians narrative exculpates nationalists by linking all leftist political ideals to the horrors of Stalinism. Anticommunism legitimates resurgent nationalisms. Such a rhetorical move seems all the more potent when coupled with the idea that there is a moral equivalence between Jewish victims of the Holocaust and Eastern European victims of communism.

This anticommunist political project requires the production of a certain story about the communist past, and in this project, both Western and Eastern European academics have perhaps unwittingly obliged, as long as the European Union provides the funds. With the tacit support of Brussels, there exists today in many Eastern European countries (not just Ukraine) an institutionally sanctioned prohibition on thinking about the everyday lived experiences of communism. In an era of supposed free speech and freedom of conscience, politicians, scholars, and activists try to drown out other stories about the past by focusing exclusively on the crimes of communism. Organizations associated with or influenced by the Platform of European Memory and Conscience try to manipulate history—by rewriting, for instance, official history textbooks—and stifle public debate using methods that mimic those once deployed by the very communist regimes they are so keen to criticize and discredit, such as the 2015 Ukrainian decommunization laws.[24]

To explain how the Ukrainian law grew out of broader European memory politics, it is instructive to go back and revisit something called the Historikerstreit, or the Historians' Battle. This Historikerstreit was a major public debate between right-leaning and left-leaning historians in West Germany in the late 1980s. The conflict was sparked by U.S. President Ronald Reagan's May 1985 visit to the Bitburg Military Cemetery. Together with West German Chancellor Helmut Kohl, Reagan spent eight minutes in a graveyard that contained the final resting places of forty-nine Waffen ss soldiers. The following day, Bernard Weinraub of the *New York Times* reported, "White House aides have acknowledged that the Bitburg visit is probably the biggest fiasco of Mr. Reagan's Presidency. The visit, which was made at the insistence of Mr. Kohl, was overwhelmingly opposed by both houses of Congress, Jewish organizations, veterans' groups and others."[25] The Bitburg visit, and Reagan's explicit commemoration of Nazi soldiers and Holocaust victims on the same day, set off a firestorm of controversy that precipitated the Historikerstreit. Public intellectuals took to the broadsheets of their country's major newspapers to exchange views on the enduring legacies of the Nazi past.

The West German historian Ernst Nolte launched the first salvo in the Historian's Battle on June 6, 1986, with an article that appeared in the center-right newspaper *Frankfurter Allgemeine Zeitung*. The article, "Vergangenheit, die nicht vergehen will" (The past that will not pass) was an abridged missive from his forthcoming book, *Der europäische Bürgerkrieg* (The European Civil War). In the article, Nolte argued against a reigning paradigm that viewed the Holocaust as a unique product of German history and asserted that Hitler's embrace of National Socialism was an understandable reaction to Russian Bolshevism. Nolte catalogued early Soviet crimes, and he employed traditional right-wing terms such as "Asiatic deeds" to do so. In addition, he proposed that fascism was a counterrevolution against communism—that communism was the original totalitarianism. He wrote, "Wasn't the gulag archipelago more original than Auschwitz? Wasn't Bolshevik 'class murder' the logical and actual predecessor to National Socialist 'race murder'?"[26] According to Nolte, the Nazis only made more efficient the mechanisms for mass murder previously invented by the Soviets.

An immediate rebuttal came from the sociologist and philosopher Jürgen Habermas, who attacked Nolte for trying to relativize the Holocaust: "Nolte's theory offers a great advantage. He kills two birds with one stone: the Nazi crimes lose their singularity in that they are understood to be an answer to Bolshevik threats of destruction (which are apparently still present today); and Auschwitz shrinks to the dimensions of a technical innovation and is to be explained through an 'Asiatic' threat from an enemy who still stands before our gates."[27] The opposing views espoused by these two articles ignited a vitriolic public debate among German intellectuals, pitting the conservative Nolte and a handful of colleagues against Habermas, and eventually against the majority of West German public opinion.[28]

In a twenty-year retrospective on the Historikerstreit, historian Norbert Frei argued that the conflict was an intergenerational tussle initiated by those German historians born during the Weimar Republic. These men lived through the Nazi period as teenagers, "often as members of the Hitler Youth or as young soldiers."[29] Frei argued that the Historikerstreit was the product of "a generation of researchers and individuals who had a specific autobiographical agenda and were facing retirement at the start of the 1990s."[30] Thus, the Historikerstreit reflected a wider West German generational shift that was taking place in the late 1980s as younger Germans who had never participated as soldiers or members of the Hitler Youth replaced those scholars with personal memories of the war. Frei argued that the Historikerstreit was part of a "protracted political farewell" on the part of those Germans born during the Weimar Republic.[31]

For almost three years, fierce barbs were traded in West Germany's mainstream newspapers. Nolte's continued insistence that Hitler's anti-Semitism was a rational extension of his anti-Marxism (because Marxists were supposedly Jews), and his unwillingness to distance himself from right-wing activists eager to use his arguments to exonerate Hitler, swayed the debate in favor of Habermas and those who believed it preposterous that Nazi crimes could be excused if they were reimagined as a sensible response to Stalinism. In a 1980 lecture, Nolte said, "It is hard to deny that Hitler had good reason to be convinced of his enemies' determination to annihilate long before the first information about the events in Auschwitz became public. . . . [Zionist leader] Chaim Weizmann's statement in the first days of September 1939, that in this war the Jews of all the world would fight on England's side . . . could lay a foundation for the thesis that Hitler would have been justified in treating the German Jews as prisoners of war, and thus interning them."[32] Ernst Nolte emerged from the Historikerstreit isolated in his opinions.[33] It was the centrist and left-wing intellectuals who triumphed at the end of the Historikerstreit, and Habermas believed that the extended public debate had permanently subverted the historiographical exoneration of Adolf Hitler. But neither Habermas nor Nolte could imagine that the Berlin Wall would fall before the end of the decade. The terms of the debate would suddenly and unexpectedly tip in Nolte's favor.

The second act in the Historikerstreit drew in scholars from across the globe. In 1993, Francis Fukuyama claimed that the collapse of Eastern European communist regimes in 1989 and the eventual implosion of the Soviet Union in 1991 represented "the end of history."[34] In his view, liberal democracy and free market capitalism were the pinnacles of human social achievement, and the collective dreams of the left were crushed in the maelstrom of anti-Marxist triumphalism. As the Federal Republic of Germany swallowed the German Democratic Republic, and Eastern European countries rushed headlong into the arms of the West, the once-settled issues of the Historikerstreit were thrown open for a new round of debate.

Although many intellectual skirmishes followed the events of 1989, perhaps the best example of the Historikerstreit 2.0 was a conflict between two eminent historians in the 1990s, one British and the other French. In 1994, the unrepentant Marxist historian Eric Hobsbawm published *The Age of Extremes: The Short Twentieth Century, 1914–1991*, a book that followed his popular trilogy on the "long nineteenth century": *The Age of Revolution*, *The Age of Capital*, and *The Age of Empire*. *The Age of Extremes* was an instant international success, translated into twenty languages in about thirty countries, and hailed as a masterpiece by critics on all points of the political spectrum.[35] The remarkable success of the book in nations as disparate as Taiwan, the United States, and Bulgaria came despite the scandal caused when Hobsbawm suggested in a 1994 BBC interview with Michael Ignatieff that the many crimes of the Soviet Union would have been forgiven if they had given birth to a functioning communist society:

> IGNATIEFF: In 1934, millions of people are dying in the Soviet experiment. If you had known that, would it have made a difference to you at that time? To your commitment? To being a Communist?
>
> HOBSBAWM: . . . Probably not.
>
> IGNATIEFF: Why?

HOBSBAWM: Because in a period in which, as you might imagine, mass murder and mass suffering are absolutely universal, the chance of a new world being born in great suffering would still have been worth backing. . . . The sacrifices were enormous; they were excessive by almost any standard and excessively great. But I'm looking back at it now and I'm saying that because it turns out that the Soviet Union was not the beginning of the world revolution. Had it been, I'm not sure.

IGNATIEFF: What that comes down to is saying that had the radiant tomorrow actually been created, the loss of fifteen, twenty million people might have been justified?

HOBSBAWM: Yes.[36]

Hobsbawm's defense of Stalinism initially prevented his book's translation into French. Even as the book was being read in German, Spanish, Portuguese, Chinese, Japanese, Arabic, Russian, and almost every language of the former Eastern Bloc, not a single French publisher—not even Fayard, the publisher of Hobsbawm's trilogy on the nineteenth century—was willing to invest in it. Given the book's commercial success outside of France, it seemed clear that the French publishing establishment was trying to silence Hobsbawm. Writing for *Lingua Franca* in November 1997, Adam Shatz argued that three trends were preventing the translation of Hobsbawm's book: "the growth of a vituperative anti-Marxism among French intellectuals; a budget squeeze in humanities publishing; and, not least, a publishing community either unwilling or afraid to defy these trends."[37]

Hobsbawm's book appeared just two years after Tony Judt's *Past Imperfect: French Intellectuals 1944–1956*, published in French as *Un passé imparfait* by Fayard in October 1992. Judt's book contributed significantly to the growing "vituperative anti-Marxism among French intellectuals."[38] In *Past Imperfect*, Judt eviscerated the left politics of Albert Camus, Jean-Paul Sartre, and Simone de Beauvoir. Judt argued that their experiences of World War II and the French Resistance convinced them that the world was divided into communists and imperialist-fascist anticommunists and there was no space to occupy in between. They believed that it was their existential imperative to make a choice. Choosing the communist side of this dichotomy apparently reflected a fatal flaw in French intellectual culture, and Hobsbawm may have been seen as reproducing that flaw.

In January 1997, in an introduction to a one-hundred-page symposium in the French journal *Le Débat*, Pierre Nora—the founding editor of *Le Débat* and the editor of France's most distinguished history series at Éditions Gallimard—justified his refusal to publish a translation of *The Age of Extremes* by citing budgetary constraints and the shrinking proportion of the French population interested in scholarly history books.[39] The length of *The Age of Extremes* (627 pages in English) rendered the cost of translation prohibitive, and Nora argued that his press would surely lose money on such an undertaking.

But Nora also admitted to having some ideological reservations about the book. In his introduction to the symposium, Nora argued that France was "the longest and most deeply Stalinised country" in Europe and that Hobsbawm's book appeared at a moment when French public culture was just shaking off its attachment to communist idealism.[40] This "decompression" followed the collapse of the Soviet Union and "accentuated hostility to anything that could from near or far recall that former pro-Soviet, pro-communist age, including plain Marxism. Eric Hobsbawn cultivates this attachment to the revolutionary cause, even if at a distance, as a point of pride. . . . But in France at this moment, it goes down badly."[41] Nora continued by saying that all publishers, "whether they want to or not, are obliged to take into account the intellectual and ideological circumstances in which they publish. There are serious reasons to think . . . that [Hobsbawm's] book would appear in an unfavourable intellectual and historical climate."[42]

Part of the problem was that *The Age of Extremes* was also published just before François Furet's highly successful *Le Passé d'une illusion*, a book asserting that Nazism and communism were the twin scourges of the twentieth century.[43] Furet's book was more in line with the reigning intellectual fashion in Paris, and French publishers perhaps feared that Hobsbawm's tome would not find an audience. Furet dedicated an extended footnote to Ernst Nolte's work, blaming the communist illusion for producing a romanticized culture of antifascism among European intellectuals. According to Furet, this led to a misreading of the Spanish Civil War and prevented the acknowledgment of the fundamental similarities between fascism and communism.

Furet's *Le Passé d'une illusion* itself was the subject of an extended symposium in *Le Débat*. There, none other than Ernst Nolte himself contributed an essay supporting Furet's indictment of communism and its equivalence with Nazism.[44] The success of *Le Passé d'une illusion* in Germany led to a partial rehabilitation of Nolte's views. In a series of letters later exchanged between the two historians, Nolte acknowledged that Furet's book had helped the international historical community to see the legitimacy of his approach, "despite a number of individual differences of opinion."[45]

The ongoing refusal to translate *The Age of Extremes* was further buttressed by the political storm unleashed in France after the 1997 publication of *Le Livre noir du communisme: Crimes, terreur, répression* by Éditions Robert Laffont. This tome—over eight hundred pages—was a collection of essays attempting to produce a worldwide tally of communist victims. Furet had initially been tapped to write the introduction to the book, but after his death in July 1997, the task fell to the editor Stéphane Courtois, who asserted that there were 100 million victims of communism worldwide, a number four times that of the victims of Nazism. Courtois inveighed against all twentieth-century communist leaders and argued that the "single-minded focus on the Jewish genocide" had impeded the accounting of communist crimes.[46] Given the revelations contained in newly opened Soviet and East European archives, Courtois argued that *Le Livre noir du communisme* definitively exposed the criminal nature of all communist regimes and claimed that Western intellectuals who supported communist ideals were no better than "common prostitutes."[47]

Almost immediately after the book's publication, however, two of the prominent historians contributing to the volume, Jean-Louis Margolin and Nicolas Werth, attacked Stéphane Courtois in an article published in *Le Monde*, stating that they disagreed with his vitriolic introduction and its overt political agenda.[48] Margolin and Werth disavowed the book, claiming that Courtois was obsessed with reaching a figure of 100 million and that this led to sloppy and biased scholarship. They further claimed that Courtois wrote the book's introduction in secret, refusing to circulate it to the other contributors. They rejected Courtois's equation of Nazism and communism, with Werth telling *Le Monde* that "death camps did not exist in the Soviet Union."[49] Indeed, in a 2000 review of *Le Passé d'une illusion* and *Le Livre noir du communisme*, the Soviet historian J. Arch Getty pointed out that over half of the 100 million worldwide deaths supposedly attributed to communism were "excess deaths" resulting from famine. Regarding the numbers in the Soviet Union, Getty wrote, "The overwhelming weight of opinion among scholars working in the new archives (including Courtois's co-editor Werth) is that the terrible famine of the 1930s was the result of Stalinist bungling and rigidity rather than some genocidal plan. Are deaths from a famine caused by the stupidity and incompetence of a regime . . . to be equated with the deliberate gassing of Jews?"[50]

Despite the inhospitable climate in France for *The Age of Extremes*, Hobsbawm did not back down. He fought for the French translation, which was finally undertaken through a joint effort of the Belgian publisher Editions Complexe and the French newspaper *Le Monde diplomatique*. In a December

5, 1999 introduction to an article by Hobsbawm, the editors of *Le Monde diplomatique* lashed out at Pierre Nora and the French publishing establishment:

> With France having undergone a long period of "Stalinisation" from which it had finally emerged, it was felt that the ideological and intellectual climate was not right for its [*The Age of Extremes*] publication. Publishers preferred books defending the ideas of French writer François Furet who held that the century boiled down to communism and nazism [*sic*], and that both were equally dangerous forms of totalitarianism. . . . In deciding to translate Hobsbawm's book, Editions Complexe and Le Monde diplomatique have refused to reduce history to a single official theory. French-speaking readers have applauded this stand.[51]

Five years after its publication in English, the French translation appeared and was an instant success, particularly given the context of the broader French debates about memory after the publication of Pierre Nora's *Lieux de Memoire* project. One month after the French release of *The Age of Extremes*, forty thousand copies were in print and the book was climbing to the top of bestseller lists. Yet despite its commercial success in France in 2000, the book continued to spark debate. Michele Tepper argued in *Lingua Franca* that the "continuing backlash in Paris against the Marxist leanings that shaped French intellectual culture for most of the twentieth century may well continue to keep publishing house doors barred against the next Hobsbawm."[52]

Indeed, in the same year that Hobsbawm's *The Age of Extremes* was finally available in French, the Germany Foundation—an organization associated with the center-right German Christian Democratic Union—awarded Ernst Nolte the prestigious Konrad Adenauer Prize, prompting Robert Cohen in the *New York Times* to proclaim, "Hitler Apologist Wins German Honor."[53] An immediate controversy ensued in Germany, particularly given the context of the far right's political ascendance in several local elections in the five states of the former GDR as well as increases in violent neo-Nazi activity against asylum seekers and other immigrants. With the National Front gaining popularity in France and Jörg Haider and the *Freiheitliche Partei Österreichs* ascending in Austria, right-wing parties were creeping back onto the political scene across the Continent. The recognition of Nolte's work by prominent German historians precipitated fierce accusations that Nolte was a Holocaust denier. Many Jewish organizations decried the Germany Foundation's decision to award Nolte a prize that had previously been bestowed on Helmut Kohl. Nolte's rehabilitation, they argued, would embolden scholars who questioned the so-called cult of the Holocaust.

An excellent example of the far-reaching legacy of the renewed Historik-erstreit is an article that appeared in the *Journal of Historical Review* in 2000. Mark Weber, director of the conservative Institute for Historical Review, argued that Nolte's receipt of the Adenauer Prize might be a portent for "greater historical objectivity":

> A Jewish view of 20th-century history—which includes what even some Jewish intellectuals call the "Holocaust cult" or "Holocaust industry"— is obviously incompatible with a treatment that is objective and truthful. . . . As the recent award to Ernst Nolte suggests, there are signs that the intellectual climate is changing. Not just in Germany, but across Europe, there is growing acknowledgement that the historical view imposed by the victorious Allies in 1945, as well as the Judeocentric view that now prevails, is a crass and even dangerous distortion. Contributing to this "historicization" has been the end of the Soviet empire, with its outpouring of new revelations about the grim legacy of Soviet Communism, and the collapse of a major pillar of the "anti-fascist" view of 20th-century history. Although powerful interests may succeed for a time in stemming the tide, in the long run a more "revisionist" treatment of history, even Third Reich history, is inevitable.[54]

Weber's article was prescient of a later wave of American popular histories derived from Nolte's revisionist position. For instance, the journalist Anne Applebaum's two books, *Gulag: A History* and *Iron Curtain: The Crushing of Eastern Europe 1944–56*, both support the idea that the horrors of communism were equal to or worse than the terrors of Nazism. It is no surprise, therefore, that Applebaum was awarded the Hungarian Petőfi Prize at the Budapest Terror House Museum on December 14, 2010, for her "outstanding efforts made to advance freedom and democracy in Central-Eastern Europe."[55] More importantly, Weber suspected that Nolte's recognition would have a real impact on the "Judeocentric" historiography of World War II. One might say that Nolte's positions in the German Historikerstreit laid the intellectual foundations for the Prague Declaration and eventually paved the way for the Ukrainian government to venerate fascists by vilifying communists in 2015.

These various public battles between European historians about the nature of twentieth-century communism, and Stalinism in particular, influenced the focus of historical scholarship in the former Eastern Bloc countries.[56] The European Union and the Visegrád Group—Hungary, Poland, Slovakia, and the Czech Republic—provided funding for anticommunist scholarship through the Platform of European Memory and Conscience. In museums such as the Hungarian House of Terror and the Lithuanian Museum of Genocide Victims, more space was allocated to the victims of communism than to the victims of the Holocaust.[57] Historical institutes, such as the Institute for Studies of the Recent Past in Bulgaria and the Institute for the Investigation of Communist Crimes and the Memory of the Romanian Exile, focus on the crimes of communism against domestic Eastern European populations and downplay the effects of the local alliances with Nazi Germany.[58]

So was it a coincidence that the institutionalization of the twin totalitarianisms narrative occurred in the wake of the global financial crisis that began in 2008? As markets plunged and the Eurozone economies teetered on the edge of collapse, the European Parliament passed the resolution establishing the European Day of Remembrance for Victims of Stalinism and Nazism. As neoliberal capitalism faltered, European leaders, facing devastated economies, a migrant crisis, and growing wealth inequality, gravitated toward an intellectual paradigm that linked leftist politics with the worst crimes of Stalinism and equated those crimes with the Final Solution. Not surprisingly, the renewed focus on the victims of communism allowed Eastern European governments to exonerate or rehabilitate known fascists, a process that led directly to the 2015 Ukrainian laws making it a crime to criticize any national figure who fought for Ukrainian independence, even if these men collaborated in the slaughter of Poles or Jews.

Eastern European examples of this rehabilitation process abound. For example, in 2009, a Bulgarian website dedicated to honoring the victims of communism (Victims of Communism in Bulgaria, victimsofcommunism.bg) included the name of the minister of interior who personally signed the deportation orders for over eleven thousand Jews from Bulgarian-occupied Thrace and Macedonia.[59] In March 2015, a Hungarian court rehabilitated Bálint Hóman, clearing him of all charges of war crimes against Hungary's Jewish minority, despite the fact that he was one of the architects of Hungary's anti-Semitic laws and pushed for the murder of Hungarian Jews by the Nazis. Hóman claimed that Jews did not belong in Hungary because of their "spirit opposing the ideas of Christianity" and their "leading role in subversive movements and the spread of destructive ideologies."[60] In May 2015, the Serbian high court rehabilitated Dragoljub "Draza" Mihailovic, the leader of the Serbian nationalist Chetniks, executed by the Yugoslav communists in 1946 for high treason and Nazi collaboration.[61] In the same month, just as the Ukrainians passed their decommunization laws legislating the veneration

FIGURE 10.2. "Fear is the path to the Dark Side."

of right-wing fighters for Ukrainian independence, the president of Croatia, Kolinda Grabar Kitarovic, paid a visit to the controversial Bleiburg cemetery, where she laid flowers at the graves of Nazi-allied Croatian soldiers.[62]

Although these recent rehabilitations have precedents, the current spate of rehabilitations and commemorations for the victims of communism coincides with a strong rightward turn in European politics.[63] In the two years I lived in Europe between 2014 and 2016, I witnessed political parties such as Hungary's Fidesz, Poland's Law and Justice, and Germany's Alternative for Deutschland finding mass support from populations suffering from years of stagnant wages and economic austerity, particularly after the onset of the European migrant crisis. In cities and towns in eastern Germany, angry mobs resist the resettlement of refugees fleeing the Syrian civil war.[64] The governments in Poland, Hungary, Slovakia, and the Czech Republic staunchly rejected quotas for accepting Muslim refugees, and new fences were erected around many national borders, jeopardizing the European Schengen free-travel zone.[65]

While the European project imploded, the European Commission, the European Central Bank, and the International Monetary Fund continued to dismantle social supports in Europe's periphery for the sake of stabilizing global financial markets. Faced with catastrophic youth unemployment, slashed pensions, and insecurity about the future, an increasing number of men and women gravitated to the far left and right. Since the evils of communism were, according to the now-dominant narrative, so incredibly grave, one need not worry too much about fascist elements, so long as they opposed communism. On the twin totalitarianisms thesis, the extremes of fascism proved no worse than the supposedly inevitable outcome of leftist demands to nationalize banks, expand state employment, and impose new global wealth taxes on the rich.[66]

As more EU populations become polarized, abandoning the liberal democratic center for the far left or the far right, it is only a matter of time before political and economic elites face a choice between supporting one side or the other in countries destabilized by the ongoing global financial crises. If both sides of this spectrum are equally evil, then there will be no moral qualm in choosing the side more likely to serve their interests, even if this means the institutionalization of new nationalist xenophobias. If communism and fascism are moral equivalents, threats to the private property of the superrich or political acts that challenge elite interests become equal to the systematic murder of immigrants and undesirable internal others. If history is any guide, we already know which side the rich will choose.

So I'm lucky that I write about Bulgaria and Germany, and not Ukraine. For now.

PART IV. "Democracy Is the Worst Form of Government, Except All Those Other Forms That Have Been Tried from Time to Time"

11. Three Bulgarian Jokes

QUESTION: What did Bulgarians use to light their houses before they started using candles?
ANSWER: Electricity.

Sometime after midnight in Sofia, a woman screams and jumps out of bed, eyes filled with terror. Her startled husband watches her rush into the bathroom and open the medicine cabinet. She then dashes to the kitchen and inspects the inside of the refrigerator. Finally, she flings open a window and gazes out onto the street below their apartment. She takes a deep breath and returns to bed.

"What's wrong with you?" her husband says. "What happened?"

"I had a terrible nightmare," she says. "I dreamed that we had the medicine we needed, that our refrigerator was full of food, and that the streets outside were safe and clean."

"How is that a nightmare?"

The woman shakes her head and shudders. "I thought the communists were back in power."[1]

QUESTION: What was the worst thing about communism?
ANSWER: The thing that came after it.

12. Post-Zvyarism: A Fable about Animals on a Farm

(FICTION)

Donkeys live a long time, and in his middle age Sivo began to contemplate his own mortality. Sivo believed that life was miserable for all beasts, and nothing in his own experience challenged his cynicism. For one brief moment, in the days before the great April Uprising, he allowed himself the small hope that a farm ruled by fellow animals would improve his lot—less work, more food, warmer stalls in the winter. But once the pigs asserted control of Zvyaria Farm, replacing their old human master, living conditions worsened.[1] Sivo would die as he had lived: a slave.

Few of the animals left remembered those days before the Uprising, only Pesho the old raven and Zdravka the mare. Before Krum imposed the travel restrictions, Sivo used to wander into town and meet Lilli, the lovely but frivolous mare who had fled from Zvyaria in the days following the Uprising.

"Hello, Lilli," Sivo said on his last trip away from the farm. "You're looking well."

"Why, Sivo, thank you. Sugar is wonderful for a horse's complexion."

Sivo studied his old barnmate: her white coat sleek and shiny, her hooves polished and clean, her forelock coifed, and green ribbons plaited in her lustrous mane. She was only three years younger than Zdravka, but she looked a decade fresher.

"How are you?" Lilli said.

"Same as always."

Lilli bowed her head. "It must be hard for you now that Stakhanski is gone."

Sivo nodded.

"Those pigs worked that old stallion to death. Why don't you leave?"

"Zvyaria is my home." Sivo clopped a hoof. "And at least I don't work for humans."

Lilli huffed. "Not all humans are like Simeonov. There are good humans who take care of their animals and treat them with respect. These days there are even humans that call themselves animal rights activists."

"What's an animal rights activist?"

"Humans who put the needs of animals before the needs of other humans."

Sivo shook his head. "Sounds like foreign nonsense to me."

Lilli stared at Sivo, pitying his sunken flanks. "You know what's foreign nonsense? The idea that animals can run their own farm."

Sivo twitched his ears. Lilli was there at those early meetings in the barn so long ago. The pigs had heard tales of an animal-run farm somewhere in a faraway land, and began to spread the idea among the horses, goats, cows, hens, and sheep. "In other nations," they said, "beasts work for themselves. They band together and form special animal collectives where humans do not profit from their toil." Few believed the pigs at first, but Krum and Botev, the two biggest and smartest boars, kept insisting that another farm was possible if they all worked together to overthrow the farmer Simeonov.

Stakhanski convinced Sivo that it could work. When the time came, Sivo joined Stakhanski and the other animals in the great April Uprising against Simeonov and rejoiced when they ran him out. Krum and Botev reorganized the farm as an animal cooperative. Stakhanski trusted Botev, and even Krum, and poured more effort into building the first Zvyaria Dam than any other beast. But now Botev and Stakhanski were gone.

"It's all nonsense," Sivo said to Lilli. "Nothing changes."

Sivo recalled this conversation with Lilli a few days later when the youngest mare disappeared from Zvyaria, and the pigeons reported that she was seen in the company of another farmer across town. Since the pigs provided no sugar or ribbons to the mares, Sivo thought it natural that some would leave the farm to pursue a life with more creature comforts, even if this meant being owned by a human. But Krum was furious with the mare's defection. It came just two months after five hens conspired to immigrate to a human-owned farm where the egg quotas were less demanding.

On the day Krum announced that no animal could leave the farm without the special permission of the pigs' council, a young boar named Chervenio paid a visit to the old donkey. "Hello, Sivo," he said.

"Hello, Chervenio. Shouldn't you be in school?"

Chervenio snorted. "No point. They never teach us anything useful. I want to learn about the great April Uprising."

"Don't they teach about it in school?"

"Not the truth," Chervenio said, lowering his voice. "They never say anything about Botev."

"Nothing?"

"They say he was an enemy of the beasts."

Sivo huffed.

"Did you know him?" Chervenio said.

Sivo studied the young boar. "Why are you so interested in Botev?"

Chervenio lowered his voice to a whisper. "I found some of his poems," he said. "They were buried in a box, and I dug them up."

"That could be dangerous," said Sivo.

"I don't think he was an enemy of the beasts. I think he was a great revolutionary," Chervenio said. "He talked about cooperation and the equality of all animals. He never wore clothes and never slept in beds, and he didn't need the dogs to get his way."

"That's how I remember him," Sivo said.

"So it's true." Chervenio stared at the ground and stood in silence for a moment. "Is it also true that Krum murdered other pigs?"

Sivo closed his watery eyes and opened them. "Krum never murdered any beast. The dogs did the murdering."

"But on his command?"

Sivo simply nodded. It had been a long time since those dark days after the Uprising.

Chervenio came closer to Sivo and motioned for the old jack to lower his head. "Sivo, Zvyaria farm is in trouble. Krum and the senior pigs have borrowed money from the humans, and are thinking of selling some of the cows to pay their debts."

Sivo shuddered as he remembered his friend Stakhanski, sold off to the knackery when he could no longer work.

"Some of the younger pigs think it's time for Krum to go. He's betrayed the

Uprising, and compromised all the original principles of Zvyarism. We want to restore equality to Zvyaria, and we want your help."

Sivo tilted his head.

"The animals respect you. They know you were there at the great April Uprising. That you helped Stakhanski build the dams, and that you sometimes leave the farm and know about the outside world."

"I can't leave the farm anymore."

"That's why we have to take back Zvyaria from Krum. He's made it a prison. He's turned us into his property, to dispose of as he wishes. Just like a human."

"What about the dogs?" Sivo whispered. "There are so many of them now."

Chervenio's voice was so low now that Sivo could barely hear. "The dogs . . . tired . . . want . . . change."

Sivo heard hoof falls outside of the barn, and lifted his head. Zdravka returned from her day in the fields. "Hello, Chervenio," she said. "Shouldn't you be in school?"

"Hello, Zdravka," Chervenio said. "Sivo was just helping me with a school project."

Chervenio turned toward the barn door. "Thanks, Sivo. Is it okay if I come back for more help tomorrow?"

Sivo hesitated. But for the sake of the poor cows, and in memory of his friend Stakhanski, he nodded.

And so it came to pass that Chervenio and some of his schoolmates spread dissent among the beasts of Zvyaria. Yes, he told them, they should stay proud that they lived and worked on a farm run by animals, but he also argued that the senior pigs had become no better than the humans and it was time to return to the original ideals of the great April Uprising. The animals didn't need much convincing. Chervenio organized secret readings of Botev's poetry, verses that gave the animals courage to stand up to the fearsome dogs.

Of course, the dogs knew what was happening. They had informers among every group of animals on the farm and got regular updates on the doings of the hens, sheep, cows, goats, and horses. The report that the young boar Chervenio was meeting with the old ass in the barn caught the attention of a junior pup named Muttro. Muttro worked as a lower-ranking officer in the internal affairs department of Canine Security. He disliked the senior pigs, whom he saw as lazy and undisciplined, but admired their ability to work with humans. Muttro heard about the plan to sell the cows, and the dog commanders warned that there would be unrest on the farm. Muttro, like many of his fellow officers, understood that the pigs could not run the farm without them. Dogs were generally loyal, and the pigs treated them well, but some pups like Muttro resented the pigs for not giving the dogs a voice in how the farm was run. Taking the loans was a stupid idea, Muttro thought, and selling the cows to pay them off was worse.

The second great Uprising required no violence. When the day came, Chervenio and the other reformist pigs appeared in the dining room of the pigs' house with representatives of all the other animals on the farm. Sivo and Zdravka represented the equines. Chervenio demanded Krum's immediate resignation. Krum called the dogs, but the dogs did not come. Instead, Muttro appeared and stood with the other animals. Dumbfounded and confused, Krum and the other senior pigs tried to negotiate, but Chervenio gave them an hour to leave the farm, taking nothing with them but the clothes on their back.

"Everything else," Chervenio said, "belongs to the beasts of Zvyaria."

Krum looked to Muttro. "Junior officer, how can you stand there and allow this treason?"

"The treason began with you, Krum, long ago," Muttro said.

"You violated all of the laws of Zvyarism and betrayed the spirit of the great April Uprising, all for your own gain," Chervenio said. "The beasts of Zvyaria will tolerate this tyranny no longer."

When Krum and the other pigs realized they had no choice, they marched out of the big house in a single file. All of the animals of Zvyaria lined up to watch them leave. When the last of the senior pigs passed through the gate, Muttro closed it behind them, and shouted, "Never return. You are welcome here no longer."

The animals cheered.

Chervenio suggested an immediate meeting in the barn.

As the animals filed into the barn, the remaining pigs, all of whom were young and born after the great April Uprising, interspersed themselves among the other beasts, ensuring that no two pigs sat together. The pigeons and Pesho, the raven, perched in the rafters. Because it was their habit, the hens sat together opposite the cows. The goats and the sheep clustered in front of the bovine contingent. The dogs came in last, and Muttro motioned for them to disperse like the pigs. The dogs hesitated, and then obeyed, even those senior dogs that felt uncomfortable with the recent turn in events. Muttro himself sauntered to Chervenio's side, resting on his haunches, as the others settled in.

Chervenio cleared his throat. "Today, fellow beasts, we have returned to the true spirit of the April Uprising. Beginning today we can return to the original principles of Zvyarism. All animals are equal and all animals deserve their fair share of the wealth created at Zvyaria."

The animals hooted, cooed, and snorted their approval.

"From now on, all decisions will be made in common, at weekly meetings here in the barn."

Muttro waited until the jubilation died down before he spoke. "And who," he said, "will be in charge of implementing the decisions?"

Chervenio eyed Muttro. "We'll all implement the decisions. Collectively."

Muttro stood and addressed the animals. "But someone must be in charge of Zvyaria, if only to coordinate our trade with the humans. We can't produce everything we need here at the farm. There will have to be some contact with the outside world."

The animals listened.

"And there is the issue of the debts owed to the humans," Muttro continued. "The senior pigs took the loans as the leaders of the farm, but the money owed doesn't disappear because the pigs are gone."

"We don't need any leaders," Chervenio said. "We can make all decisions collectively."

"It won't work," Muttro said. "We need to have someone in charge, but we can choose that person collectively."

Sivo, standing in the back, snorted. "What do you mean, Muttro?"

Muttro pricked up his ears, and made eye contact with the donkey. He inhaled. "We must hold elections: free, open, zoocratic elections. All of the animals on Zvyaria farm will elect their leader. And we will hold elections every two years, and no one animal will be able to remain leader of Zvyaria for more than six years."

A murmur spread among the beasts. Muttro waited until they settled down.

"Under our Zvyarian zoocracy every animal will have one vote each, and you will vote on paper ballots in an enclosed stall so no one else can see who you are voting for. After you vote, you will put your ballot in a box until everyone has voted. Then the votes will be counted in the open, and whoever has the most votes will be the leader of Zvyaria."

"Why is an election better than a weekly meeting?" Chervenio said. "A meeting where every animal can have his say."

"Weekly meetings take too much time," Muttro said, addressing the animals. "We all have so much work to do and Sunday is our day of rest. Do we really want to spend every Sunday in a meeting that could take hours, to decide how many eggs to sell?"

"How can we ensure the elected leader will not become like Krum?" Sivo said.

"Because," Muttro said, "in our zoocracy, the leader will have to stand for reelection in two years. If the leader doesn't do a good job, he'll be voted out of office. This way he is accountable to his fellow animals. If we want to have true equality and freedom, we have to have elections."

At this moment, Muttro made eye contact with his informant among the sheep, and the informant repeated the word "elections." The sheep bleated the word "elections" until the other sheep joined in. "Elections. Elections. Elections. Elections. Elections." The sheep's voices filled the barn for two minutes.

"Are we agreed then," Muttro said to the animals, "that we will have elections?"

"Can we have them right now?" Chervenio said.

"No. We must first have candidates and those candidates must have time to prepare their campaign."

Chervenio eyed Muttro. "What is a campaign?"

"A campaign is how a candidate explains to voters why he is the best choice. All candidates must explain to the voters what he will do for Zvyaria, and convince them to vote for him when the day of the election comes."

The sheep bleated the word "election."

"And who chooses the candidates?" Chervenio said.

"They are nominated," Muttro said, "or they may volunteer."

"I nominate Chervenio," Sivo said, and the other animals nodded.

"Do you accept this nomination?" Muttro asked the young boar.

Chervenio paused. "I still think weekly meetings would be better."

"And if you are elected," Muttro said, "you can have weekly meetings with all of the animals."

"Then I accept."

"Are there other nominations?" Muttro said to the assembled beasts. "What about you, old Sivo? Would you consider running for president of Zvyaria?"

Sivo shook his head. "I've already nominated Chervenio. I think he will make a fine leader."

"An endorsement," Muttro said. "And the campaign hasn't even begun. Do you have other nominations?"

No animal spoke.

"We must have at least two candidates to have a proper election."

"Why?" Sivo said. "Why can't we all vote for Chervenio and be done with it?"

Muttro shook his head. "Because that's a coronation, not an election."

The sheep bleated the word "election."

"We need another candidate to oppose Chervenio so that we animals have a choice." Muttro studied the faces of the young pigs scattered among the crowd, and then rested his eyes on a cluster of dogs lingering in the back of the barn. "Surely, there must be some animal among you who will contest Chervenio."

"What about you, Muttro?" shouted one of the dogs. "Maybe it's time we had a president from a different species. Why does it always have to be a pig?"

Another murmur spread throughout the barn, and Muttro nodded. "I accept this nomination, and I would be honored to contest Chervenio in the first free zoocratic elections on Zvyaria."

The sheep bleated the word "elections" until Muttro motioned for them to stop. The animals discussed the election procedures and agreed that they would vote in one month's time. Meanwhile, all animals would work double shifts to raise the money necessary to pay off Zvyaria's debts. Everyone agreed that no cows would be sold. The animals decided to lift the travel ban and restore freedom of speech. Banned songs, books, and poems could all be read and discussed openly. Even old Pesho the Raven could resume his preaching about the afterlife that awaited all beasts in Baklava Valley.

The campaigning began the next day. Chervenio called meetings in the barn, read selections from the poems of Botev, and discussed his plans for running the farm through consensus. The weekly meeting was the centerpiece of Chervenio's campaign. In order to return to the true spirit of the great April Uprising, the animals needed to work together and always treat each other as equals. Krum had granted unfair privileges to the pigs and dogs, but Chervenio would ensure those privileges came to an end. Old Sivo accompanied the young boar for all of his poetry readings and speeches, and they drew a good cross section of the animals who were not working.

Muttro the dog had a different strategy in mind. Muttro knew about the outside world, and was savvy in the ways of the human equivalent of zoocracy. He hired a pretty hen to be his campaign manager and began negotiations with some pro-zoocracy humans to fund his campaign. Even the humans had heard about the terrible abuses of the pigs, and hoped to improve the living standards of the animals at Zvyaria. They were eager to support experiments with zoocracy, and happily obliged to help Muttro in his campaign for the presidency, although the dog insisted that their involvement remain a secret.

Muttro's first strategy was to activate his old network of informants among the different animals on the farm. Each of these informants was funded to create a special association to promote the interests of their own species. Within days they formed the Organization for Bovine Rights (OBR), the Association for the Advancement of Poultry (AAP), the Union of Sheep and Goats (USG), and the High Council of Pigeon Affairs (HCPA). Each of these groups was charged with asking the candidates tough questions about how their leadership of Zvyaria would help their specific constituents. The dogs, out of loyalty, would vote for Muttro, and formed no association. The young pigs, not wanting to appear speciesist, joined the associations of the other animals, becoming honorary members. This caused a split in the OBR, with the original faction accepting pigs as members, and a rival faction, the Bovine Rights Organization, refusing to accept nonbovine members. After a week, a similar schism occurred among the poultry. The original organization changed its name to the Association for the Advancement of Poultry and Pigs (AAPP), and those who disagreed created the Poultry First Coalition (PFC).

Muttro ran a two-pronged campaign, helped by his human backers and his charismatic and coquettish campaign manager. The first prong of his campaign consisted of two key buzzwords that few of the animals understood: "modernization" and "decollectivization." In his campaign speeches and the meetings he organized on the outdoor steps of the still-vacant big house, Muttro told the sheep, goats, cows, and hens that their farm was hopelessly out of date: their equipment was old, and they lacked access to the miraculous new fertilizers and pesticides that would improve their crop yields. He spoke of the wonders of the machines that could milk the cows with the softest touch, and the special conveyor belts that could be installed in the hen house.

"On other farms, animals have not only heat in the winter, but also machines that keep them cool and dry in the summer months," Muttro said.

The animals oohed at the idea of a cool and dry August.

"But all of these things require access to human money, and we cannot afford to take any more loans."

"So how can we buy them?" said a cow, enamored by the idea of the automatic milking machines.

"We have to increase productivity," Muttro said. "Our productivity on this farm is poor because we do not have the right incentives. If the hens produce more eggs, they do not benefit directly. If the cows produce more milk, it gets shared among all of the animals. The idea is that every animal will do his fair share, but we all know that some animals produce more than other animals on the farm. Why should we all benefit from the efforts of a few hard workers?"

The animals nodded.

"If you vote for me," Muttro said, raising his voice and waving his paws about the air, "I will decollectivize Zvyaria farm. Ownership of the hen house will pass to the hens, and only hens will reap the profits from their eggs. Full ownership of the dairy works will be divided between the cows and the goats in proportion to their productivity. All profits from milk sales will accumulate to those who produce milk. Similarly, all profits from wool sales will go to the sheep. If animals profit from their own labors, there will be greater incentives to produce more."

"What about the horses?" said a young mare.

"The horses plow the fields and do many essential tasks around the farm. If you elect me, they will be paid a wage in proportion to the work that they do. The same goes for the pigs and pigeons. The independent enterprises will pay them a salary for their services."

"And what about the dogs?" said a goat.

"If you elect me and we modernize Zvyaria, our farm will be the envy of all farmers, not to mention that Krum and his senior cronies might try to return. The dogs will provide security. The independent enterprises will pay them a salary for their services when they are required."

"What about the dams and the electricity they generate? How will we share the electricity? The dams belong to all of the animals since we all helped to build them. And the farmland: we all helped to clear and weed and sow the land," said a young pig in the audience.

Muttro paused, studying the faces of the beasts gathered around him. "It is true that the dams and the farmland belong to all of us, but sharing the electricity and the corn is inefficient. The names of Krum and the pigs are written on the deeds to the land and the dams. The only fair way to distribute the ownership of these assets is to divide them equally among all the beasts that helped to build them."

"How?" said Kafiava, the campaign manager.

"We will create a system of vouchers dividing up the land and the dams on paper. If you elect me, each animal will receive his or her fair share of Zvyaria's assets, becoming shareholders of the farm."

"What is a shareholder?" said a pigeon.

"If you elect me, you will all be part owners of the farm through your shares. When the land or the dams generate income, you will share in the profits after the wages of the other animals have been paid," Muttro said. "This is how the most efficient farms are run, and this system will allow us to modernize our farm and bring wealth and prosperity to all of the beasts of Zvyaria!"

At that moment, the sheep got excited and began to bleat the word "elections."

When Chervenio heard of Muttro's plans, he redoubled his efforts to maintain the true spirit of Zvyarism, reading the poems of Botev and trying to convince the animals that only collective decision making would ensure their welfare. But once the animals understood that they would have full control over the fruits of their own labors, and that their farm would have heat in the winter and cooling in the summer, and that they would become shareholders of the lands and the dams, the various associations began to endorse Muttro. The first to back him were the OBR and the USG. With some persuasion, the PFC and the HCPA also endorsed Muttro and his plans for modernization and decollectivization.

But Chervenio had a stalwart group of supporters who viewed Muttro's plans for Zvyaria with suspicion. Chervenio continued to hold his meetings in the barn, discussing the theoretical basis for the equality of all animals. A week before the election, Muttro, Kafiava, and the leaders of the associations appeared at Chervenio's barn meeting.

"Welcome, Muttro," Chervenio said. "Welcome, fellow beasts. All are welcome at these meetings."

Muttro strode to the middle of the circular congregation and pointed his paw at Chervenio. "After everything that we beasts have been through on Zvyaria," Muttro said. "You would cast your one precious vote for a pig?"

Sivo stepped forward. "Pigs are animals," he said.

"Pigs are oppressors," Muttro said. "The pigs want to keep us ignorant. They want us to live in the past."

Chervenio stared at Muttro, dumbfounded. "What are you talking about? We all believe in the original principles of Zyvarism that pigs like Botev died to defend."

"It's a lie!" Muttro said, addressing the animals. "No pig can be trusted with the welfare of his fellow animals. They are out to oppress you. Once Chervenio is elected president, he will become just like Krum. Pigs cannot be trusted!"

Sivo brayed at the top of his lungs, drowning out the words of Muttro, who cowered at the force of Sivo's voice.

"You dogs," Sivo said, "you dogs were the real oppressors. The pigs never murdered anyone, because you dogs always did it for them."

Sivo turned to the animals. "Don't you remember who you were all afraid of? The pigs may have owned the farm, but the dogs beat us into submission. I was alive then. I remember. Those dogs murdered hens and sheep, and they even murdered four young pigs who dared to oppose Krum."

At Sivo's words, all of the animals in the room, even Muttro's supporters, felt sickened. They feared the dogs to be sure, but they never imagined that the dogs had once killed pigs.

"Lies!" Muttro bellowed. "We dogs were the slaves of the pigs, just like all of you. Those evil pigs held our puppies captive and threatened to kill them if we did not do their bidding. We hated violence, but we feared the power of the pigs! Pigs are the real enemy!"

At that, Muttro stormed out of the barn, followed by Kafiava and the sheep. The leaders of the hens, cows, pigeons, and goats stayed behind to hear Chervenio and Sivo speak about the original principles of Zvyarism.

Within a day, Muttro had secured the funds necessary to print a thousand campaign posters, which plastered almost every inch of Zvyaria. The poster showed an image of Chervenio and Krum's faces side by side in profile. A red circle enclosed the image and a thick red line slashed diagonally across it. At the bottom of the poster in blue letters were the words "VOTE MUTTRO" accompanied by the outline of a dog's paw.

Because Chervenio didn't have any money for posters, some of his supporters simply scratched out the word "Chervenio" in the dirt around the farm. A handful of industrious spiders also spun his name into their webs, but these could only be seen in the early morning when the dew hung on the thin fibers.

With the funding from his secret human backers, Muttro distributed free ribbons to the mares and gave away imported French seed to the hens. He made promises of the newest electric shears to the sheep, and swore to the cows that the private profits from their milk would allow them to import the tastiest gourmet grasses from Scotland. When a mare dropped a foal, Muttro was the first one to congratulate her. When new chicks hatched from their eggs, Muttro celebrated with the hens, never missing an opportunity to remind them of the previous tyranny of the pigs.

But Muttro's greatest convert was old Pesho the Raven, who still babbled in the rafters about the future paradise of Baklava Valley. Pesho had a particularly strong following among the sheep and pigeons, and he initially preached that the election meant nothing in the grander scheme of things. What really mattered was whether or not an animal had lived a worthy enough life to earn passage to Baklava Valley. But two days before the election, old Pesho suddenly started castigating those who had stopped him from preaching his gospel during their rule. For years, Pesho said, he kept his bill shut for fear of persecution by the pigs. "Baklava Valley," Pesho said to the assembled beasts and birds, "is the ultimate destination, but while we live on this earth we must live in a world that allows for the freedom of spiritual expression."

Election Day came with great pomp and circumstance. Ballots contained a rough drawing of a pig and a dog, and all animals were to dip their hooves, paws, or talons in a pot of ink and step on the drawing of the candidate they wanted to vote for. The animals agreed that the three oldest beasts, Sivo, Pesho, and Zdravka, would stand over the ballot box to ensure that each animal deposited his own vote. At the end of the day, the three senior beasts would open the box and count the votes in front of a full assembly in the barn.

Almost every animal on the farm voted, save for a handful of fundamentalist pigeons that spent the day praying for passage into Baklava Valley. The sheep bleated the word "elections," and the various associations organized private parties to pass the time while the voting was completed. Chervenio set up his headquarters in the horse shed and Muttro splurged for a lavish HQ on the steps of the big house. Young attractive hens provided voters with overflowing fresh water troughs. Muttro greeted the animals, shaking paws and hooves with confidence.

When the sun set, Zdravka opened the ballot box with her hoof. Pesho flew into the box and picked out the first ballot and showed it to Sivo who said, "Chervenio."

Chervenio and his supporters gave a cheer.

Pesho flew in and got the second ballot, showing it to Zdravka, who announced, "Muttro."

Muttro smiled and pumped his paws in the air toward his followers. The sheep bleated "elections."

The procedure continued, with Pesho taking out each ballot for either Zdravka or Sivo to read out loud. A goat kept track of the tally. When all of the votes were counted, Chervenio had 124 and Muttro had 132. The goat declared Muttro the winner, and Muttro led a procession to the big house. Muttro opened the doors and revealed a feast waiting inside. His supporters celebrated the first zoocratic elections with great vigor, while Chervenio, Sivo, and Zdravka sulked in the barn.

"Are you sure you counted them right?" Chervenio said.

Sivo nodded and placed a hoof gently on Chervenio's back. "He won fairly."

A silence filled the barn. Some of Chervenio's supporters slipped out to investigate the festivities at the big house.

Within days, Muttro made good on his campaign promises. The farm was broken up into different enterprises: the egg production enterprise, the milk production enterprise, the wool production enterprise, and so on. Ownership of these enterprises was transferred to the animals in charge of production. Ownership of the rest of the farm (the farmland and the dams) was divided equally among all of the animals through a system of vouchers. Whatever money the farm made, minus the wages paid to the farm workers, would be equally distributed to the owners of the vouchers. The electricity generated by the dams would also be distributed among voucher owners. Muttro, as the zoocratically elected president, was in charge of making all decisions regarding the farmland and the dams. He would organize trade with the human world and pay off the debts of Krum and the deposed pigs.

The first managerial decision Muttro made was to lay off all of the pigeons and pigs. Neither animal, he argued, had a productive use on the farm. The laid-off pigeons begged Muttro for some work, but he told them that there was little they could do on a modern farm. He only needed one or two of them to carry messages back and forth to the outside world. Then he offered them food in exchange for their Zvyaria vouchers, and the pigeons gladly exchanged the pieces of paper for seed. But once Muttro had the last of their vouchers, he stopped feeding the pigeons. They turned to old Pesho for help. Pesho received a special food allowance from Muttro, but Pesho refused to share it with the pigeons and advised that they go off in search of Baklava Valley.

Some of the laid-off pigs found work with the hens and the cows, but the rest turned to Chervenio for help. "Can we set up our own enterprise?" said a now unemployed pig.

"The truth is," Chervenio said, "most of us pigs only have value to the farm when we are slaughtered for meat. A few of the stronger boars might become studs, but I'm afraid we have no future on Zvyaria if we want to stay alive."

"I have piglets," said an older male porker. "I would happily sacrifice myself for their sake."

"Me, too," said another pig. "If it helps the other pigs survive, I am happy to be slaughtered. We have to stick together."

"No," said Chervenio. "We have to try to make ourselves useful on the farm. Together we own enough of the vouchers that we should be able to survive on the income from the dams and the land. We are clever and can help the other animal enterprises. Or we can leave Zvyaria and look for a better life elsewhere."

"This is our home," said the old porker.

"But they don't want us here," said another pig.

In the end, about half of the pigs left Zvyaria, transferring their vouchers to Chervenio in the hopes that they might someday return to a pig-run enterprise that would create a future for their piglets that didn't include being eaten by humans.

For a while, none of the enterprises employed a dog since Zvyaria was a tranquil farm with few disturbances. But less than a month after the elections, someone broke into the hen house and stole eggs. A few days later, milk disappeared from the dairy. When two lambs went missing, a general panic seized the farm. The dogs offered their protective services to the various enterprises, promising to guard against any future acts of theft or vandalism. Every enterprise hired a dog. But as the mysterious attacks continued, they hired five or six dogs until all of the dogs were employed on the farm. Once they had work, Muttro convinced the dogs to trade in their vouchers for designer Italian dog beds imported from Rome.

The hens' enterprise was doing a booming business, and their nine dogs guarded the henhouse twenty-four hours a day. But the hens dreamed of a modern conveyor belt that would make it easier to gather and package their goods for sale. Muttro promised to broker a deal for the hens if they exchanged their Zvyaria vouchers for money, which could be used to buy the necessary equipment. The hens happily agreed since they had their own enterprise and cared little for the doings of the farmland and the dams. They kept only enough vouchers to ensure that they had electricity to run the lights and their future conveyor belt.

A similar deal was made with the cows and goats. Since the animals took over Zvyaria, the pigs had been milking the cows, and this arrangement continued now that the cows had their own dairy enterprise. But the cows and goats were desperate for the chance to get their hooves on a sparkling new automated milking machine, and exchanged their vouchers for the necessary capital when Muttro offered them the possibility.

The sheep grew their wool and hired some pigs to shear them with the old tools, but the idea of electric shears seduced them. A clever sheep suggested that they wait to buy the electric shears out of the profits of the first year's wool sales. One more year of manual shears wouldn't make such a difference in the long run. But the sheep were impatient for the modernization that Muttro had promised, so they traded in their vouchers for money just as the hens, cows, and goats had done before them.

The horses and old Sivo the donkey had more work than they could handle. They were the sole mode of transport for the goods of the other animals. The horses plowed the fields, hauled rocks to repair the dams, harvested the apples, and fixed broken things. Several horses from neighboring farms joined the Zvyaria horses since the wages were so good, and they could afford to buy ribbons and sugar cubes in town. Some of the remaining pigs worked with the horses, but Muttro offered them lower wages because he argued that they weren't as efficient. Sivo and the other horses formed a union with the pigs to try to force Muttro to pay the pigs a better wage, but Muttro just hired different horses from neighboring farms. The horses also refused to hire dog security until a one-month foal was kidnapped from the farm. Then the mares insisted on hiring a few dogs to look after the young ones while the horses were away in the fields. The horses held onto their vouchers, pooling them with those of the pigs to ensure that they received their fair share of electricity.

After six months, Muttro raised the price of electricity by 400 percent. The president claimed he needed to increase electricity production to plan for the future needs of the farm. This required "new capital investments." The animal enterprises that had sold their vouchers protested that the new prices were too high. But Muttro argued that he was only looking out for their long-term interests. Since he had full control over the dams, they had no choice but to pay the price he set.

At the same time, crime increased in Zvyaria: theft, assault, even murder. Much of this was blamed on foreign wolves, and the animal enterprises hired ever more dogs for security. Trade disputes also broke out between the different animal enterprises, and between the enterprises and their pig and horse laborers, who always demanded higher wages to keep up with the skyrocketing costs of food and dog security. The common areas of the farm fell into disrepair since none of the animals cared for anything but their own enterprises. Rather than resting on Sundays, the animals worked harder than they had worked under Krum, hoping they could earn more money to purchase the next piece of modern farm equipment. Only the horses and the pigs surrounding Chervenio continued to meet in the old barn, wondering what would happen to Zvyaria Farm until the next elections.

A year into Muttro's term as president of Zvyaria, several cars full of human men in business suits drove into the farm and filed into the big house. The animals hadn't seen humans on the farm since Krum and the senior pigs left. For five hours the humans stayed in the house, and all of the animals wondered if Muttro was finally purchasing the machines they needed to make the farm modern. When the humans left, Muttro announced that there would be an important meeting on Sunday in the barn.

Sunday came and all of the beasts assembled, but Muttro and the dogs never appeared. Instead several humans came, waving formal-looking documents at the animals. Sivo tried to understand what was happening, but it was Chervenio who finally managed to communicate with the humans. After the humans explained the situation to the pig, they left the farm.

Chervenio returned to the barn to address the animals. "My fellow beasts," he said. "The farm has been sold to these humans. All of the land and the dams."

"But how?" said Zdravka.

"It seems that Muttro owned 80 percent of the farm," Chervenio said.

The animals murmured in confusion.

Chervenio pointed at them. "He bought all of your vouchers."

"But we were supposed to get a conveyor belt," said a hen.

"And we were supposed to have electric shears," said a sheep.

"And what about our automatic milking machines?" said a cow.

"I don't know what he promised you," Chervenio said, "but Muttro is gone, and he has taken all of the money the humans paid him."

"What about the horses and the pigs who still own vouchers?" Sivo said.

"They are going to buy us out."

"And what about our enterprises?" said a hen.

"The humans are giving you sixty days to relocate."

"Why can't we stay here?" said a cow.

Chervenio looked down at the hay on the floor of the barn. "The humans are going to build a shopping mall next door. They need our land."

"For what?" several animals said at once.

"A parking lot," Chervenio said.

Sivo brayed. "What about Zvyaria?"

Chervenio did not answer. He hung his head and walked slowly out of the barn.

And so within sixty days, Pesho the Raven flew off to preach his gospel of Baklava Valley to other beasts. The hens left to find another farm where they might lay their eggs. The cows wandered into town and sold themselves to the highest human bidder. The goats decided to strike out into the wild. They disappeared into the mountains. When the humans came to bulldoze the buildings and flatten the farmland, the sheep wandered around in a daze, bleating the word "elections" to no one in particular.

The humans kept their promise and paid money for the remaining Zvyaria vouchers. Some of the younger horses and more adventurous pigs set off to find work on other farms. Chervenio took his money and said his farewells, telling Sivo and the horses that he planned to travel abroad until he found another collective farm to join.

On the day the humans came to pave, only a few animals remained: three black sheep, one old goat, Zdravka the horse, and Sivo the donkey, who still had a long time to live. They stood together on a hill watching the machines spread thick black sheets of tarmac over the land where the big barn once stood.

A human in a car driving past shook his head and said to his companion, "Aren't those the animals from Zvyaria Farm?"

The companion nodded.

"Can you believe that some of those poor beasts are actually nostalgic for the pigs?"

13. Interview with a Former Member of the Democratic Party of the United States

(FICTION)

17 October 2029

FROM: Thomas Müller, Federal Ministry of Immigration and Resettlement
TO: Office of the Rector, Friedrich Schiller Universität, Jena
RE: Frau Professor Doctor Kristen Ghodsee

I have been asked by your office to provide a report on the suitability of Frau Professor Doctor Kristen Ghodsee for employment at the University of Jena in the capacity of visiting lecturer or guest researcher. As you know, I represent the special department within the Federal Ministry of Immigration and Resettlement charged with integrating political refugees with high qualifications into German society. After the passage of the 2028 amendment to the U.S. Constitution allowing President Daniel Drumph, Jr. to remain in office indefinitely, the Federal Republic of Germany has granted political asylum to many highly educated Americans fleeing the continued persecution of intellectuals and political dissidents who resisted the constitutional amendment.

Frau Prof. Dr. Ghodsee is an established scholar, with many publications and years of university teaching experience, and she has expressed interest in finding employment at a German university or research institute. Despite her considerable qualifications, Frau Prof. Dr. Ghodsee was for many years a registered member of the Democratic Party of the United States, and questions have been raised regarding her suitability for work with young adults. As you know, the Federal Republic of Germany has twice in its history investigated the suitability of its citizens for important roles in society, once after 1945 and once again after 1989 when thousands of our compatriots, former members of the Socialist Unity Party, were expelled from their university positions due to their association with, and presumed support of, communist ideology.

This report is based on two interviews that I conducted with Frau Prof. Dr. Ghodsee in September and October of this year. Both interviews were recorded and transcribed in English. Full German translations of these interviews are appended to this report. I base my recommendation to you on these interviews and on my extensive review of Frau Prof. Dr. Ghodsee's case files.

In late 2028, Frau Prof. Dr. Ghodsee's life partner was shot and killed when the U.S. National Guard opened fire on a peaceful demonstration during the so-called December Massacre. Frau Prof. Dr. Ghodsee survived the violence and managed to avoid arrest for three weeks. She fled the United States after her name was included on a published government list of "state enemies," and she was threatened with imprisonment in one of the political internment camps in Alaska. She escaped into Canada with the assistance of underground operatives in Maine. She spent two months in a refugee facility outside of Quebec City, where she applied for political asylum in Germany. Frau Prof. Dr. Ghodsee lived and worked in Germany for several years over the course of her career, and she has a twenty-eight-year-old daughter who is married to a German citizen and lives in Jena. Frau Prof. Dr. Ghodsee arrived in Germany in April 2029, and spent four months in a refugee settlement facility in Erfurt before the ministry granted her permission to live with her daughter.

My first interview with Frau Prof. Dr. Ghodsee occurred on 23 September at the ministry regional office in Erfurt. Our conversation lasted ninety-two minutes. This was a formal interview where she confirmed basic facts about her biography and previous career in the United States. Prof. Dr. Ghodsee grew up in San Diego and attended the University of California, Santa Cruz, from 1988 to 1993, where she earned her bachelor of arts degree. According to our records, she participated in political demonstrations against the first Gulf War in 1990, and spent the 1991–1992 academic year as an exchange student at the University of Ghana at Legon. Upon graduation, she lived and worked in Japan from 1993 to 1996, whereupon she returned to California to pursue her PhD degree at Berkeley. Ghodsee confirmed that she received a Fulbright grant from the U.S. federal government to fund her dissertation research in Bulgaria in 1999–2000, but insisted that this grant carried no subsequent work requirements. Our own databases corroborate that unlike the Boren Fellowships of the U.S. National Security Education Program, Fulbright fellowships granted in the 1990s and 2000s did not commit recipients to work for the U.S. Departments of Defense or State, or any other federal agency.

Although Frau Prof. Dr. Ghodsee never held an elected office in the United States, she was a registered member of the Democratic Party. Our records show that she made regular financial contributions to Democratic candidates for the last thirty years, and that she actively campaigned for several Democratic presidential candidates. Given the recent transformations within the Democratic Party and its support for the constitutional amendments and innumerable international treaty violations, her continued membership casts grave doubts on the nature of her political and ideological commitments.

After the introductory formalities, I began by asking Frau Prof. Dr. Ghodsee about the 2000 presidential election. She stated that she was a registered member of the Democratic Party and that she voted for Al Gore, but like many Americans she accepted the Supreme Court decision in *Bush v. Gore* on 12 December 2000. What follows is a partial transcript of our conversation:

Thomas Müller (TM): Were you not suspicious that the younger brother of George W. Bush governed the contested state? And the father of George W. Bush appointed two of the Supreme Court justices involved in deciding the case?

Kristen Ghodsee (KG): Of course, I was suspicious. We were all suspicious at the time, but it was a complicated issue because of the confusing nature of the ballots in Florida. Different versions of the statewide recount produced different outcomes.

TM: But the recount was not allowed to continue.

KG: In our system, at that time, the Supreme Court had the right to make that decision.

TM: And the fact that Al Gore won the popular vote?

KG: [subject sighs] As I'm sure you know, Herr Müller, back then the United States had an electoral college system, and the president was not elected by popular vote. Although I did not like it, I accepted the outcome at the time. Those were the rules.

TM: You are aware that conclusive evidence of electoral tampering in Florida was found in 2022. Republican operatives spoiled more than 50,000 ballots in favor of Al Gore.

KG: Yes. The uncounted overvotes. I've read the reports.

TM: Given what you now know about the true circumstances in 2000, do you think you would have acted differently?

KG: Of course I would have acted differently. But none of us had the information at the time.

TM: Can we talk about 11 September 2001 and the subsequent Uniting and Strengthening America by Providing Appropriate Tools Required to Intercept and Obstruct Terrorism Act of 2001?

KG: The Patriot Act?

TM: Exactly. You are aware that the majority of the elected representatives of your party voted in favor of a drastic decrease in American civil liberties, directly undermining the principles of democracy upon which the United States was founded?

KG: Some Democrats voted against it. There were some.

TM: All Democratic senators excepting Senator Feingold voted in favor. And 123 members of the Democratic Party voted in favor in the House of Representatives. The vast majority of the elected Democrats supported the Patriot Act.

KG: The legislation was passed right after the September 11 attacks. It was rushed through with little time for debate.

TM: I believe the ordinary rules of the House of Representatives were suspended.

KG: Yes, that's right.

TM: Did you agree with this legislation?

KG: No.

TM: Did you take any action against this legislation? Did you protest?

KG: I was eight and a half months pregnant with my daughter when it was passed in October 2001. I lost my best friend on September 11, and my father died unexpectedly two weeks later. You could say that I had other things on my mind.

TM: Did you leave the Democratic Party at that time?

KG: No.

TM: Why not?

KG: I was opposed to Bush and opposed to the Iraq War. In a two-party system, I felt that remaining with the Democratic Party was the only way to effect political change.

TM: You were opposed to the Iraq War?

KG: Yes. I organized demonstrations against the war on my campus. You should have records on that.

TM: You are aware that 58 percent of Democratic senators voted in favor of the Iraq War Resolution? And eighty-two congressmen and women.

KG: Yes, but there was also Democratic opposition in both houses. Many Democrats spoke out against the war.

TM: Did you take any action in support of these dissenting Democrats?

KG: They were elected representatives, and I felt they represented my interests at the federal level.

TM: Even after it was discovered that there were no weapons of mass destruction in Iraq?

KG: [subject sighs] Yes. Members of the Democratic Party were increasingly outspoken and critical of the Bush administration's policies.

TM: You and your husband at that time, a dual Bulgarian-American citizen, worked for the presidential campaign of John Kerry. You contributed both time and money to the Kerry campaign. I am assuming that you voted for Senator Kerry in the 2004 presidential election.

KG: Yes. I was opposed to George W. Bush.

TM: But you knew that Senator Kerry voted in favor of the Iraq War, as did his vice presidential running mate, Senator John Edwards.

KG: Yes, I knew. I initially caucused for Congressman Dennis Kucinich in Maine, who opposed the Iraq War. But I felt I had little choice but to support Kerry once he won the Democratic nomination. After Ralph Nader's candidacy hurt Gore in the 2000 election, many of us were fearful of being divided. I voted against Bush more than I voted for Kerry. I had few options.

TM: Many Americans abstained from voting.

KG: Kerry was the lesser of two evils.

TM: You were aware that your country acted in blatant violation of international law when it invaded Iraq unilaterally without a second resolution from the United Nations Security Council. Kofi Annan, the UN Secretary General, declared the war illegal and the International Commission of Jurists in Geneva found that the Iraq invasion constituted an illegal war of aggression.

KG: Yes, I was aware of the reports.

TM: Millions of people around the world protested this war, including citizens of the Federal Republic of Germany.

KG: [subject nods.]

TM: Between 2003 and 2010, many Americans engaged in acts of civil disobedience against the Iraq War. Did you participate in any way?

KG: [Subject shakes her head.]

TM: Why did you not participate? Did you become a supporter of the illegal war and the continued American occupation of Iraq?

KG: Of course not.

TM: But you did not resist in any way. How are we supposed to interpret that?

KG: Herr Müller, it's always easier to see what you should have done in hindsight. But you must understand the circumstances. I was working full time and had a toddler in the house, with limited support from my husband, who was often in Europe for work. When we divorced in the summer of 2005, I became a single mom trying to finish a book and earn tenure. I had financial problems and didn't feel like there was anything I could do to change things after Bush was reelected. I was trying to just get on with life.

TM: And the hundreds of thousands who died in Iraq? Prof. Dr. Ghodsee, your government placed an eighteen-year-ban on photographs of flag-draped coffins (in direct contravention of the first amendment of your own constitution) so it could hide from the public the human costs of an illegal war, and you were just trying to get on with your life?

KG: I didn't believe there was anything I could do at the time. When the financial crisis hit, I stopped thinking about the war. There was so much going on in those years. I was working very long hours, and I had limited resources. I know this sounds like I'm making excuses. And when I look back on that time now, I don't know how I could have been so blind to the changes going on around me. But I had classes to teach, a daughter to raise, bills to pay, and personal problems that seemed much more immediate to me than what was happening in Iraq or anywhere else in the world. It was easy to tune it all out, to ignore it, to pretend it wasn't happening, or that it didn't concern me. I was just one person in a country of over 300 million, and the thing about the system back then was that it made you feel like you couldn't do anything to change it.

At this point I could tell that Frau Prof. Dr. Ghodsee was growing tired. I asked her some short questions about gun control and the situation of black Americans, and she reiterated that she was always in favor of gun control and opposed to institutionalized racism and state persecution of racial minorities. When I asked how she expressed her political opinions to her government, she insisted that voting in what she considered free and open democratic elections constituted active participation at the time.

I will admit that I find Frau Prof. Dr. Ghodsee's case perplexing. Since arriving in Germany, she has been a tireless critic of the Drumph regime, penning almost daily articles for all of the major German newspapers. With her daughter, she is active in providing legal and material assistance to American refugees, and teaches weekly classes in the resettlement camps outside of Erfurt. Despite her age and ill health, her demeanor is energetic and committed, and I have a difficult time reconciling her current level of political activity with her previous apathy.

When I asked her why she remained a registered member of the U.S. Democratic Party and continued to vote in what were clearly no longer free and fair elections after the 2010 Supreme Court decision of *Citizens United v. Federal Election Commission*, she gave no answer. Furthermore, at a time when legions of Americans refused to vote in the fraudulent elections of 2024 and 2028 I remain incredulous that a woman of Frau Prof. Dr. Ghodsee's experience and seeming intelligence continued to legitimate the U.S. government through her ongoing electoral participation, and perhaps more worryingly, her continued admonition to her university students to participate in these elections. Either she was incredibly naive or she tacitly supported the totalitarian drift of her country.

My second interview with Frau Prof. Dr. Ghodsee occurred on 7 October, once again in the ministry regional office in Erfurt. The interview lasted sixty-seven minutes. I began the interview by explaining to Frau Prof. Dr. Ghodsee that German history requires us to be vigilant against those who support state violence by their inaction, and that we must by necessity hold university professors to higher moral standards than ordinary citizens. I reminded her of the twin German totalitarianisms of the twentieth century, and she made no protest at my comparison between the politics of the National Socialists and the Socialist Unity Party with the politics of the current regime in the United States. Once again, I pressed her on several key issues relating to the ongoing deterioration of civil rights in her country between 2001 and 2028.

> Thomas Müller (TM): I'd like to discuss the surveillance provisions of the 2001 Patriot Act, which eventually authorized the National Security Agency to conduct illegal electronic surveillance of innocent Americans, surveillance which was later used by federal agents to blackmail or intimidate opponents of the Drumph regime. You were aware of the extent of the surveillance?
>
> Kristen Ghodsee (KG): Yes, after the Edward Snowden revelations in 2013, I was aware of the full extent of the surveillance.
>
> TM: President Barack Obama, a member of the Democratic Party of the United States, continued to authorize this surveillance, which violated domestic protections of the Fourth Amendment regarding unreasonable searches and seizures. Internationally, the leaders of countries which were at that time the allies of the United States, including the chancellor of Germany, had their personal mobile phones tapped by the National Security Agency. You campaigned and voted for President Obama, correct?
>
> KG: That is correct.

TM: Did you support his extension of the Patriot Act?

KG: No, I didn't.

TM: Did you at any time during the Obama administration consider leaving the Democratic Party of the United States of America?

KG: No. I supported President Obama.

TM: The Obama administration charged Edward Snowden with treason under a 1917 Espionage Act that would limit his access to due process. You supported this?

KG: No.

TM: What about Obama's policy of regime change in the Middle East?

KG: In those years, ordinary citizens had no idea of the extent of CIA involvement in the democratic uprisings of the Arab Spring. Had I understood the full extent of American covert operations, I would not have supported this policy.

TM: Frau Professor Ghodsee, you will forgive me if I have a difficult time understanding you. You say that you did not support his policies and yet you continued to support President Obama and the Democratic Party. All of the evidence was there before your eyes and you chose not to act in any way in opposition to the growing surveillance state and the suspension of basic civil liberties. Were you ill? Was there some other personal crisis?

KG: Herr Müller, I don't know what to tell you.

TM: Were you aware that you were the subject of ongoing government surveillance?

KG: I assumed that all of my Internet records, e-mail and voice communications, mobile phone location data, and social media accounts were not private, regardless of my privacy settings.

TM: Were you not disturbed by the extent of the surveillance and the threat to your constitutionally guaranteed right of freedom of speech and conscience?

KG: Yes, it bothered me sometimes, but mostly I didn't think about it. I didn't think I had anything to hide. I wasn't doing anything wrong.

TM: Did you begin to censor yourself?

KG: Sure. It wasn't intentional at first, but I definitely thought twice about everything I wrote electronically. Of course, I feared the Internet Twitter mobs before I feared the government. The witch hunts started from the grassroots. Only later did the government start manipulating them.

TM: Did you resist in any way?

KG: The surveillance?

TM: Yes.

KG: Well, I started using my typewriters a lot more, but in general, no, I didn't really do anything. Like I said, I didn't think I had anything to hide. They say that if you throw a frog into a pot of boiling water, it will jump out. But if you put a frog in a pot of tepid water and heat the water to a boil, the frog will not move. The gradual change is the hardest to perceive. I was just living an ordinary life—work, family, friends. I don't know. After the eleventh of September, I felt scared, and maybe I believed that the extra surveillance measures were actually there to protect ordinary people from terrorists. I know that sounds stupid, but it's hard to explain what it was like back then.

TM: I know these things are easier to see in hindsight, but if you could go back in time now, knowing what you know about the 2024 amendment and the collapse of American democracy, what do you think you would have done differently?

KG: [Long pause] I'd like to say that I would do everything differently, and I know that's what I should tell you. Of course if I could have seen the future, maybe I would have fought harder, maybe I would have more actively protested the things I saw going wrong. But people were protesting, people were out on the streets, and it made no difference. I was complacent because everyone else was complacent. We never imagined things would get as bad as they did. Maybe I should've known better, knowing what I know about European history, but I just didn't think it could happen in the United States. Certainly, I'm glad my daughter left when she did, and I wish I'd left sooner, too. My partner might still be alive.

But to be truthful, and I want to be truthful here, Herr Müller, because I understand that you are using this interview to make a decision about my suitability to teach in the university classroom. The truth is that things never felt that bad. No matter what was happening in Washington, the grind of my ordinary life just went on. There were more wars and there was more surveillance and I understood that our democracy was threatened, but in those early years it was just easy to ignore because it didn't directly impact me. It's not that I supported the government; I was too damn busy to support anything really. I just plodded through life like I thought I was supposed to. I'm certainly no hero, but I also don't think that people like me can be held accountable for the things the government did while we were busy living our lives. Maybe that's the wrong answer, but it's the truth, Herr Müller. I don't know what else to say.

At this point I had no further questions for Frau Prof. Dr. Ghodsee. We exchanged pleasantries, and she inquired how long it might be before an official decision was reached. I informed her that the decision rested with the university and that I had no clear timeline for her case.

Overall, I had hoped that my conversations with Frau Prof. Dr. Ghodsee would be less confrontational. But given the ongoing violence in the United States, and the fact that both interviews were conducted at a time of increasing anxiety among the German people about the influx of American refugees, I felt obliged to challenge her directly. In particular, there are concerns that libertarian terrorists may be entering our country under the guise of political asylum seekers.

Frau Prof. Dr. Ghodsee is not a terrorist, nor do I believe that she poses any threat to the German nation or its people. She has clearly been persecuted by her government for her recent political activities, and there remains no doubt that she should be granted full political asylum if she does not pursue a family reunification permit through her daughter. Her current journalistic writing is of great value to the public, but I understand that it provides no financial remuneration, and that she desires to find some form of employment.

Frau Prof. Dr. Ghodsee is a highly qualified and experienced scholar, but I maintain reservations about her political commitments and her suitability for university teaching. It is my firm belief that her long association with the Democratic Party of the United States will compromise her effectiveness in the classroom. No educators tainted with this previous ideology should have an opportunity to corrupt the minds of the young.

Although we have no evidence that Frau Prof. Dr. Ghodsee was a direct collaborator with the American government, she clearly suffers psychological damage from the long years she lived in the United States of America. Given the many challenges facing the Federal Republic of Germany today, our educators must be men and women willing to question authority and resist tyranny in all its forms. It is therefore my official recommendation that Frau Prof. Dr. Ghodsee be denied a position at F. Schiller Universität Jena and, indeed, at any other German university.

Yours respectfully,

Thomas Müller
Federal Ministry of Immigration and Resettlement

14. Democracy for the Penguins

It was nearing midnight on Christmas Eve 2015, and much wine and Johnny Walker had been consumed when the conversation turned to contemporary politics. My former brother-in-law, a Bulgarian who had lived for many years in the United States, turned to me and said, "You know, if the Americans discovered oil near the South Pole, they would send an army to end the cruel tyranny of the Emperor Penguin and bring democracy to Antarctica."

This comment elicited raucous laughter from the assembled Bulgarians, and even my often dour ex-mother-in-law allowed herself a genuine smile. But the joke haunted me for days afterward because of my brother-in-law's genuine suspicion of the motives of those who claim to want democracy. His cynicism recalled for me three other vexed conversations about the problems of liberal democracy after the Cold War.

The first was a tense debate following a presentation by the renowned Jamaican anthropologist David Scott in the School of Social Sciences Monday lunch seminar at the Institute for Advanced Study on February 8, 2007. Back then, I was an untenured assistant professor unaccustomed to the intellectual sparring of my academic elders, so the rancorous tone of the discussion that followed Scott's talk surprised me. Even a decade later, I remember David Scott's seminar in the Dilworth Room as the most controversial of all that I attended that year, inspiring weeks of verbal jousting in the IAS dining hall and in the corridors of the West Building.

The title of his talk was something like "Norms of Democratization." Scott proceeded to mount a careful but nevertheless scathing critique of how former colonial powers now deployed the idea of democracy, in much the same way as they had once mobilized the concept of civilization, to justify violations of the sovereignty of developing countries. In other words, European powers, he argued, once legitimated their imperial entanglements in Asia, Africa, and Latin America by claiming that subjugated peoples lacked the civilized culture necessary for joining the modern age. In Scott's view, the Third World independence movements threw off colonial domination by asserting rights of national self-determination with the direct or indirect support of the Soviet Union and its allies.[1] Cold War superpower rivalries between East and West created a space for the countries of the Global South to chart their own courses to modernization, whether under the leadership of monarchs, military dictatorships, vanguard parties, or freely elected liberal parliamentarians.

The end of the Cold War precipitated a return to the civilizational discourse of the past, but this time, the United States and its Western allies employed a normative concept of democracy to delegitimize Third World leaders they disliked and justify foreign interventions into the sovereign internal political landscapes of developing countries. A narrow definition of democracy as a system of multiparty elections, and the elevation of the idea of a consolidated democracy as a yardstick against which the success or failure of sovereign nations is determined, was, in Scott's opinion, a new justification for First World imperialism in the countries of the Third World. The principles of sovereignty and national self-determination required Western nonintervention in the internal affairs of developing countries, even when those countries were ruled by monarchs, theocrats, or unelected secular leaders. "Democracy is the contemporary political name of an old civilizing project: it is now a regulating principle in the political rationality of international order by which the political prospects of (especially, if not only) the Third World are governed."[2]

When David Scott finished reading his presentation, hands shot up like missiles. The Pakistani-British political scientist Farzana Shaikh bounced with agitation in her seat. I sat processing the lecture, feeling convinced that Scott had put his finger on something very important, and that his periodization of the ascent of this "norm of democratization" following the collapse of Soviet communism was accurate. During the Cold War, the United

States and its Western allies had indeed lambasted the communist countries for lacking free elections and liberal political rights, but the East had always countered with arguments about the lack of social and economic rights in the West. Where the United States guaranteed rights such as freedom of speech, religion, assembly, and private property, the Soviet Union guaranteed rights such as full employment and state provision of a basic social safety net through which (at least theoretically) no one would be allowed to fall. Each side argued that their protected categories of rights were more important, and often viewed the two categories as mutually exclusive. These debates about abstract categories of rights underpinned the ideological conflicts of the Cold War. While the West accused the East of countless human rights violations, the East pointed to the West's hypocrisy regarding civil rights for African Americans and its support of pro-American military dictatorships in Latin America.

In the context of a bipolar world, many Third World nations followed a state socialist path to modernization and development by limiting political rights to avoid the internal instabilities often created by multiparty elections in newly independent states. Instead, the leaders of developing countries, many of them former fighters for national independence, concentrated attention and resources on providing basic social and economic rights. They nationalized former colonial enterprises and used the revenues to build necessary infrastructure, raise the literacy rate, expand educational opportunities, and increase access to health care, among many other projects. In their view, the electoral process could too easily be manipulated by former colonial powers to perpetuate their economic interests. Great Britain, for instance, had a long history of using divide-and-rule tactics to subjugate local populations, and former British subjects were rightly suspicious of British and American championing of democracy given the latter's unwavering support for the apartheid regime in South Africa, which curtailed black political rights to bolster the power of a white minority. It should come as no surprise, therefore, that Marxism-Leninism influenced many Cold War–era Third World leaders; Nelson Mandela, the first president of postapartheid South Africa, for instance, was a prominent member of the South African Communist Party.[3]

Back at the seminar in Princeton, David Scott took a few questions before finally acknowledging Farzana Shaikh, who said, in a most proper British tone of voice, something like, "While I understand the nature of your critique, and I commend you on your analysis, I am perturbed by its implications. Are you suggesting that we brown people aren't good enough for democracy?"

Before David Scott had a chance to answer, Shaikh's husband, the late Africanist and political scientist Patrick Chabal, launched into a polite diatribe opposing the idea that African dictators should be allowed to terrorize their populations without fear of international intervention. I remember listening to Shaikh and Chabal and suddenly doubting my previous certainty in Scott's conclusions. Shaikh and Chabal argued, in essence, that democracy could not be an ideal only suitable for the enlightened countries of the West but was, at least in principle, the form of government that guaranteed the maximum number of people some type of political enfranchisement. Particularly when there existed local social movements demanding reform, the international community had a responsibility to support the forces of democratization.

At that point the Dilworth Room exploded with conversation as the other members, visitors, and guests of the School of Social Science lunch seminar grappled with the thorny issues David Scott's lecture had raised. The historian Joan Wallach Scott, our seminar leader, tried to impose order, but passions ran high. Although I stayed for the rest of the discussion, it was Shaikh's incisive question that has lingered with me over the years. Of course, David Scott gave his talk in the aftermath of the Iraq War to depose Saddam Hussein and continued U.S. hostility toward Latin American populist leaders like Hugo Chavez in Venezuela and Evo Morales in Bolivia. But it was still a few years before the beginning of the Arab Spring, when the West supported local democratic forces against secular dictators in Middle Eastern countries like Egypt, Libya, and Syria. As global events unfolded over the next decade, I found myself always returning to the two opposing positions staked out that afternoon in 2007. Was democracy a tool for continued imperialism or a universal ideal requiring unfaltering international support? Could it be both?

The second conversation I recalled after my brother-in-law suggested that the U.S. government would try to bring democracy to the penguins if it suited American economic interests occurred about three years after David Scott's lunch seminar. It was January 2010 and I met a Bulgarian friend for dinner in a Georgetown restaurant. This friend, whom I will call Svetozara, had just immigrated to the United States and was looking for a job in the capital. She had been a lawyer in Bulgaria, and one of a core of prodemocracy activists involved in Bulgaria's transition from communism.

With her liberal colleagues, Svetozara had fought hard to banish communist influences from the Bulgarian government and economy. She believed that democracy and the institution of free markets would improve the lives of her compatriots after more than four decades of communist rule and worked to ensure free and fair elections after 1989. She helped reorganize local governments to make them more responsive to citizens' needs and had supported legislation to make the national government less bureaucratic and more open and transparent. Western democracy promoters loved her.

During the first glass of wine, we caught up on each other's personal lives; after the second glass, the conversation turned to politics. I remarked that nothing had been done in Bulgaria to mark the twentieth anniversary of the fall of the Berlin Wall.

She nodded. "That's because there's nothing to celebrate."

"What do you mean?"

Svetozara lowered her glass, staring down at the table.

"I can't tell you how disgusted I am, Kristen. I feel like such an idiot. I thought we were fighting on the right side," Svetozara said. "I thought we were fighting for freedom, for democracy, for principles that I believed in. But it was all a lie. What we have now is worse than what we had before. I used to think that maybe we did something wrong, but now I realize that the whole thing was rotten from the start; 1989 was not about bringing liberty to the people of Eastern Europe; it was about expanding markets for Western companies. They used the language of freedom and democracy, but it was all about money. I was so stupid."

"You were idealistic," I said. "That's different."

"No, it's worse." Svetozara shook her head. "I never understood how people could have supported a terrible system like communism, but now I see that they made the same mistake that I made. They believed in something that they thought was good, but that turned out to be very bad. I did the exact same thing."

A few months after that conversation with Svetozara, the East German writer Daniela Dahn gave a lecture at the American Institute for Contemporary German Studies at Johns Hopkins University in Baltimore titled, "The Legacy of Democratic Awakening: Twenty Years after the Fall of the Berlin Wall." Dahn had been a political activist in the GDR, and had helped draft new laws to eradicate state censorship and guarantee a free press. With her fellow dissidents, Dahn participated in the process of imagining a new future for East Germany, a new democratic socialist future. She explained, "As I grew up in the GDR, I always longed to live in a democracy. But not in capitalism. I had no illusions about its tendency to economic and financial crises, its power to create a social divide between the rich and poor, and its inclination to military solutions."[4]

Dahn cited an opinion poll taken at the end of November 1989 that showed that 89 percent of East Germans preferred to take "the path to better, reformed socialism," with only 5 percent supporting the "capitalist path."[5]

Dahn and other East Germans longed for greater political rights and Western prosperity, but they also wanted to keep some of the public supports of socialism in place: guaranteed employment, free education and health care, state-supported maternity leave, and kindergartens that allowed women to better combine work and family life. New East German constitutions were drafted, but it soon became clear that their efforts would be in vain. With lightning speed, the West German Constitution became the new constitution of a unified Germany. Dahn reflected, "Many in the oppositional civil movements would have been grateful for more time to consider how the advantages of both sides could be retained. How the dictatorship could be overcome without subjecting the defenseless population to the rough climate of the market economy. How a humane balance between the market and the planned economies could be achieved. How the GDR's defects could be corrected by the strength of its own grassroots democracy."[6]

My ex-brother-in-law's joke about the penguins, David Scott's lecture, Svetozara's regrets, and Daniela Dahn's reflections all take issue with the use of democracy as a tool of Western economic elites. Although in theory, democracy should increase personal freedoms, too often it arrives linked to an economic system that disempowers and disenfranchises. Since 2005, I have written four books about communism and postcommunism in Eastern Europe, and I believed for a long time that I was researching the lived experiences of the transition from communism to capitalism, exploring the impacts on ordinary lives. On some level, I accepted that this transitional period was temporary. Once the culture of democracy took hold, the former communist nations would flourish like their new Western allies. But today, after twenty years of research on the region, I realize that things are not improving and, like my friend Svetozara, I was naive. Without intending to, I've been documenting the failures of liberal democracy in the aftermath of the Cold War. Francis Fukuyama famously claimed that the collapse of world communism was the end of history, because liberal democracy and free market capitalism had triumphed and proved themselves to be the best political and economic systems available for organizing human affairs. But today, capitalism threatens to destroy democracy, and the world stands on the precipice of a post-democratic age.

The year 2017 marks the centennial of the Russian Revolution, and this provides an opportune moment to turn our analytic attentions to the problem of democracy and the ways it has been used and abused by those nations that crowned themselves the victors of the Cold War. Both communism and democracy must be understood as political systems embedded in particu-

FIGURE 14.1. Graffiti in Sofia, February 2016.

lar historical contexts, but which can be detached from those contexts to offer different ideals to guide us toward alternative futures. As we update and adapt historically rooted political ideals to the twenty-first century, we must reflect upon the way democracy has been violently deployed to further the interests of a particularly destructive form of neoliberal capitalism in the same way we understand how the ideals of communism were used to justify various forms of state repression. Political theories must be allowed to exist as ideal types even after they have become tainted by the histories of their failed applications.

Back in 2002, the Slovenian philosopher Slavoj Žižek published a selection of Vladimir Lenin's letters written between February and October 1917.[7] In his lucid afterword to the collection, Žižek considered the factors that pushed Lenin to abandon parliamentary democracy and embrace revolution. Žižek railed against what he calls the *Denkverbot* (prohibition on thinking) imposed by the contemporary political insistence on the primacy of liberal parliamentarianism. If the West truly embraces the values of freedom of speech and of conscience, Žižek argued, this must include the right to question the desirability of democracy and the right to reconsider Lenin's vision of why bourgeois democracy had always been, and would remain, the handmaiden of capitalist economic elites. Justifying his sustained interrogation of Lenin's pre-October psyche, Žižek asserted that "repeating Lenin does not mean a return to Lenin—to repeat Lenin is to accept . . . that his particular solution failed, but there was a utopian spark in it worth saving."[8]

Everywhere I look today, scholars, politicians, and activists are trying to reinvent the democratic ideal as an ally in the fight against unfettered free markets and rapacious global capitalism, to excavate its own "utopian spark worth saving." In October 2009, twenty years after the fall of the Berlin Wall, the world wallowed in the aftermath of the global financial crisis caused by reckless Wall Street trading and collateralized debt obligations. Surveying the carnage, former U.S. secretary of labor Robert Reich penned a fierce article in *Foreign Policy*: "How Capitalism Is Killing Democracy."[9] "It was supposed to be a match made in heaven," Reich wrote. "Capitalism and democracy, we've long been told, are the twin ideological pillars capable of bringing unprecedented prosperity and freedom to the world." Instead, Reich catalogued evidence of their growing divergence—as investors and consumers benefited from the unchallenged dominance of global capitalism, citizens suffered from increasing economic marginalization. Growing inequalities caused deep fissures in democratic societies as voters lost hope in the electoral process, feeling powerless in a system that privileged the interests of the rich. Reich lamented that the West had blurred the responsibilities of capitalism and democracy; the former should concern itself with generating wealth while the latter sees to it that the wealth is distributed equitably. Free markets, Reich argues, were never intended to look after the common good. That is the job of democracy. But capitalist interests had led to a weakening rather than the strengthening of democracy predicted in the triumphalist aftermath of the end of the Cold War. Reich explained, "Democracy has become enfeebled largely because companies, in intensifying competition for global consumers and investors, have spent ever greater sums for lobbying, public relations, and even bribes and kickbacks, seeking laws that give them a competitive advantage over their rivals. The result is an arms race for political influence that is drowning out the voices of average citizens."[10] Reich wrote these words before the January 2010 *Citizens United* Supreme Court decision that invoked First Amendment guarantees for free speech to allow unlimited corporate campaign spending in American elections. The Supreme Court decision rolled back federal legislation to clean up campaign finance in the United States, prompting former President Jimmy Carter to proclaim, "We've become now an oligarchy instead of a democracy. And I think that's been the worst damage to the basic moral and ethical standards of the American political system that I've ever seen in my life."[11]

Scholars also noted the enfeeblement of democracy in reunified Ger-

FIGURE 14.2.
A reminder
of video
surveillance
on a German
train.

many, a country where concepts such as freedom and elections have justified a quarter of a century of outsourcing, job cuts, stagnant wages, and growing income inequality. In 2014, the German political scientist Wolfgang Merkel asked, "Is capitalism compatible with democracy?"[12] Merkel, a member of the Brandenburg Academy of Sciences and an expert on democracy and democratization, echoed the earlier sentiments of Reich and worried that the answer to his question would soon be "no." Like Thomas Piketty, Merkel points out that capitalism might be producing inequality rather than mitigating it. In the decades immediately following World War II, the rising tide did raise all boats. State commitments to welfare and redistribution ensured that all citizens benefited from growing the economic pie. But since the 1980s, the twin forces of deregulation and globalization have undermined the governing power of democratic states:

Capitalism and democracy are guided by different principles that create tensions between the two. This is expressed primarily in the different relations to equality and inequality. The level of inequality that defines specific variants of capitalism and supposedly secures productivity and profits is hardly compatible with the democratic principle of equal rights and opportunities for political participation. Socioeconomic inequality challenges the core democratic principle of equality in participation, representation and governance. . . . If these challenges are not met with democratic and economic reforms, democracy may slowly transform into an oligarchy, formally legitimized by general elections.[13]

In her 2015 book *Undoing the Demos*, the political theorist Wendy Brown blamed the ideology of neoliberalism for the erosion of democratic societies in Europe and North America, and rooted the rise of neoliberalism in the ideological vacuum created by the fall of the Berlin Wall. For Brown, the idea of neoliberalism captures the marketization of everyday life so that everything we do (every activity we engage in) becomes governed by the laws of supply and demand, something to be valued for potential sale within a market made up of other individuals offering similar commodities. Sex, for instance, no longer serves as an act we engage in for pleasure or for building and maintaining relationships. Sex and sexuality are things to be valued and measured in terms of market metrics (How often? How good? For what purpose?), in terms of opportunity costs (What could I be doing with my time if I weren't having sex?), or in terms of strategic investments in the future (What will I get by having sex with this person? How will this sex benefit me in the long run?).

These neoliberalizing tendencies have also changed the way most Americans think about exercise or about pursuing higher education. No longer do we go for a run for the pleasure of being outside or merely moving our bodies; now we wear bracelets to track every step and minute fluctuation in our heart rates. No longer do students attend university to expand their minds or increase their knowledge of the arts and sciences. Instead, college has become a personal investment for the improvement of future success in competitive labor markets. Even dogs have been neoliberalized. No one gets a dog just because they like dogs. Now we get dogs because it's good for the kids, or good for the parents, or good for our limbic brains because some study has told us that people with dogs live longer and healthier lives. Finally, time spent with our family and friends has become a form of social capital to be measured and managed. Jodi Dean uses the term "communicative capitalism" to describe how social networks have become commodities to be gathered, packaged, and sold to corporate interests without our consent.[14]

Similarly, Brown argues that democracy has been stripped of any meaning beyond the economic, and this neoliberalization of democracy portends its doom. "Liberty is disconnected from either political participation or existential freedom, and is reduced to market freedom unimpeded by regulation or any other form of government restriction. Equality as a matter of legal standing and of participation in shared rule is replaced with the idea of an equal right to compete in a world where there are always winners and losers."[15] But the equal right to be a winner or loser ignores the real advantages that the rich have in playing the game, and the valorization of personal liberty masks the way that economic elites deploy the language of the inalienability of political rights as a smoke screen for a system that is rigged in their favor.

A wonderful example of the marketization of American politics and the slow drift toward oligarchy can be found in journalist Jane Mayer's 2016 book on the campaign influence of the Koch brothers and other conservative billionaires, *Dark Money*. Mayer showed how the private funds of individuals could be used to promote policies to protect or increase their wealth despite the costs to the planet or the democratic process. Mayer found that the Koch brothers used the freedom of speech guaranteed by *Citizens United* to advocate for lower taxes, business deregulation, and climate change denial. "It's very worrisome to many Americans to think that the whole ideal of one man, one vote might be overwhelmed by 400 of the richest people of any political persuasion picking the next leader for them. That's just not how democracy is supposed to work."[16]

On January 19, 2016, just a week after I attended the Liebknecht-Luxemburg Demonstration in Berlin, the British charity Oxfam released a report stating that only sixty-two people owned as much wealth as the lower 50 percent of humanity combined.[17] This was a dramatic change from 2010, when the 388 richest individuals owned an amount equivalent to that owned by the poorest 50 percent. Mark Goldring, the chief executive of Oxfam in the United Kingdom, commented, "It is simply unacceptable that the poorest half of the world population owns no more than a small group of the global super-rich—so few, you could fit them all on a single coach."[18] Two days later *Guardian* columnist Jeff Sparrow urged readers to express their rage at Oxfam's recent findings and their implications for the future of democracy: "The notion that our 62 god-kings can be in any way constrained or controlled by Joe and Jane Citizen dropping their votes in a ballot box is too ludicrous for serious contemplation. On the contrary, the multibillionaire relates to the pauper as predator does to its prey, with the vast human flock simply a re-source that, in Pushkin's phrase, can be 'either slaughtered or shorn.'"[19]

The former Greek finance minister Yanis Varoufakis recorded a TED talk in December 2015 called "Capitalism Will Eat Democracy—Unless We Speak Up," which was viewed by over 1.5 million people in just three months.[20] On February 9, 2016, Varoufakis launched a pan-European citizens' initiative called DiEM25, hoping to use democracy as a tool to rescue Europe from disintegration.[21] To initiate this new left-wing movement, Varoufakis sym-bolically chose Berlin, the city once divided by the Wall. Progressive politi-cians from a variety of EU countries attended the opening event, including Slavoj Žižek, musician Brian Eno, and WikiLeaks founder Julian Assange (by video). DiEM25's "manifesto for democratizing Europe" argues that democ-racy is the only weapon ordinary citizens have to defend themselves against the "democracy-free zone" supported by the EU bureaucracy in Brussels.[22] Varoufakis argues that European leaders rule in the name of democracy while simultaneously doing everything to undermine its true power. The long version of the DiEM25 Manifesto argues, "For all their concerns with global competitiveness, migration and terrorism, only one prospect truly ter-rifies the Powers of Europe: Democracy! They speak in democracy's name but only to deny, exorcise and suppress it in practice. They seek to co-opt, evade, corrupt, mystify, usurp and manipulate democracy in order to break its energy and arrest its possibilities."[23]

Like Rosa Luxemburg and Karl Liebknecht railing against the betrayal of the German Social Democrats who voted in favor of World War I, Varoufakis and his allies have lost patience with "political parties appealing to liberal-ism, democracy, freedom and solidarity to betray their most basic principles when in government" and "bailed out bankers, fund managers and resurgent oligarchies perpetually contemptuous of the multitudes and their organised expression."[24] The European initiative seeks to disentangle democracy and capitalism in order to build a future where Europeans are not tempted to retreat into their nation-states and reenact a history that will benefit no one save the arms dealers (like Germany's Rheinmetall).

Back in the pages of *Foreign Policy*, Thomas Carothers of the Carnegie Endowment for International Peace argued that the United States could no longer be held up as a beacon of democracy. Working around the world in the 1990s, Carothers and others could feel secure that they represented a nation that lived up to the principles it exported abroad: "Giving advice to people in another country about how to organize their political life is al-ways a sensitive endeavor. But in those earlier decades, the United States was emerging victorious from its long ideological rivalry with the Soviet Union and exuding political confidence at home and abroad. The health of its own democracy seemed almost beyond question. In the ensuing decades, that has greatly changed."[25]

Today Carothers argues that the legions of overseas democracy promoters once dispatched to the far reaches of the planet should "look homeward" and try to fix a crumbling system before it is too late. Of course, Carothers remains deeply committed to the democratic project, as do Reich, Merkel, Brown, Varoufakis, and others who have argued that capitalism and democracy are becoming incompatible. Even after the 2016 election of Donald Trump, who won the Electoral College but lost the popular vote by almost 3 million votes in an election influenced by Russian hackers and an FBI director intent on undermining the campaign of Trump's rival, few pundits dared to suggest we revisit the basic premises of democracy. Almost everyone seems to accept the old adage often attributed to Winston Churchill, "Democracy is the worst form of government, except for all others."[26]

But I think we should pause and consider how often democracy is seen as the only way to fight capitalism even as critics accept that capitalism has deeply wounded the democratic ideal. Mainstream discussions about the erosion of democracy still insist that some uncorrupted form of democracy is the only legitimate system of government for the future. Within the corridors of power, it proves heresy to discuss possible alternatives to liberal democracy, such as those hinted at by David Scott, or advocated in the works of Jodi Dean (*The Communist Horizon*) or of Slavoj Žižek and others in the 2009 volume *The Idea of Communism*, a provocative set of essays arguing that the communist ideal must be detached from the history of twentieth-century Eastern Europe.[27] Instead, we should endeavor to detach the democratic ideal from its historically specific link with neoliberal capitalism. And while I agree that the ideals of both communism and democracy should be separated from specific instances of their implementation, we must also face the possibility that proponents of global capitalism (in its current form) might be suppressing any real challenge to their continued hegemony by limiting our political imaginations to what Žižek has called the "liberal parliamentary consensus."[28] David Scott describes this as "the new 'blackmail' of democracy," which has "come to frame the political discussion: either democracy frames your horizon of expectation, or you are ruled unqualified to participate in the language game of legitimate political discourse."[29] Jodi Dean, too, argues that in order to push forward with real political change, we must be willing to uncouple our minds from the straitjacket of liberal democracy.[30] As

FIGURE 14.3. A communist-era Lada in storage in a back courtyard.

Audre Lorde once said, "The Master's tools will never dismantle the Master's house."[31]

In other words, how convenient is it that a political system easily (and legally) manipulated by the top 1 percent of the income distribution happens to be the only one we are allowed to consider legitimate? When the Supreme Court of the United States justifies unlimited corporate campaign contributions by citing free speech protections, not only are the inherent tensions between capitalism and democracy exposed, but political rights such as freedom of speech become a rhetorical tool for extending the privileges of the superrich. To paraphrase George Orwell in *Animal Farm*, "All men are created equal, but some are more equal than others."

If we can save the democratic ideal from its specific historical deployment by neoliberal capitalism, then by all means we should do so, but if democracy serves as a convenient ideological shield for the abuses and excesses of capitalism, then we should not be surprised when citizens feel compelled to abandon it. Indeed, Jodi Dean argues that conservative political forces have manipulated the twentieth-century history of communism to support the hegemony of neoliberalism.[32] For too long, the horrors of communist dictatorships of Eastern Europe have legitimated the horrors of democro-capitalism.

This is not to deny the crimes of communism, but to call attention to the ways in which the end of the Cold War and the triumphalism of the

West legitimated the military, political, and economic violence inflicted on millions of men and women across the globe in the name of promoting democracy. Yes, there were labor camps, travel restrictions, secret police, and consumer shortages. Those were the pathologies of twentieth-century state socialist regimes. But we must also consider the pathologies of democracy in the twenty-first century: the misery, illness, and premature deaths of the unemployed; the commodification of sex and sexuality; the black markets for human organs and child trafficking; the desperate hopelessness of those willing to set themselves on fire to protest the failed promises of freedom after 1989. Isn't detaching the democratic ideal from the horrors and abuses of global neoliberalism the same intellectual project as detaching the communist ideal from the crimes of past communist regimes? Why are we being admonished to do one, but not the other?

More importantly, as I wrote these words in the spring of 2016, populations in both Europe and the United States were being polarized and radicalized toward the left and right. In Poland, one of the few political and economic success stories of the post-1989 transitions in Eastern Europe, a populist, right-wing government was attempting to undermine the power of the constitutional court in the name of national interests. Even as the European Union launched an unprecedented inquiry into the rule of law in Poland, popular support for the Law and Justice Party continued to increase, with ordinary men and women supporting moves to create an illiberal democracy similar to that taking shape in Hungary.

On March 13, 2016, the far-right Alternative for Germany (AfD) party beat the pollsters' expectations and increased its influence in all three German states where elections were held. Most strikingly, however, was the AfD success in Saxony-Anhalt, one of the five former states of the GDR, where the nationalist party picked up 24.2 percent, much of it from voters who had previously not participated in regional elections. These 2016 results foreshadow the fate of the future German political landscape when elections are held at the federal level in 2017. AfD will build on its regional triumphs to mount a more successful national campaign, capitalizing on the rightward, anti-EU, anti-immigrant drift of the German electorate. Indeed, the AfD and Marine Le Pen's National Front party in France received a huge boost after the Brexit vote in the United Kingdom and the election of Donald Trump, a billionaire real estate mogul with no governmental experience, who reached out to angry and disenfranchised Americans with the promise to "make America great again." As I copyedited this manuscript in early February 2017 (my last chance to make changes to the final text), many Americans were reeling from events of the first three weeks of the Trump presidency after a series of controversial tweets and executive orders deepened the divisions in an already polarized electorate. Trump and his aides attacked the mainstream media for being dishonest and openly questioned the objectivity of the judiciary, claiming that both judges and journalists were thwarting his efforts to keep Americans safe from terrorists and "bad people." Trump's surprise election sparked fear and foreboding across the nation. A January 30 article in *The New Yorker* investigated the preparations already being taken by America's superrich in the event of a civil war or a total breakdown of law and order in the United States; they were stockpiling food, hoarding guns and ammunition, and buying remote underground properties and motorcycles to zoom through the inevitable traffic jams that will occur when citizens need to evacuate major cities.[33] George Orwell's dystopian novel *1984* had leaped to the top of Amazon.com's bestseller's list, with Hannah Arendt's *The Origins of Totalitarianism* not far behind.[34]

It is not a coincidence that all of this political upheaval and polarization in the consolidated democracies happened in the wake of the Great Recession of 2008 and the accelerating global economic inequality that made it possible for sixty-two people to own the same wealth as 50 percent of the rest of humanity. Some may argue that these political trends are just anomalies, but they may also be the canaries in the coal mine, warning us of impending disaster. In theory, the democratic process should be able to check the excesses of global capitalism, but in practice, electorates are powerless to effect change within an international system that is fundamentally undemocratic. Wealth can no longer be tied to any one nation-state (as the April 2016 Panama Papers leaks so clearly revealed), and political leaders are too closely allied with economic elites to defend their domestic constituents. There will be populists on both the left and the right who will try to challenge the increasing power of the oligarchy using either class-based anger or nationalist fury to mobilize frustrated voters. Ordinary men and women will be increasingly drawn to radical alternatives as they grow frustrated with a political system that no longer represents their interests.

But wherever radical elements achieve power (even if done through the ballot box), threatened elites will deploy the language of democracy, human rights, and rule of law to selectively protect their economic interests. Just as the United States conveniently overlooks egregious human rights abuses in oil-rich but nondemocratic Saudi Arabia while supporting prodemocracy forces in Syria, the ideal of democratization is only useful as a tool when it does not interfere with the needs of capital. Moreover, we know from history

that commitment to the democratic ideal breaks down quickly when people succumb to fear about the future or about preserving their way of life in the face of a menacing other. If we look around the United States and Europe today, this process of letting our civil rights be eroded for the sake of national security has already begun. We have compromised the democratic process with decisions like *Citizens United* and with various and ongoing efforts that can only be seen as undemocratic: gerrymandering voting districts, the preservation of Tuesday voting to suppress turnout among workers (most consolidated democracies vote on Sundays), the introduction of voter ID cards, and so on. The National Security Agency vacuums up the private communications of innocent citizens while whistleblowers like Edward Snowden

FIGURE 14.5. "Not a meter to the fascists."

are accused of treason and forced to seek political asylum in (of all places) postcommunist Russia. At what point do we stop and accept that our current forms of democracy are so broken that they are useless as a vehicle for choosing a government ruled by and for the people?

Again, if history is any guide, it will probably be the far right that abandons democracy first, to save democracy and our way of life. Someone like Donald Trump could easily justify limiting democracy to make America great again. At the end of the day, the internationalist and secular humanist ideals of the left are perhaps too aspirational, too utopian, and too inchoate to provide a real platform for a political revolution from below. Moreover, even if they managed to achieve some electoral victory, intraleft struggles would cripple the movement from the inside, fracturing the solidarity necessary to resist the inevitable opposition. For better or worse, too many of us are too committed to some ideal of democracy to take the difficult steps necessary (repealing the speech protections of the First Amendment for corporations in the U.S. case) to purge it of the pervasive influence of the rich.

Fear is much more immediate. Fear of other people trying to take things away from you, from your children, from your community, or from your nation; that kind of fear mobilizes people. Fear is unifying; we are all being attacked by the same other: illegal immigrants, refugees, Muslims, Jews,

Bolsheviks, terrorists, Mexicans, Canadians—insert your bogeyman here. We're willing to make sacrifices to protect ourselves. When we are afraid, it becomes easy to justify exceptional means of protecting the nation, like the Patriot Act, or the curtailment of the Fourth Amendment, or the erosion of civil liberties, or the declaration of martial law. If the right is willing to use fear (as they are in Poland, in Germany, and in the United States in 2017), then they have a much better chance of realizing a political revolution from below and defending that revolution by all means necessary.

But nationalists are nationalists, and they can embrace the interests of the domestic economic elite, as long as the elite pledges to support the interests of the nation. When presented a choice between the left and the right, those with wealth and property have always thrown in their lot with the right, using the language of patriotism to defend (and increase) their privileges. At some point in the near or distant future when democracy falters, I hope the battered, disorganized, and ragtag left can set aside our differences (no matter how important) and find a way to unite in resistance to the angry, hate-filled politics of the far right. Despite all of our internal divisions, those who still believe that people should be treated with equal respect and accorded the same opportunities to live and thrive in a peaceful, diverse, and sustainable world must be able to stand together to fight a common enemy.

From where I was sitting in Germany in April 2016, the world looked chaotic and confused, and I couldn't help but draw parallels with the fate of the fragile Weimar Republic after the stock market crash of 1929. The polarization in German society in the 1930s looks an awful lot like the polarization in Europe and the United States today, with voters flocking to the left and the right in the wake of continued economic upheaval and uncertainty. The Nazis came to power slowly, mobilizing their supporters within the framework of a liberal parliamentary democracy before suddenly abandoning it for a dictatorship. Of course the world is a very different place today than it was in the early twentieth century, but our human frailties remain the same. When faced with growing poverty, economic inequality, and bleak prospects for the future, it is all too easy to blame some visible population of imagined outsiders than to challenge the invisible hand of an economic system that benefits a cluster of well-concealed insiders. In this, the world has changed very little.

Maybe I'm too sensitive. Maybe I'm a bit paranoid. Maybe, like any other parent, I just worry about what kind of future our children will have. But there are a lot of smart people out there warning us that things could get a hell of a lot worse before they get better, and if there is one lesson to learn from the history of twentieth-century communism, it's that massive political change can occur with little warning. In less than a year after the Berlin Wall fell, the GDR ceased to exist as a country. The Soviet Union dissolved almost overnight. Democracy promised freedom and liberty, but brought unexpected hardships, hardships that have been little acknowledged by those who continue to spread the democracy gospel.

Today, a quarter of a century of unfettered global capitalism has produced misery, unemployment, inequality, and hopelessness, pushing people to the far right and left. But as I consider the political situation on the ground, I can't help but conclude that the scales are tipped in favor of the far right. Those on the right are willing to fight dirty and find ways to circumvent or abandon the principles of democracy, for instance, capitalizing on fear as an excuse to limit civil liberties and rigging the system to reduce voter participation. In the new post-truth era, they are also willing to spread fake news and deploy an ever more consolidated media to manipulate popular opinion, conflating a caricatured version of the worst aspects of twentieth-century state socialism in practice with even the most moderate form of democratic socialism where Joe and Jane citizen use the ballot box to limit the power and privilege of the superrich.

Since the right will attempt to construe any move toward serious redistributive politics as a return of the great mustachioed Soviet monster, it is essential that those fighting to reign in the excesses of capitalism promote a more realistic view of twentieth-century state socialism, which cannot be reduced to Stalinism. Despite the many shortcomings of really existing socialism, the communist ideal (even in its most undemocratic forms) was based on a humanistic, egalitarian vision of the future, one that may have been corrupted and badly implemented in practice, but which is nevertheless opposed to the racist, xenophobic nationalism of the far right (ideals that were quite effectively realized during World War II). Furthermore, we have to accept that really existing democracy, especially as experienced in the former Eastern Bloc countries after 1989, was far from the democratic ideal. Like the example of Americans bringing democracy to the penguins, post–Cold War democratization served as a tool to promote the economic interests of Western elites who stood the most to gain from access to previously inaccessible consumer markets and vast new populations of cheap labor.

None of this is to say that we should tackle twenty-first-century problems with nineteenth-century solutions—fomenting a violent revolution to institute a dictatorship of the proletariat—but we do need to start having a serious conversation about how to make democracy great again. We should also be open to discussing the point at which we give up (at least temporarily) on

FIGURE 14.6. A sign in Frankfurt Airport in March 2016: spend 75 euros and receive a free piece of the Berlin Wall.

representative democracy in its current form, and begin a sustained program of civil or uncivil disobedience, hacktivism, or whatever technologies of citizen resistance emerge in the future. What is that breaking point? When we have definitive evidence of electoral tampering? When the only speech we hear is that controlled by the corporations? When deliberate disinformation, alternative facts, and fake news render it impossible to hold elected leaders responsible for unconstitutional actions? When our democratic governments suspend our civil liberties to protect us from the terrorists? How bad does it have to get before ordinary people stand up and oppose the drift into xenophobic oligarchy? Or are we all like frogs in the pot of slowly boiling water, incapable of perceiving these incremental changes that will ultimately lead to the dismantling of democracy altogether?

Finally, to prevent the ascendance of a resurgent far right, we need to get past our red hangover and recognize the pros and cons of both liberal democracy and state socialism in an effort to promote a system that gives us the best of both. Like the sudden collapse of communism, the days of liberal democracy may be numbered, and the West could soon face its own equivalent of November 9, 1989. Twentieth-century communism failed because the ideals of communism had been betrayed by the leaders who ruled in its name. When the reform efforts came, they came too late: ordinary people had already given up on the system. Today, democratically elected leaders too often betray the ideals of democracy and those who are calling for reform may also be too late. Citizens across Europe and the United States have lost faith in the system, and global capitalism's final crisis could be just around the corner. Perhaps in this moment of dramatic rupture, we will have the opportunity to rethink the democratic project and finally do the work necessary to either rescue it from the death grip of neoliberalism, or replace it with a new political ideal that leads us forward to a new stage of human history.

ACKNOWLEDGMENTS

The vast majority of these essays and stories were written between December 2015 and April 2016, although the research and experiences that inspired them have been accumulating for decades, since I first set foot in Eastern Europe in June 1990. A lot of institutions, foundations, and individuals have supported my research over the years, but I especially want to thank those who made possible a two-year sabbatical leave, which allowed me to live and work in Bulgaria, Germany, Finland, and the United Kingdom from August 2014 to August 2016. First and foremost, I am grateful to Bowdoin College for giving me the time away and for supporting me with a variety of small faculty research grants to travel in Eastern Europe. I also benefited from a 2012 John Simon Guggenheim Memorial Foundation Fellowship, which helped to fund one of my years in Europe.

In Baden-Württemberg, I must thank Bernd Kortmann and Cartsen Dose at the Freiburg Institute for Advanced Studies (FRIAS) for agreeing to host me as a senior external fellow for the 2014–2015 academic year. The FRIAS staff—especially Britta Küst, Helen Pert, and Petra Fischer—was exceptionally helpful in getting my family and me settled in Freiburg and navigating the bureaucracy of Freiburg University. In addition to the vibrant intellectual program organized by FRIAS, I also benefited from the lunchtime conversations I shared with other FRIAS fellows, particularly David Kauzlaric, Maja Temerinac-Ott, Spyridon Skourtis, Brook Bolander, and Evanghelia and Christopher Stead. Jörn and Marlies Ambs were wonderful landlords, upstairs neighbors, and friends, and I am endlessly thankful that neither of them complained about the noise of my typewriters.

In Thüringen, I spent five months as a fellow at the Imre Kertesz Kolleg at the F. Schiller University in Jena, where I was surrounded by brilliant scholars immersed in the twentieth-century culture and history of Eastern Europe: Stanislav Holubec, Elena Marushiakova, Roumen Daskalov, Ana Dević, Grzegorz Krzywiec, Karolina Szymaniak, Kateřina Lišková, James Ward, and Łukasz Mieszkowski. Special thanks to Joachim von Puttkamer and Włodzimierz Borodziej for welcoming me into their community, and especially to Joachim for taking the time to share his opinions on and perceptions of contemporary German politics. His insights proved invaluable to helping me understand the social upheavals and protests of the winter and spring of 2016. I am even more indebted to my many conversations with Gerd Koenen, who enlightened me on the complex history of the German left. Gerd was writing a history of communism when in residence in Jena, and while we often found ourselves in disagreement, I valued Gerd's vast knowledge and wide-ranging personal experiences of what Eric Hobsbawm called the "short twentieth century." Finally, Raphael Utz, Daniela Gruber, and Diana Joseph went above and beyond the call of duty when it came to supporting the fellows, and for their many efforts I am grateful.

I was also fortunate to spend almost three months at the Aleksanteri Institute at the University of Helsinki in Finland, with special thanks to Markku Kivinen, Anna Korhonen, and Sari Autio-Sarasmo. Finally, Mathew and Diana Webster lent me their home in London while I was making revisions to the manuscript, and I benefited greatly from the sustained solitude necessary to complete the book.

Many colleagues in Eastern and southeastern Europe contributed insights that are reflected in these pages, including Krassimira Daskalova, Mihaela Miroiu, Adriana Zaharijević, Libora Oates-Indruchova, Tanja Petrović, Agnieszka Koscianska, Ljubica Spaskovska, and Katerina Dalakoura. Susan Neiman at the Einstein Forum in Berlin was a major interlocutor, and helped me to think through a wide variety of sticky issues with regard to the German public memory of communism. I credit Susan with first convincing me of the continued relevance of the Historikerstreit and the need to critically reassess the events of November 1989. An earlier version of chapter 10, "Venerating Nazis to Vilify Commies," appeared as "A Tale of Two Totalitarianisms: The Crisis of Capitalism and the Historical Memory of Communism," in *History of the Present: A Journal of Critical History* 4 (2) (fall 2014): 115–142, and for that I am deeply indebted to Joan Wallach Scott for encouraging me to explore the politics of public memory in Eastern Europe.

Many thanks to those who read through the manuscript in its entirety: Scott Sehon, Kristiana Filipov, and Anne Clifford. My colleagues at Bowdoin—especially Jennifer Scanlon, Rachel Connelly, Page Herrlinger, Susan Faludi, and Jill Smith—were wonderfully supportive, as were the members of my writing group: Sarah Braunstein, Pope Brock, and Annie Finch. I am also thankful to Courtney Berger at Duke University Press for her editorial insights, and the two anonymous reviewers whose critical comments helped me reorganize the essays and stories into a more coherent narrative arc. Sandra Korn, Christine Riggio, Laura Sell, Helena Knox, Sara Leone, Karen Fisher, and the rest of the editorial team at Duke University Press deserve much credit and praise for their hard work.

It goes without saying that my partner and my daughter deserve the lion's share of my thanks for the many hours of my time and attention that I stole from them to write the essays and stories in this book. Scott often held the fort while I traveled to deliver lectures or attend seminars, but he was also willing to sneak into an AfD demonstration, spend hours in a local museum, or march with me in the freezing cold through the streets of Berlin. Scott provides a sounding board for my crazy ideas and creative impulses, and his critical insights and expert editing enrich and improve my work. Most importantly, without his prodding I would probably not have agreed to spend a year in Germany in the first place, which turned out to be one of the best professional decisions I ever made. My daughter has become quite the intrepid research assistant, and I am eternally grateful to her for allowing me to transplant her from Maine and place her in a German school with minimal language training. Although she struggled at first, she persevered, learning German and spending the seventh and eighth grades in two different schools.

My daughter turned thirteen in Germany, and for the first time I felt like I could share with her my personal passions regarding art, film, theater, and music. In October 2015, we caught the *David Bowie Is . . .* exhibition at the Australian Centre for the Moving Image (ACMI) in Melbourne, where we immersed ourselves for several hours in the world of all things Starman. For ten days following the exhibition, we listened to a nonstop Bowie playlist, and when we returned to Melbourne she demanded that we visit the ACMI to see it a second time before we returned to Germany. I recall November and December 2015 as a kind of ongoing festival of Bowie, as my now fourteen-year-old daughter discovered the songs that I had once loved as a fourteen-year-old. It was the first time we really bonded over the love of an artist, and we waited impatiently for the next Bowie album to be released in January.

The U-Bahn stations in Berlin were plastered with ads for *Blackstar* on January 9 and 10 when we traveled up from Jena to attend the Liebknecht-Luxemburg Demonstration, and I was sitting in a seminar in Jena on Monday the eleventh when I heard the sad news of Bowie's death. *Blackstar* soundtracked the writing of this book, interrupted only occasionally by *Hunky Dory, Aladdin Sane, Diamond Dogs, Low, "Heroes," Let's Dance,* and some songs from the film *Labyrinth*. But mostly it was *Blackstar* on auto repeat, and I will forever associate these essays and stories with those cold, dark months in Jena, bashing out prose to the voice of a "hero" no longer with us. When Suzanne Moore proposed in the pages of the *Guardian* in July 2016 that perhaps the world was "going to hell in a handcart" because it had actually been David Bowie's "presence in the universe that was holding everything together," I couldn't help but agree.[1] Of course, I had no idea how much worse things were about to get. My last chance to edit this manuscript occurred in early February 2017, which coincided with the first weeks of the Trump presidency. I was now living back in Maine, and every day brought more evidence of President Trump's authoritarian tendencies and the maniacal support of his alt-right popular base. Right-wing parties in Europe looked on with glee, hoping that the same popular discontent would fuel their own electoral victories. I realized that some of the arguments in this book might be overtaken by events before it was published, but I thought it still important to try to capture the zeitgeist of the changes I felt in Germany during those early months of 2016 when David Bowie's sudden and unexpected death became the harbinger of what felt like the looming unraveling of the world order.

Finally, I dedicate this book to my maternal grandmother, Cristina Lugo. She came to the United States in 1947 during the Great Puerto Rican Migration and settled in New York, where she worked as a seamstress for almost three decades, making dresses for the ladies who shopped at Sax Fifth Avenue. A longtime member of the International Ladies Garment Workers Union and a zealous supporter of the Democratic Party, my grandmother immigrated to an America where it was still possible for a woman with a third-grade education to have a granddaughter who earned a PhD. My childhood is filled with memories of her standing over the stove frying *platanos, yuca, empanadas,* or *sorullos* or sitting at her sewing machine to make clothes for my dolls even as she held down a full-time job. My grandmother taught me to believe that hard work and dedication pay off in the end, and that girls don't have to be satisfied with only being wives and mothers. Although she only had one daughter, she has five great-grandchildren, and recently became a great-great-grandmother. The years have worn her body, but her spirit remains indomitable. She will probably never read this book, but I hope that every word stands as a testament to her refusal to let life kick her down. I hope I have inherited some of her strength. I will need it in the years to come.

NOTES

Prelude. *Freundschaft*

1. "Concerned citizens" is the description for PEGIDA supporters used by Dresden's mayor in a 2016 interview with *Deutsche Welle*: Hildegard Michel-Hamm, "Xenophobia in Germany: Interview," *Deutsche Welle*, February 2, 2016, http://dw.com/p/1I3f7.

2. Maximillian Gerl, "Neonazi-Krawalle in Leipzig: Verwüstet," *Der Spiegel*, January 12, 2016, http://www.spiegel.de/politik/deutschland/leipzig-connewitz-viele-scherben -viele-fragen-a-1071665.html. Russia Today also covered the event and posted videos of the violence: "Over 100 Arrested, Shops Vandalized in Leipzig amid LEGIDA Birthday Demonstrations," Russia Today, January 12, 2016, https://www.rt.com/news /328586-legida-anti-migrant-demonstration-rampage/.

3. Christoph Titz, "Busattacke in Clausnitz: Ein Dorf wundert sich," *Der Spiegel*, February 21, 2016, http://www.spiegel.de/politik/deutschland/clausnitz-und-die -attacke-auf-fluechtlinge-jetzt-will-es-keiner-gewesen-sein-a-1078492.html. Video of the event can be seen here: "'Shameful' Video of Mob Blocking a Refugee Bus in Germany Sparks Outrage," *Deutsche Welle*, February 19, 2016, http://www.dw.com/en /shameful-video-of-mob-blocking-a-refugee-bus-in-germany-sparks-outrage/a -19062019. Tobias Dorfer, "Nach Clausnitz und Bautzen: Auf die Straße!," *Zeit Online*, February 28, 2016, http://www.zeit.de/gesellschaft/zeitgeschehen/2016–02 /clausnitz-bautzen-reaktionen-engagement.

4. Dirk Pilz, "Rechte Gewalt Kein schlimmer Land als Sachsen," *Berliner Zeitung*, February 28, 2016, http://www.berliner-zeitung.de/politik/rechte-gewalt -kein-schlimmer-land-als-sachsen-23636326.

5. "Really existing socialism" or "actually existing socialism" was a term embraced during the Brezhnev era to refer to the realities of Soviet-style central planning as opposed to Marxist ideals of socialism as a step on the way to pure communism.

6. Timothy Garton Ash, "As an English European, This Is the Biggest Defeat of My Political Life," *Guardian*, June 24, 2016, http://www.theguardian.com/politics /commentisfree/2016/jun/24/lifelong-english-european-the-biggest-defeat-of-my -political-life-timothy-garton-ash-brexit.

7. Winston Churchill, speech, House of Commons, November 11, 1947, in *Winston S. Churchill: His Complete Speeches, 1897–1963*, ed. Robert Rhodes James (New York: Chelsea House, 1974), 7:7566.

8. Kristen Ghodsee, *Lost in Transition*: *Ethnographies of Everyday Life after Communism* (Durham, NC: Duke University Press, 2011).

1. Fires

1. Linda Geddes, "Body Burners: The Forensics of Fire," *New Scientist*, May 20, 2009, https://www.newscientist.com/article/mg20227091.300-body-burners-the -forensics-of-fire.

2. Kristen Ghodsee, "Bulgarians Take to the Streets," *Anthropology News*, February 24, 2013.

3. "Десетина души запалиха свещи пред президентството в памет на самозапалилите се" Darik News, March 24, 2013, http://dariknews.bg/view_article .php?article_id=1059736.

4. "Почетоха Траян, който се самозапали във Велико Търново," Blitz, March 15, 2013, http://www.blitz.bg/news/article/188215.

5. "Майката: От сина ми Траян остана едно парче пластмаса с формата на гълъб," 24chasa, March 17, 2013, http://www.24chasa.bg/Article.asp?ArticleId =1847633.

6. "Почетоха Траян, който се самозапали във Велико Търново."

7. "Самозапалванията посочват нуждата от промяна към добро," Btvnovinite, March 17, 2013, http://btvnovinite.bg/article/bulgaria/samozapalvaniyata-posochvat -nuzhdata-ot-promyana-kam-dobro.html.

8. Yavor Siderov, "What a Terrible Time for Europe to Show Bulgaria the Cold Shoulder," *Guardian*, March 6, 2013, http://www.theguardian.com/commentisfree /2013/mar/06/bulgaria-europe-plamen-goranov; and Matthew Brunwasser, "With Many Despairing, Bulgaria Heads to Polls," *New York Times*, May 10, 2013, http://www.nytimes.com/2013/05/11/world/europe/a-spate-of-self-immolations .html.

9. Tsvetelia Tsolova and Angel Krasimirov, "Bulgarian Mayor Resigns after Man Sets Himself on Fire," Reuters, March 3, 2013, http://www.reuters.com/article /2013/03/06/us-bulgaria-mayor-idUSBRE9250RF20130306.

10. Caritas Europa, "Crisis Monitoring Report 2015: Poverty and Inequalities on the Rise: Just Social Models Needed as the Solution," February 9, 2015, 90–92, http://www .caritas.eu/news/crisis-report-2015.

11. Caritas Europa, "Crisis Monitoring Report 2015," 90–92.

12. "Венцислав от Раднево се самозапалил, за да призове за помощ," Darik News, March 11, 2013, http://dariknews.bg/view_article.php?article_id=1052896.

13. "Венцислав от Раднево се самозапалил."

14. "Bulgaria's Suicide Rate 'among Highest in Europe'—Experts," Novinite, April 1, 2013, http://www.novinite.com/view_news.php?id=149144.

15. "Sixth Bulgarian Sets Himself on Fire to Protest Poverty," Public Radio Inter-

national, March 25, 2013, http://www.pri.org/stories/2013–03–25/sixth-bulgarian-sets
-himself-fire-protest-poverty.

16. Katie Harris, "A Bulgarian Spring? Entrenched Protests Challenge Eastern Europe's Status Quo," *Time*, July 26, 2013, http://world.time.com/2013/07/26/a-bulgarian
-spring-entrenched-protests-challenge-eastern-europes-status-quo/.

17. The Bulgarian Wikipedia page for self-immolations has a comprehensive list of suspected self-immolations between 2013 and 2015: "Самозапалвания в България
(2013–2015)," bg.wikipedia.org/wiki/Самозапалвания_в_България (2013–2015).

18. "Георги от Димитровград се запалил пред децата си заради дълг," 24chasa,
June 5, 2013, http://www.24chasa.bg/Article.asp?ArticleId=2032978.

19. "Присадиха кожа на самозапалилия се Георги от Димитровград," 24chasa,
June 7, 2013, http://www.24chasa.bg/Article.asp?ArticleId=2039050.

20. See, for example, the case of Sylvia Miskova: Vanjo Stoilov, "Ето къде се самозапали 32-годишната Силвия Мишкова от Стара Загора (снимки)," 24chasa,
December 8, 2014, http://www.24chasa.bg/Article.asp?ArticleId=4467648.

21. "Почина жената, която се самозапали пред президентството," Nova.bg,
November 10, 2014, https://nova.bg/news/view/2014/11/10/92076/почина-жебата
-която-се-самозапали-пред-президентсвото/.

22. "Погребаха жената факла от Перник Деси Колева, остави предсмъртно писмо: Правя го от бедност, ще се запаля в гаража, за да не повредя имуществото на хората, в чиято къща живея," Viara News, November 23, 2014,
http://viaranews.com/2014/11/23/погребаха-жената-факла-от-перник-дес/.

23. Wes Enzinna, "Wave of Immolation: Bulgarians Are Setting Themselves on Fire in Record Numbers," Vice, accessed March 9, 2016, http://www.vice.com/video
/burning-men-of-bulgaria.

24. Enzinna, "Wave of Immolation."

25. Enzinna, "Wave of Immolation."

26. Enzinna, "Wave of Immolation."

27. Tom Esslemont, "Poverty in Bulgaria Drives More to Make Ultimate Sacrifice,"
BBC News, May 8, 2013, http://www.bbc.com/news/world-europe-22439961.

28. Enzinna, "Wave of Immolation."

29. Esslemont, "Poverty in Bulgaria Drives More to Make Ultimate Sacrifice."

2. Cucumbers

1. See, for instance, Gerald Creed, Domesticating Revolution: *From Socialist Reform to Ambivalent Transition in a Bulgarian Village* (University Park: Penn State University Press, 1997).

3. Pieces (Fiction)

1. This is the text of an actual article in the Bulgarian press. The original text in English is available here: "Organ Traffic Ring 'Used Bulgarian Kids,'" Novinite, May 13, 2004, http://www.novinite.com/view_news.php?id=34608.

5. #Mauerfall25

1. For the official website of the event see 25 Years Fall of the Wall, December 1, 2014, http://www.berlin.de/mauerfall2014/en/.

2. For the curious among you, I tell this story in great detail in the first chapter of my 2011 book, Kristen Ghodsee, *Lost in Transition: Ethnographies of Everyday Life under Communism* (Durham, NC: Duke University Press, 2011).

3. Melissa Eddy, "Lights and Celebration Where a Wall Divided Berlin," *New York Times*, November 8, 2014, http://www.nytimes.com/2014/11/09/world/europe/where -berlin-wall-once-stood-lights-now-illuminate.html?ref=topics.

4. My video from that morning can be found here: LiteraryEthnography, "Sunrise in Berlin—9 November 2014 (The 25th Anniversary of the Fall of the Berlin Wall)," YouTube, November 9, 2014, https://www.youtube.com/watch?v=9AjnKfGCiFU.

5. Wolfgang Münchau, "Eurozone Crisis: Why German Unification Was a Mistake," VoxEurop.eu, October 3, 2012, http://www.voxeurop.eu/en/content/article/2799441 -why-german-unification-was-mistake.

6. Chris Johnston, "Mikhail Gorbachev: World on Brink of New Cold War over Ukraine," *Guardian*, November 8, 2014, http://www.theguardian.com/world/2014 /nov/08/gorbachev-new-cold-war-ukraine-soviet-union-us-russia.

7. Gorbachev has written three books since 1991. See Mikhail Gorbachev, *Memoirs* (New York: Doubleday, 1996); Mikhail Gorbachev, *On My Country and the World* (New York: Columbia University Press, 2005); and Mikhail Gorbachev, *The New Russia* (London: Polity, 2016).

8. After the defeat of the Nazis in World War II, Germany was divided into two zones: the Western Zone, which became the Federal Republic of Germany (occupied by British, American, and French forces), and the Eastern Zone, which became the German Democratic Republic (GDR) (under the control of the Soviets). As the Cold War progressed, two key mutual defense treaties were ratified on either side of the Iron Curtain. Western nations created NATO in 1949, and signatories to the treaty agreed to act collectively in the defense of any member attacked by a nonmember state (i.e., if the Soviet Union or one of its new East European allies attempted to invade). In response to NATO, the Soviet Union formed the Warsaw Pact in 1955, a similar military alliance that promised the collective defense of the GDR, Bulgaria, Czechoslovakia, Romania, Hungary, Poland, and Albania. With the fall of the Wall in 1989, the proposal to unify the two Germanies into one state meant combining a NATO country with a Warsaw Pact country, an unprecedented situation that neither the Western nor Eastern Bloc leaders prepared for.

9. See for instance the April 3, 2014, blog post of Jack Matlock, the last U.S. ambassador to the Soviet Union: "NATO Expansion: Was There a Promise?," http://jackmatlock .com/2014/04/nato-expansion-was-there-a-promise/.

10. For more details on the negotiations, see the interesting exchange between Mary Elise Sarotte and Mark Kramer in the pages of *Foreign Affairs*: Mark Kramer and Mary Elise Sarotte, "No Such Promise," *Foreign Affairs*, November/December 2014, https:// www.foreignaffairs.com/articles/eastern-europe-caucasus/no-such-promise; and Mary Elise Sarotte, "A Broken Promise? What the West Really Told Moscow about NATO

Expansion," *Foreign Affairs*, September/October 2014, https://www.foreignaffairs.com /articles/russia-fsu/2014–08–11/broken-promise. On *Der Spiegel*'s investigation, see Uwe Klußmann, Matthias Schepp, and Klaus Wiegrefe, "NATO's Eastward Expansion: Did the West Break Its Promise to Moscow?," *Spiegel* Online International, November 26, 2009, http://www.spiegel.de/international/world/nato-s-eastward-expansion-did -the-west-break-its-promise-to-moscow-a-663315.html.

11. Charles Shaar Murrey, "David Bowie: Who Was That (Un)Masked Man?," *New Musical Express*, November 12, 1977, http://www.bowiewonderworld.com/press /press70.htm#77CSM.

12. The official program of the Lichtgrenze event: *Mauergeschichten/Wall Stories*, 2014, 12. http://www.berlin.de/mauerfall2014/en/highlights/wall-stories/.

13. *Mauergeschichten/Wall Stories*, 26–27.

14. For a detailed narrative of the events leading up to the fall of the Berlin Wall, see Mary Elise Sarotte, *Collapse: The Accidental Opening of the Berlin Wall* (New York: Basic Books, 2014); Mary Elise Sarotte, *1989: The Struggle to Create Post-Cold War Europe*, 2nd ed. (Princeton, NJ: Princeton University Press, 2014). Also useful is Eric D. Weitz, *Creating German Communism, 1890–1990: From Popular Protests to Socialist State* (Princeton, NJ: Princeton University Press, 1997).

15. Alison Smale, "In a United Germany, the Scars of the East-West Divide Have Faded," *New York Times*, October 2, 2015, http://www.nytimes.com/interactive/2015 /10/02/world/europe/germany-unification-anniversary.html.

16. Smale, "In a United Germany."

17. Smale, "In a United Germany."

18. Of these, one hundred were East German fugitives shot trying to escape, thirty were East or West Germans killed by accident, and eight were East German border guards killed in the line of duty. See the website of the Berlin Wall Memorial, http:// www.berliner-mauer-gedenkstaette.de/en/todesopfer-240.html.

19. Website of the Berlin Wall Memorial, accessed March 11, 2016.

20. Klaus F. Zimmermann and Regina T. Riphahn, "The Mortality Crisis in East Germany," IZA Discussion Paper Series, no. 6 (1998): 40, http://www.econstor.eu /dspace/bitstream/10419/20852/1/dp6.pdf.

21. Eric Kirschbaum, "The Dark Side of German Reunification," Reuters, September 29, 2010, http://blogs.reuters.com/global/2010/09/29/the-dark-side-of-german -reunification/.

22. See, for instance, Daniela Dahn, *Vertreibung ins Paradies: Unzeitgemäße Texte zur Zeit* (Berlin: Rowohlt Verlag, 1998); Daniela Dahn, *Westwärts und nicht vergessen: Vom Unbehagen in der Einheit* (Berlin: Rowohlt Verlag, 1997); Daniela Dahn, *Wenn und Aber: Anstiftungen zem Widerspruch* (Berlin: Rowohlt Verlag, 1997); Jana Hensel, *Zonenkinder* (Berlin: Rowohlt, 2004); Thea Dorn, Jana Hensel, and Thomas Brussig, *Sind wir ein Volk?* (Berlin: Verlag Herder, 2015).

23. Smale, "In a United Germany."

24. Branko Milanovic, "For Whom the Wall Fell? A Balance-Sheet of Transition to Capitalism," Global Inequality, November 3, 2014, http://glineq.blogspot.de/2014/11 /for-whom-wall-fell-balance-sheet-of.html.

25. Milanovic, "For Whom the Wall Fell?"

26. Milanovic, "For Whom the Wall Fell?"

27. Of course, David Brooks sees no fault with capitalism or democracy, but blames the situation on the damaged psyches of communism's victims and the "the corrosive power of distrust, and how long it would take to heal the mental scars caused by it." David Brooks, "The Legacy of Fear," *New York Times*, November 10, 2014, http://www .nytimes.com/2014/11/11/opinion/david-brooks-the-legacy-of-fear.html?ref=topics.

28. David Stuckler, Lawrence King, and Martin McKee, "Mass Privatisation and the Post-Communist Mortality Crisis: A Cross-National Analysis," *Lancet* 373, no. 9661 (2009): 399–407.

29. Stuckler, King, and McKee, "Mass Privatisation and the Post-Communist Mortality Crisis."

30. Nicholas Kulish, "In East Germany, a Decline as Stark as a Wall," *New York Times*, June 18, 2009, http://www.nytimes.com/2009/06/19/world/europe/19germany .html?_r=2.

31. Smale, "In a United Germany."

6. The Enemy of My Enemy

1. Sara Ann Sewell, "Mourning Comrades: Communist Funerary Rituals in Cologne during the Weimar Republic," *German Studies Review* 32, no. 3 (2009): 530.

2. Jens Blankennagel, "Demonstration in Berlin: Gedenken an Rosa Luxemburg, Karl Liebknecht und Rio Reiser," *Berliner Zeitung*, January 10, 2016, http://www .berliner-zeitung.de/berlin/demonstration-in-berlin-gedenken-an-rosa-luxemburg --karl-liebknecht-und-rio-reiser-23459338.

3. Logistical information about the yearly demonstration can be found on the organizers' website: Liebknecht-Luxemburg Demo, http://www.ll-demo.de/. Accessed March 9, 2016.

4. Annelies Laschitza, *Die Liebknechts: Karl und Sophie—Politik und Familie* (Berlin: Aufbau Taschenbuch, 2009).

5. Dietmar Dath, *Rosa Luxemburg* (Berlin: Suhrkamp Verlag, 2010).

6. Kate Evans, *Red Rosa: A Graphic Biography of Rosa Luxemburg* (New York: Verso, 2015).

7. Eric D. Weitz, "'Rosa Luxemburg Belongs to Us!' German Communism and the Luxemburg Legacy," *Central European History* 27, no. 1 (1994): 27–64.

8. Werner van Bebber, "Ein Hoch auf Karl und Rosa," *Der Tagesspiegel*, January 11, 2014, http://www.tagesspiegel.de/berlin/demonstration-auf-dem-sozialistenfriedhof -ein-hoch-auf-karl-und-rosa/9319240.html.

9. For a brief overview of 2013 German election results see "German Election Results: Who's in the Haus?" *The Economist*, September 23, 2013, http://www.economist .com/blogs/charlemagne/2013/09/german-election-results.

10. Alison Smale and Melissa Eddy, "German Rivals Reach Pact for Coalition Government," *New York Times*, November 27, 2013, http://www.nytimes.com/2013/11/28 /world/europe/merkel-and-rivals-strike-deal-on-new-german-government.html; and

Roland Nelles, "Coalition Stalemate: SPD and Greens Balk over Merkel Alliance," *Der Spiegel*, September 23, 2013, http://www.spiegel.de/international/germany/social -dems-wary-of-grand-coalition-with-cdu-as-are-greens-a-924009.html.

11. For 2005 election results, see electionresources.org, "September 18, 2005 Bundestag Election Results—Federal Republic of Germany Totals."

12. See the history section of the SPD website, https://www.spd.de/partei/. Accessed March 9, 2016.

13. For a scholarly history of the SPD, see Eric D. Weitz, *Creating German Communism, 1890–1990: From Popular Protests to Socialist State* (Princeton, NJ: Princeton University Press, 1997).

14. David Priestland, *Red Flag: A History of Communism* (New York: Grove, 2009).

15. Andreas Conrad, "Tausende gedenken Liebknechts und Luxemburgs," *Der Tagesspiegel*, January 10, 2016, http://www.tagesspiegel.de/berlin/sozialistenfriedhof -in-berlin-friedrichsfelde-tausende-gedenken-liebknechts-und-luxemburgs/12810722 .html.

16. Klaus Taubert, "Gdenkzug in eigener Sache," *Spiegel* Online, January 6, 2011, http://www.spiegel.de/einestages/luxemburg-liebknecht-demo-a-946963.html.

17. The full text of Khrushchev's speech condemning Stalin can be found here: Nikita Khrushchev, "Speech to 20th Congress of the C.P.S.U.," February 24–25, 1956, Nikita Khrushchev Reference Archive, https://www.marxists.org/archive/khrushchev /1956/02/24.htm.

18. See, for instance, Chris Bellamy, *Absolute War: Soviet Russia in the Second World War* (London: Vintage, 2008).

19. Taubert, "Gdenkzug in eigener Sache."

20. William Taubman, *Krushchev: The Man and His Era* (New York: Norton, 2004).

21. Rosa Luxemburg, "The Problem of Dictatorship," in *The Russian Revolution*, Marxists Internet Archive, https://www.marxists.org/archive/luxemburg/1918/russian -revolution/ch06.htm.

22. UPI NewsTrack, "East German Police Arrest 120 Dissident Protestors," January 18, 1988. All UPI NewsTrack articles were accessed using the electronic database NewsBank made available through the Bowdoin College library.

23. UPI NewsTrack, "East German Court Sentences Three Dissidents," February 1, 1988; UPI NewsTrack, "East German Dissidents Released," February 2, 1988; UPI NewsTrack, "East Germany Expels Three More Dissidents," February 5, 1988 (NewsBank).

24. *New York Times* News Service, "Communist Martyrs Hailed/Huge Turnout in East Berlin a Surprise to Many Observers," January 16, 1995 (NewsBank).

25. Associated Press, "Police Use Water Cannons against Communist Demonstrators," January 9, 2000 (NewsBank).

26. DDP News Agency, "Germany: 200 Held at Berlin Demo" (in German), January 9, 2000 (NewsBank); Associated Press, "Police Use Water Cannons against Communist Demonstrators."

27. Deutsche Press-Agentur, "Thousand Join Memorial Service for Communist Leader Rosa Luxemburg," January 10, 2010 (NewsBank).

28. "Programme of the Die Linke Party," Die Linke, December 2011, http://en.die
-linke.de/die-linke/documents/party-programme/.

29. Daniil Turovsky, "Russian City Opens Cultural Centre Celebrating Stalin,"
Guardian, January 11, 2016, http://www.theguardian.com/world/2016/jan/11/stalin
-russia-penza-cultural-centre-meduza.

30. On Stalin as an effective manager, see Peter Pomerantsev, *Nothing Is True and
Everything Is Possible: The Surreal Heart of the New Russia* (New York: Public Affairs,
2014).

7. A Tale of Two Typewriters

1. Leonhard Dingwerth, *Historische Schreibmachinen Sammlerträume: Geschichte,
Technik und Faszination* (Regenstauf: Battenberg Verlag, 2008). "Olympia original,"
56; "Olympia Werke," 65–66; "VEB Optima, 67–68"; and "Rheinmetall," 69.

2. "The Story of Our History," Rheinmetall Defence, accessed March 9, 2016, http://
www.rheinmetall-defence.com/en/rheinmetall_defence/company/corporate_history
/index.php.

3. "The Story of Our History."

4. Eberhard Lippmann, AEG—*Olympia*—*Optima: Büromaschinen aus Erfurt
1924–2004* (Erfurt: Sutton Verlag, 2010).

5. "Olympia Werke" [in German], Wikipedia, accessed January 29, 2015, https://
de.wikipedia.org/wiki/Olympia_Werke.

6. "Rheinmetall" [in German], Wikipedia, https://de.wikipedia.org/wiki
/Rheinmetall.

7. See for instance the biography of Charlotte (Sari) Ickovics, who was a Hungarian
Jew and a supervisor at the Sömmerda factory in 1944: "Sommerda Labor Camp Auf-
sicht [Supervisor] Armband Worn by a Czech Jewish Female Inmate," United States
Holocaust Memorial Museum, accessed March 9, 2016, http://collections.ushmm.org
/search/catalog/irn36928.

8. "The Story of Our History."

9. Rheinmetall Defence, accessed March 9, 2016, http://www.rheinmetall-defence
.com/en/rheinmetall_defence/index.php.

10. Simon Doing, "Appropriating American Technology in the 1960s: Cold War
Politics and the GDR Computing Industry," *IEEE Annals of the History of Computing*
32, no. 2 (April–June 2010): 32–45.

11. Dietmar Grosser, Hanno Müller, and Paul-Josef Raue, eds., "Robotron
2003–2009," in *Treuhand in Thüringen: Wie Thuringen nach der Wende ausverkauft
wurde* (Erfurt: Klartext-Verlag, 2013).

12. Tom Hanks, "I Am TOM. I Like to TYPE. Hear That?," *New York Times*, August 3,
2013, http://www.nytimes.com/2013/08/04/opinion/sunday/i-am-tom-i-like-to-type
-hear-that.html.

13. "In Tom Hanks' iPad App, Typewriters Make Triumphant Return (Ding!)," All
Tech Considered, National Public Radio, September 2, 2014, http://www.npr.org

/sections/alltechconsidered/2014/09/02/345254677/in-tom-hanks-ipad-app-typewriters
-make-triumphant-return-ding.

14. "Der Verein," Internationales Forum Historische Bürowelt, http://www.ifhb.de
/Verein.php. January 19, 2017.

15. Lippmann, AEG—Olympia—Optima.

16. Lippmann, AEG—Olympia—Optima.

17. Manfred Bock, "Everything Must Go! The Privatization of East German Industry," Harvard International Review 14, no. 1 (fall 1991).

18. Heather M. Stack, "The 'Colonization' of East Germany? A Comparative Analysis of German Privatization," Duke Law Journal 46, no. 5 (March 1997): 1211–1253.

19. Tomáš Ježek, "The Czechoslovak Experience with Privatization," Journal of International Affairs 50, no. 2 (winter 1997): 477–489.

20. Bock, "Everything Must Go!"

21. Bock, "Everything Must Go!"

22. Grosser, Müller, and Raue, Treuhand in Thüringen.

23. Stack, "The 'Colonization' of East Germany?"

24. Lippmann, AEG—Olympia—Optima.

25. A video of the explosion has been posted on YouTube: "1995 Sprengung
Soemtron-Haus BWS Sömmerda (ehem. VEB Robotron)," YouTube, April 27, 2014,
https://www.youtube.com/watch?v=7AWoglOXnoE.

26. Ferdinand Protzman, "Privatization in the East Is Wearing to Germans," New
York Times, August 12, 1994, D1–D2.

27. Jenny Hill, "Die Linke Triumph: Mixed Reaction as German Far-Left Gains
Power." BBC News, December 2, 2014, http://www.bbc.com/news/world-europe
-30342441.

28. "Millions of German Workers in Poverty," Deutsche Welle, January 24, 2015.
http://www.dw.com/en/millions-of-german-workers-in-poverty/a-18212765.

29. Karl Marx, The Communist Manifesto, accessed January 19, 2017, https://www
.marxists.org/archive/marx/works/1848/communist-manifesto/.

30. Jörg Grabhorn, "Das letzte Stück der Olympia-Werke ist tot," Wilhelmshavener
Zeitung, May 25, 2012, http://www.wzonline.de/nachrichten/lokal/artikel/das-letzte
-stueck-der-olympia-werke-ist-tot.html.

8. Gross Domestic Orgasms

1. The full film can be streamed at: http://www.dailymotion.com/video/x222wlo
_do-communists-have-better-sex_shortfilms.

2. Dagmar Herzog, Sex after Fascism: Memory and Morality in Twentieth-Century
Germany (Princeton, NJ: Princeton University Press, 2005).

3. Josie McLellan, Love in the Time of Communism: Intimacy and Sexuality in the
GDR (Cambridge: Cambridge University Press, 2011). When I lived in Rostock in
the summers of 2008 and 2009, I witnessed for myself the totally nonerotic nature
of German nudism on the beach at Warnemünde, where pink-skinned toddlers and

potbellied grandfathers frolicked happily in the ice-cold and jellyfish-filled waters of the Baltic Sea.

4. Herzog, *Sex after Fascism*, 8.

5. Kayleigh Dray, "Is Shopping REALLY Better Than Sex?," *Cosmopolitan UK*, June 6, 2013, http://www.cosmopolitan.co.uk/love-sex/sex/tips/a20363/sex-versus-shopping/.

6. Paul Betts, *Within Walls: Private Life in the German Democratic Republic* (Oxford: Oxford University Press, 2013).

7. Andrew I. Port, "Love, Lust, and Lies under Communism: Family Values and Adulterous Liaisons in Early East Germany," *Central European History* 44, no. 3 (2011): 478–505.

8. Dagmar Herzog, "Post Coitum Triste Est . . . ? Sexual Politics and Culture in Postunification Germany," *German Politics and Society* 94, no. 28 (spring 2010): 111–140.

9. Agnieszka Kościańska, "Beyond Viagra: Sex Therapy in Poland," *Czech Sociological Review* 20, no. 6 (2014): 919.

10. Kościańska, "Beyond Viagra."

11. Kościańska, "Beyond Viagra."

12. Katherine Verdery has a wonderful discussion about the socialist experience of time in her book *What Was Socialism and What Comes Next?* (Princeton, NJ: Princeton University Press, 1996).

13. Herzog, "Post Coitum Triste Est . . . ?"

14. Elizabeth Wood, *The Baba and the Comrade: Gender and Politics in Revolutionary Russia* (Bloomington: Indiana University Press, 1997).

15. Richard Stites, *The Women's Liberation Movement in Russia: Feminism, Nihilism, and Bolshevism, 1860–1930* (Princeton, NJ: Princeton University Press, 1978).

16. Wendy Z. Goldman, *Women, the State and Revolution: Soviet Family Policy and Social Life, 1917–1936* (Cambridge: Cambridge University Press, 1993).

17. Rebecca Balmas Neary, "Mothering Socialist Society: The Wife-Activists' Movement and the Soviet Culture of Daily Life, 1934–1941," *Russian Review* 58, no. 3 (July 1999): 396–412.

18. Kateřina Lišková, "Sex under Socialism: From Emancipation of Women to Normalized Families in Czechoslovakia," *Sexualities* 19, nos. 1/2 (2016): 211–235.

19. Kristen Ghodsee, "Pressuring the Politburo: The Committee of the Bulgarian Women's Movement and State Socialist Feminism," *Slavic Review* 73, no. 3 (fall 2014): 538–562.

9. My Mother and a Clock

1. This was the title of an October 11, 1948, *Time* magazine article on Soviet architecture and art: http://content.time.com/time/magazine/article/0,9171,887936,00.html.

2. Quoted in Frances Stonor Saunders, "Modern Art Was CIA 'Weapon,'" *Independent*, October 21, 1995, http://www.independent.co.uk/news/world/modern-art-was-cia-weapon-1578808.html.

3. Quoted in Saunders, "Modern Art Was CIA 'Weapon.'"

4. Taylor Littleton and Maltby Sykes, *Advancing American Art: Painting, Politics, and Cultural Confrontation at Mid-century* (Tuscaloosa: University of Alabama Press, 2005).

5. Louis Menand, "Unpopular Front: American Art and the Cold War," *New Yorker*, October 17, 2005, http://www.newyorker.com/magazine/2005/10/17/unpopular-front.

6. Eric Bennet, "How Iowa Flattened Literature," *Chronicle of Higher Education*, February 10, 2014, http://chronicle.com/article/How-Iowa-Flattened-Literature/144531/.

7. Nikolai Vukov, "The Museum of Socialist Art in Sofia and the Politics of Avoidance," in Forum Geschichtskulturen, Bulgaria, November 26, 2012, http://www.imre-kertesz-kolleg.uni-jena.de/index.php?id=361#c1642.

8. Vukov, "The Museum of Socialist Art in Sofia."

9. DDR Museum, accessed March 9, 2016, http://www.ddr-museum.de/; Bulgarian National Gallery of Art, accessed March 9, 2016, http://www.nationalartgallerybg.org/index.php?1 =95.

10. See for instance *Frieze* magazine's 2005 survey, "How Has Art Changed?," no. 94 (October 2005), https://frieze.com/article/how-has-art-changed.

11. Liam Stack, "George Lucas Criticizes Latest 'Star Wars' Installment," *New York Times*, December 31, 2015, http://www.nytimes.com/2015/12/31/movies/george-lucas-criticizes-latest-star-wars-installment.html.

12. Which were owned, according to some estimates, by at least 20 percent of American households in 2012. Maura Judkis, "Thomas Kinkade's Polarizing Legacy: How Will the 'Painter of Light' Be Remembered?," *Washington Post*, April 7, 2012, https://www.washingtonpost.com/blogs/arts-post/post/thomas-kinkades-polarizing-legacy-how-will-the-painter-of-light-be-remembered/2012/04/07/gIQAov1G2S_blog.html.

13. Milan Kundera, *The Unbearable Lightness of Being* (New York: Harper Perennial Modern Classics, 2005).

10. Venerating Nazis to Vilify Commies

1. Press Office of the Vice Prime Minister, "Gov't Approved a Package of Bills on Decommunisation, Commemoration of Fighters for Ukraine's Independence and Victory over Nazism," Ukrainian Government, April 1, 2015, http://www.kmu.gov.ua/control/en/publish/article?art_id=248057658&cat_id=244314975.

2. Alec Luhn, "Ukraine Bans Soviet Symbols and Criminalises Sympathy for Communism," *Guardian*, May 21, 2015, http://www.theguardian.com/world/2015/may/21/ukraine-bans-soviet-symbols-criminalises-sympathy-for-communism; Vitaly Shevchenko, "Goodbye, Lenin: Ukraine Moves to Ban Communist Symbols," BBC Monitoring, April 14, 2015, http://www.bbc.com/news/world-europe-32267075; and Sabra Ayres, "Ukraine's Plans to Discard Soviet Symbols Are Seen as Divisive, Ill-Timed," *Los Angeles Times*, May 13, 2015, http://www.latimes.com/world/europe/la-fg-ukraine-decommunization-20150513-story.html.

3. Shaun Walker, "Ukrainians Say Farewell to 'Soviet Champagne' as Decommunisation Law Takes Hold," *Guardian*, January 4, 2016, http://www.theguardian

.com/world/2016/jan/04/ukrainians-say-farewell-to-soviet-champagne-as
-decommunisation-law-takes-hold.

4. "Проект Закону про засудження комуністичного та націонал-
соціалістичного (нацистського) тоталітарних режимів в Україні та заборону
пропаганди їх символіки," website of the Ukrainian Parliament (Verkhovna Rada)
April 6, 2015, http://w1.c1.rada.gov.ua/pls/zweb2/webproc4_1?pf3511=54670; and Per
Anders Rudling and Christopher Gilley, "Laws 2558 and 2538–1: On Critical Inquiry,
the Holocaust, and Academic Freedom in Ukraine," Political Critique, April 29, 2015,
http://ukraine.politicalcritique.org/2015/04/laws-2558-and-2538–1-on-critical
-inquiry-the-holocaust-and-academic-freedom-in-ukraine/.

5. Halya Coynash, "President Signs Dangerously Flawed 'Decommunization' Laws,"
Human Rights in Ukraine, May 16, 2015, http://khpg.org/index.php?id=1431743447.
This article also has an English translation of the relevant text from Article 6 of the
law "On the Legal Status and Honoring of Fighters for Ukraine's Independence in the
Twentieth Century": "Ukrainian nationals, foreigners and stateless persons who publicly express disrespect for those stipulated in Article 1 of this law . . . bear liability in
accordance with current Ukrainian legislation. 2. Public denial of the legitimacy of
the struggle for Ukraine's independence in the XX century is deemed desecration of
the memory of fighters for Ukraine's independence in the XX century, denigration
of the dignity of the Ukrainian people and is unlawful."

6. David R. Marples, "Open Letter from Scholars and Experts on Ukraine Re.
the So-Called 'Anti-Communist Law,'" Krytyka, April 2015, http://krytyka.com/en
/articles/open-letter-scholars-and-experts-ukraine-re-so-called-anti-communist
-law.

7. "New Laws in Ukraine Potential Threat to Free Expression and Free Media,
OSCE Representative Says," press release, OSCE, May 18, 2015, http://www.osce.org
/fom/158581.

8. "Ukraine Lawmakers Ban 'Communist and Nazi Propaganda,'" Deutsche Welle,
April 9, 2015, http://dw.com/en/ukraine-lawmakers-ban-communist-and-nazi
-propaganda/a-18372853; "New Laws in Ukraine Potential Threat."

9. "Проект Закону про засудження комуністичного та націонал-
соціалістичного (нацистського) тоталітарних режимів в Україні та заборону
пропаганди їх символіки"; Christopher Gilley and Per Anders Rudling, "The History Wars in Ukraine Are Heating Up," History News Network, May 9, 2015, http://
historynewsnetwork.org/article/159301.

10. Gilley and Rudling, "The History Wars in Ukraine."

11. J. P., "The Tragic Massacre in Volyn Remembered," Economist, July 13, 2015,
http://www.economist.com/blogs/easternapproaches/2013/07/polish-ukrainian
-relations.

12. Marples, "Open Letter from Scholars and Experts on Ukraine."

13. "Ukraine Bans Communist Party for 'Promoting Separatism,'" Guardian,
December 17, 2015, http://www.theguardian.com/world/2015/dec/17/ukraine-bans
-communist-party-separatism.

14. An English translation of the law can be found here: "Opinion on the Law on

the Condemnation of the Communist and Nazi Totalitarian Regimes of Ukraine," Venice Commission, 2015, http://www.venice.coe.int/webforms/documents/?opinion =823&year=all.

15. "Ukraine's Law on 'Decommunisation' Does Not Comply with EU Standards— Venice Commission, OSCE/ODIHR," Interfax Ukraine, December 19, 2015, http://en .interfax.com.ua/news/general/312592.html.

16. "Prague Declaration on European Conscience and Communism," June 3, 2008. http://www.voltairenet.org/article191922.html. Accessed March 11, 2016.

17. "Prague Declaration on European Conscience and Communism."

18. "Press Release Issued by the OSCE Parliamentary Assembly," OSCE, July 3, 2009, http://www.osce.org/pa/51129.

19. Platform of European Memory and Conscience, accessed March 11, 2016, http:// www.memoryandconscience.eu/.

20. Platform Members List, Platform of European Memory and Conscience, August 18, 2011, http://www.memoryandconscience.eu/2011/08/18/platform-members/.

21. "Lee Edwards, Ph.D.," Heritage Foundation, accessed March 11, 2016, http:// www.heritage.org/about/staff/e/lee-edwards.

22. Seventy Years Declaration, accessed March 11, 2016, http://www.seventyyears declaration.org/the-declaration/.

23. Monica Lowenberg, "Riga, Capital of European Culture: Waffen SS, Stags and Silence?" *Defending History*, February 4, 2014, http://defendinghistory.com/riga -capital-of-european-culture-waffen-ss-stags-and-silence/63468.

24. For an excellent study of the anticommunist bias in German history textbooks, see Augusta Dimou, "Changing Certainties? Socialism in German History Textbooks," in *Remembering Communism: Genres of Representation*, ed. Maria Todorova (New York: SSRC, 2010), 293–316.

25. Bernard Weinraub, "Reagan Joins Kohl in Brief Memorial at Bitburg Graves," *New York Times*, May 6, 1985, section A, 1.

26. Ernst Nolte as quoted in Daniel Schönpflug, "Histoires croisées: François Furet, Ernst Nolte and a Comparative History of Totalitarian Movements," *European History Quarterly* 37, no. 2 (2007): 282.

27. Habermas as quoted in Mark S. Peacock, "The Desire to Understand and the Politics of Wissenschaft: An Analysis of the Historikerstreit," *History of the Human Sciences* 14, no. 4 (2001): 95.

28. Gerhard Hirschfeld, "Erasing the Past?," *History Today* 37, no. 8 (1987): 8–10.

29. Norbert Frei, "The Historikerstreit Twenty Years On," *German History* 24, no. 4 (2006): 590.

30. Frei, "The Historikerstreit Twenty Years On," 590.

31. Frei, "The Historikerstreit Twenty Years On."

32. Ernst Nolte as quoted in Ian B. Warren, "Throwing Off Germany's Imposed History—the Third Reich's Place in History: A Conversation with Ernst Nolte," *Journal of Historical Review* 14, no. 1 (January–February 1994): 15–22, http://www.ihr.org /jhr/v14/v14n1p15_Warren.html.

33. Schönpflug, "Histoires croisées."

34. Francis Fukuyama, *The End of History and the Last Man* (New York: Free Press, 1993).

35. Adam Shatz, "Chunnel Vision," *Lingua Franca*, November 1997, http://linguafranca.mirror.theinfo.org/9711/9711.ip.hobs.html.

36. Hobsbawm and Ignatieff quoted in Alex Massle, "Eric Hobsbawm and the Fatal Appeal of Revolution," *Spectator*, October 2, 2012, http://blogs.spectator.co.uk/alex-massie/2012/10/eric-hobsbawm-and-the-fatal-appeal-of-revolution/.

37. Shatz, "Chunnel Vision."

38. Shatz, "Chunnel Vision."

39. Pierre Nora, "Sur l'histoire du XXe siecle," *Le Débat*, January–February 1997; Pierre Nora, "Traduire: nécessité et difficulties," *Le Débat* 142, no. 93 (January–February 1997): 93–95.

40. Pierre Nora as quoted in Eric Hobsbawm, "A History of the 20th Century: Age of Extremes Defies French Censors," *Le Monde diplomatique*, December 5, 1999, http://mondediplo.com/1999/12/05hobsbawm.

41. Hobsbawm, "A History of the 20th Century."

42. Hobsbawm, "A History of the 20th Century."

43. François Furet, *The Passing of an Illusion: The Idea of Communism in the 20th Century* (Chicago: University of Chicago Press, 2000).

44. "Communisme et fascisme au XXe siecle" [Communism and Fascism in the 20th Century], *Le Débat*, March–April 1996.

45. For the letters, Francois Furet and Ernst Nolte, *Fascism and Communism* (Lincoln: University of Nebraska Press, 2004). Ernst Nolte as cited in Schönpflug, "Histoires croisées," 284.

46. Stéphane Courtois as quoted in Adam Shatz, "The Guilty Party," *Lingua Franca*, October 1999, http://linguafranca.mirror.theinfo.org/br/9911/shatz.html.

47. Shatz, "The Guilty Party."

48. Jean-Louis Margolin and Nicolas Werth, "Communisme: Le Retour a l'histoire," *Le Monde*, November 14, 1997.

49. Nicolas Werth as quoted in J. Arch Getty, "The Future Did Not Work," *Atlantic Monthly* 285, no. 3 (March 2000): 114.

50. Getty, "The Future Did Not Work," 114.

51. Hobsbawm, "A History of the 20th Century."

52. Michele Tepper, "Once-Shunned History Proves 'Extreme'-ly Popular in Paris," *Lingua Franca*, February 7, 2000, http://linguafranca.mirror.theinfo.org/webonly/update-hobsbawm.html.

53. Robert Cohen, "Hitler Apologist Wins German Honor, and a Storm Breaks Out," *New York Times*, June 21, 2000, http://www.nytimes.com/2000/06/21/world/hitler-apologist-wins-german-honor-and-a-storm-breaks-out.html.

54. Mark Weber, "Changing Perspectives on History in Germany: A Prestigious Award for Nolte: Portent of Greater Historical Objectivity?," *Journal of Historical Review* 19, no. 4 (July–August 2000): 29. See Institute for Historical Review, www.ihr.org.

55. "Anne Applebaum Receives Petőfi Prize," Embassy of the United States, Buda-

pest, Hungary, December 14, 2010, http://hungary.usembassy.gov/event_12142010
.html.

56. There is also an ongoing debate about the expulsion of ethnic Germans from
the East, the Vertriebenen. Apparently, discussion of the expelled Germans used to
be limited to a handful of marginal scholars collaborating with the Association of the
Expulsed or the Sudeten Germans Day. Today, however, debates about Germans as
victims of expulsion, massacres, and rape in the East are now relatively mainstream,
and a center documenting and memorializing German expulsions opened in November
2016. There are also heated debates regarding the Allied bombings of cities such
as Dresden and Hamburg. In this discourse, Germans are now considered victims of
war crimes perpetrated by the Allies. Although these debates are more about internal
German memory politics than they are about anticommunism, they are interesting to
consider alongside the double genocide thesis. For further information on German
victims of World War II, see "Online-Ressourcen zur Debatte um das Zentrum gegen
Vetreibungen und zum Diskurs zum Thema der Flucht und Vertreibung," Zeitges-
chichte Online, January 2006, http://www.zeitgeschichte-online.de/thema/online
-ressourcen-zur-debatte-um-das-zentrum-gegen-vetreibungen-und-zum-diskurs
-zum-thema-der.

57. Hungarian Terror House, http://www.terrorhaza.hu/en; Museum of Genocide
Victims, Genocide and Resistance Research Centre of Lithuania, http://www.genocid
.lt/muziejus/en/.

58. Institute for Studies of the Recent Past in Bulgaria, accessed September 1, 2013,
http://www.minaloto.org/; Institute for the Investigation of Communist Crimes and
the Memory of the Romanian Exile, accessed September 1, 2013, http://www.iiccr.ro
/index.html/about_iiccr/institute/?lang=en&section=about_iiccr/institute.

59. Kristen Ghodsee, The Left Side of History: World War II and the Unfulfilled
Promise of Communism in Eastern Europe (Durham, NC: Duke University Press,
2015).

60. "Academic Genius and/or Unpalatable Anti-Semite?—Who Was Bálint
Hóman?," Hungary Today, December 10, 2015, http://hungarytoday.hu/news
/academic-genius-andor-unpalatable-anti-semite-balint-homan-31000.

61. Marija Ristic and Sven Milekic, "Serbia Rehabilitates WWII Chetnik Leader
Mihailovic," Balkan Insight, May 14, 2015, http://www.balkaninsight.com/en/article
/serbia-rehabilitates-wwii-chetnik-leader-mihailovic.

62. "Over 25,000 Attend 70th Bleiburg Commemorations," Croatia Week,
May 16, 2015, http://www.croatiaweek.com/over-25000-attend-70th-bleiburg
-commemorations/; and "Jakovina o obilasku Bleiburga: Predsjednica nedosljedna
i nekonkretna," HRT Vjesti, May 14, 2015, http://vijesti.hrt.hr/284507/grabar
-kitarovic-potajno-obisla-bleiburg.

63. For precedents, for instance, in the 1997 German Waldheim case (in which a
seventy-nine-year-old former East German judge was sentenced to four years in jail
for issuing thirty-two death sentences to men believed to be Nazi perpetrators), see
Rado Pribic, The Trouble with German Unification: Essay on Daniela Dahn (Berlin:
NORA, 2008), 50–52; and for the 1998 and 1999 Romanian Supreme Court acquittals

of Holocaust perpetrators Radu Dinulescu and Gheorghe Petrescu, see Alexandru Climescu, "Post-transitional Injustice: The Acquittal of Holocaust Perpetrators in Post-Communist Romania," *Holocaust: Studii si Cercetari* 6, no. 1(7) (2014): 145–157.

64. "Planned Refugee Shelter in Eastern German Town of Bautzen Catches Fire," *Deutsche Welle*, February 21, 2016, http://www.dw.com/en/planned-refugee -shelter-in-eastern-german-town-of-bautzen-catches-fire/a-19063792.

65. "Visegrad Group Opposes Germany's Refugee Policy," *Deutsche Welle*, February 15, 2016, http://www.dw.com/en/visegrad-group-opposes-germanys-refugee -policy/a-19048816.

66. Thomas Piketty, *Capital in the Twenty-First Century* (Cambridge, MA: Harvard University Press, 2014).

11. Three Bulgarian Jokes

1. I originally included a slightly shorter version of the second joke in the 2004 article, Kristen Ghodsee, "Red Nostalgia? Communism, Women's Emancipation, and Economic Transformation in Bulgaria," *L'Homme: Zeitschrift für Feministische Geschichtswissenschaft* (L'Homme: Journal for Feminist History) 15, no. 1 (spring 2004): 23–36.

12. Post-Zvyarism

1. *Zvyar* means "beast" in Bulgarian.

14. Democracy for the Penguins

1. Although it is antiquated, I use the term "Third World" because it is the term David Scott used in his lecture and subsequent article.

2. David Scott, "Norms of Self-Determination: Thinking Sovereignty Through," *Middle East Law and Government* 4 (2012): 219.

3. Stephen Ellis, "Nelson Mandela, the South African Communist Party and the Origins of Umkhonto we Sizwe," *Cold War History* 16 (1) 2016: 1–18.

4. Daniela Dahn, "The Legacy of Democratic Awakening—20 Years after the Fall of the Berlin Wall," Johns Hopkins University, Baltimore, April 7, 2010, http://www.aicgs .org/events/the-legacy-of-democratic-awakening/. An English transcript of the talk was posted on the RevLeft.com forum, http://www.revleft.com/vb/legacy-democratic -awakening-t142041/index.html. More information about Daniela Dahn can be found on her website: www.danieladahn.de.

5. Dahn, "The Legacy of Democratic Awakening."

6. Dahn, "The Legacy of Democratic Awakening."

7. Slavoj Žižek. *Revolution at the Gates: Selected Writing of Lenin from 1917* (New York: Verso, 2002).

8. Žižek, *Revolution at the Gates*, 310.

9. Robert Reich, "How Capitalism Is Killing Democracy," *Foreign Policy*, October 12, 2009, http://foreignpolicy.com/2009/10/12/how-capitalism-is-killing-democracy/.

10. Reich, "How Capitalism Is Killing Democracy."

11. Jimmy Carter, interview with Oprah Winfrey, SuperSoul Sunday TV, Season 6, episode 620, airdate September 27, 2015, accessed March 11, 2016, http://www.supersoul.tv/supersoul-sunday/jimmy-carter-on-whether-he-could-be-president-today-absolutely-not/.

12. Wolfgang Merkel, "Is Capitalism Compatible with Democracy?," *Zeitschrift für Vergleichende Politikwissenschaft* 8, no. 2 (October 2014): 109–128.

13. Merkel, "Is Capitalism Compatible with Democracy?," 123, 126.

14. Jodi Dean, "Communicative Capitalism: Circulation and the Foreclosure of Politics," *Cultural Politics*, Vol. 1. No. 1 (2005): 51–74.

15. Timothy Shenk, "Booked #3: What Exactly Is Neoliberalism?," interview with Wendy Brown, *Dissent*, April 2, 2015, https://www.dissentmagazine.org/blog/booked-3-what-exactly-is-neoliberalism-wendy-brown-undoing-the-demos.

16. "'Hidden History' of Koch Brothers Traces Their Childhood and Political Rise," interview with Jane Mayer, *Fresh Air*, National Public Radio, January 19, 2016, http://www.npr.org/2016/01/19/463565987/hidden-history-of-koch-brothers-traces-their-childhood-and-political-rise.

17. Larry Elliott, "Richest 62 People as Wealthy as Half of World's Population, Says Oxfam," *Guardian*, January 19, 2016, http://www.theguardian.com/business/2016/jan/18/richest-62-billionaires-wealthy-half-world-population-combined.

18. Elliott, "Richest 62 People as Wealthy as Half of World's Population."

19. Jeff Sparrow, "By Every Meaningful Measure, Today's Elites are Gods. This Should Make Us Angry," *Guardian*, January 21, 2016, http://www.theguardian.com/commentisfree/2016/jan/21/by-every-meaningful-measure-todays-elites-are-gods-this-should-make-us-angry.

20. Yanis Varoufakis, "Capitalism Will Eat Democracy—Unless We Speak Up," TED, December 2015, https://www.ted.com/talks/yanis_varoufakis_capitalism_will_eat_democracy_unless_we_speak_up?language=en#t-88411.

21. "Yanis Varoufakis Launches Pan-European Leftwing Movement DiEM25," *Guardian*, February 10, 2016, http://www.theguardian.com/world/2016/feb/10/yanis-varoufakis-launches-pan-european-leftwing-movement-diem25.

22. DiEM25, "Manifesto," accessed March 11, 2016, http://diem25.org/manifesto-long/.

23. "Yanis Varoufakis Launches Pan-European Leftwing Movement DiEM25."

24. DiEM25, "Manifesto."

25. Thomas Carothers, "Look Homeward, Democracy Promoter," *Foreign Policy*, January 27, 2016, http://foreignpolicy.com/2016/01/27/look-homeward-democracy-promoter/.

26. For an interesting discussion on the origin of this quote, see Richard M. Langworth, "Democracy Is the Worst Form of Government . . . ," June 26, 2009, https://richardlangworth.com/worst-form-of-government.

27. Jodi Dean, *The Communist Horizon* (New York: Verso, 2012); Costas Douzinas and Slavoj Žižek, *The Idea of Communism* (New York: Verso, 2010).

28. Slavoj Žižek, *Revolution at the Gates* (New York: Verso, 2002).

29. Scott, "Norms of Self-Determination," 219.

30. Dean, *The Communist Horizon.*

31. Audre Lorde, "The Master's Tools Will Never Dismantle the Master's House" (1984), in *Sister Outsider: Essays and Speeches*, 110–114 (Berkeley, CA: Crossing Press, 2007).

32. Dean, *The Communist Horizon.*

33. Evan Osnos, "Doomsday Prep for the Super-Rich," *The New Yorker*, January 30, 2017. http://www.newyorker.com/magazine/2017/01/30/doomsday-prep-for-the-super-rich.

34. Kimiko Freytas-Tamura, "George Orwell's '1984' Is Suddenly a Best-Seller," *New York Times*, January 25, 2017, https://www.nytimes.com/2017/01/25/books/1984-george-orwell-donald-trump.html?_r=0.

Acknowledgments

1. Suzanne Moore, "Yes, the World Seems Like It's Going to Hell in a Handcart— but This Is No Time to Disengage," *Guardian*, July 20, 2016, https://www.theguardian.com/commentisfree/2016/jul/20/world-going-to-hell-in-handcart-but-no-time-to-disengage.

Allinson, Mark. *Politics and Popular Opinion in East Germany, 1945–68*. Manchester: Manchester University Press, 2000.

Applebaum, Anne. *Gulag: A History*. New York: Doubleday, 2003.

Applebaum, Anne. *Iron Curtain: The Crushing of Eastern Europe, 1944–1956*. New York: Doubleday, 2012.

Baeva, Iskra, and Evgeniya Kalinova. *Vazroditelniyat Protses: Balgarskata Darzhava in Balgarskite Turtsi*. Sofia: Ciela, 2009.

Baeva, Iska, and Plamen Mitev. *Predizvikatelstvata na promyanata*. Sofia: Univerzitetsko Izdatelstvo "Sv. Kliment Ohridski," 2006.

Badiou, Alain. *The Communist Hypothesis*. New York: Verso, 2010.

Bellamy, Chris. *Absolute War: Soviet Russia in the Second World War*. London: Vintage, 2008.

Berdahl, Daphne. *On the Social Life of Postsocialism: Memory, Consumption, Germany*. Bloomington: Indiana University Press, 2009.

Berdahl, Daphne. *Where the World Ended: Re-unification and Identity in the German Borderland*. Berkeley: University of California Press, 1999.

Betts, Paul. *Within Walls: Private Life in the German Democratic Republic*. Oxford: Oxford University Press, 2013.

Bosteels, Bruno. *The Actuality of Communism*. New York: Verso, 2014.

Brown, Archie. *The Rise and Fall of Communism*. New York: Ecco, 2009.

Brown, Wendy. *Undoing the Demos: Neoliberalism's Stealth Revolution*. New York: Zone, 2015.

Creed, Gerlad. *Domesticating Revolution: From Socialist Reform to Ambivalent Transition in a Bulgarian Village*. University Park: Penn State University Press, 1997.

Dahn, Daniela. *Vertreibung ins Paradies: Unzeitgemäße Texte zur Zeit*. Berlin: Rowohlt Verlag, 1998.

Dahn, Daniela. *Wenn und Aber: Anstiftungen zem Widerspruch*. Berlin: Rowohlt Verlag, 1997.

Dahn, Daniela. *Westwärts und nicht vergessen: Vom Unbehagen in der Einheit.* Berlin: Rowohlt Verlag, 1997.

Dath, Dietmar. *Rosa Luxemburg.* Berlin: Suhrkamp Verlag, 2010.

Dean, Jodi. *The Communist Horizon.* New York: Verso, 2012.

Dean, Jodi. "Communicative Capitalism: Circulation and the Foreclosure of Politics," *Cultural Politics* 1, no. 1 (2005): 51–74.

Dimou, Augusta. "Changing Certainties? Socialism in German History Textbooks." In *Remembering Communism: Genres of Representation,* edited by Maria Todorova, 293–316. New York: SSRC, 2010.

Dingwerth, Leonhard. *Historische Schreibmaschinen Sammlerträume: Geschichte, Technik und Faszination.* Regenstauf: Battenberg Verlag, 2008.

Dobrenko, Evgeny. *Political Economy of Socialist Realism.* New Haven, CT: Yale University Press, 2007.

Doing, Simon. "Appropriating American Technology in the 1960s: Cold War Politics and the GDR Computing Industry." *IEEE Annals of the History of Computing* 32, no. 2 (April–June 2010): 32–45.

Dorn, Thea, Jana Hensel, and Thomas Brussig. *Sind wir ein Volk?* Berlin: Verlag Herder, 2015.

Douzinas, Costas, and Slavoj Žižek. *The Idea of Communism.* New York: Verso, 2010.

Evans, Kate. *Red Rosa: A Graphic Biography of Rosa Luxemburg.* New York: Verso, 2015.

Fowkes, Ben. *Communism in Germany under the Weimar Republic.* London and Basingstoke: The MacMillan Press, 1984

Fukuyama, Francis. *The End of History and the Last Man.* New York: Free Press, 1993.

Fulbrook, Mary. *Anatomy of a Dictatorship: Inside the GDR, 1949–1989.* Oxford: Oxford University Press, 1995.

Fulbrook, Mary. *The People's State: East German Society from Hitler to Honecker.* New Haven, CT: Yale University Press, 2005.

Furet, François. *The Passing of an Illusion: The Idea of Communism in the 20th Century.* Chicago: University of Chicago Press, 2000.

Furet, François, and Ernst Nolte. *Fascism and Communism.* Lincoln: University of Nebraska Press, 2004.

Ghodsee, Kristen. *The Left Side of History: World War II and the Unfulfilled Promise of Communism in Eastern Europe.* Durham, NC: Duke University Press, 2015.

Ghodsee, Kristen. *Lost in Transition: Ethnographies of Everyday Life after Communism.* Durham, NC: Duke University Press, 2011.

Ghodsee, Kristen. *Muslim Lives in Eastern Europe: Gender, Ethnicity and the Transformation of Islam in Postsocialist Bulgaria.* Princeton, NJ: Princeton University Press, 2009.

Ghodsee, Kristen. "Pressuring the Politburo: The Committee of the Bulgarian Women's Movement and State Socialist Feminism." *Slavic Review* 73, no. 3 (fall 2014): 538–562.

Ghodsee, Kristen. *The Red Riviera: Gender, Tourism and Postsocialism on the Black Sea.* Durham, NC: Duke University Press, 2005.

Giatzidis, Emile. *An Introduction to Postcommunist Bulgaria: Political, Economic and Social Transformation.* Manchester: Manchester University Press, 2002.

Goldman, Wendy Z. *Women, the State and Revolution: Soviet Family Policy and Social Life, 1917–1936.* Cambridge: Cambridge University Press, 1993.

Gorbachev, Mikhail. *Memoirs.* New York: Doubleday, 1996.

Gorbachev, Mikhail. *The New Russia.* London: Polity, 2016.

Gorbachev, Mikhail. *On My Country and the World.* New York: Columbia University Press, 2005.

Grosser, Dietmar, Hanno Müller, and Paul-Josef Raue, eds. *Treuhand in Thüringen: Wie Thuringen nach der Wende ausverkauft wurde.* Erfurt: Klartext Verlag, 2013.

Hensel, Jana. *Zonenkinder.* Berlin: Rowohlt, 2004.

Herzog, Dagmar. "Post Coitum Triste Est . . . ? Sexual Politics and Culture in Postunification Germany." *German Politics and Society* 94, no. 28 (spring 2010).

Herzog, Dagmar. *Sex after Fascism: Memory and Morality in Twentieth-Century Germany.* Princeton, NJ: Princeton University Press, 2005.

Herzog, Dagmar. *Sexuality in Europe: A Twentieth-Century History.* Cambridge: Cambridge University Press, 2011.

Hobsbawn, Eric. *The Age of Capital: 1848–1875.* New York: Vintage, 1996.

Hobsbawn, Eric. *The Age of Empire: 1875–1914.* New York: Vintage, 1989.

Hobsbawn, Eric. *The Age of Extremes: 1914–1991.* New York: Vintage, 1996.

Hobsbawn, Eric. *The Age of Revolution: 1789–1848.* New York: Vintage, 1996.

Jarausch, Konrad H., and Eve Duffy. *Dictatorship as Experience: Towards a Sociocultural History of the GDR.* New York: Berghahn, 1999.

Ježek, Tomáš. "The Czechoslovak Experience with Privatization." *Journal of International Affairs* 50, no. 2 (winter 1997): 477–489.

Koenen, Gerd. *Was war der Kommunismus?* Freiberg: Vandenhoeck & Ruprecht, 2010.

Kościańska, Agnieszka. "Beyond Viagra: Sex Therapy in Poland." *Czech Sociological Review* 20, no. 6 (2014): 919–938.

Kundera, Milan. *The Unbearable Lightness of Being.* New York: Harper Perennial Modern Classics, 2005.

Laschitza, Annelies. *Die Liebknechts: Karl und Sophie—Politik und Familie.* Berlin: Aufbau Taschenbuch, 2009.

Lippmann, Eberhard. AEG—Olympia—Optima: Büromaschinen aus Erfurt 1924–2004. Erfurt: Sutton Verlag, 2010.

Lišková, Kateřina. "Sex under Socialism: From Emancipation of Women to Normalized Families in Czechoslovakia." *Sexualities* 19, nos. 1/2 (2016): 211–235.

Littleton, Taylor, and Maltby Sykes. *Advancing American Art: Painting, Politics, and Cultural Confrontation at Mid-century.* Tuscaloosa: University of Alabama Press, 2005.

Maier, Charles S. *Dissolution: The Crisis of Communism and the End of the GDR.* Princeton, NJ: Princeton University Press, 1999.

McLellan, Josie. *Love in the Time of Communism: Intimacy and Sexuality in the GDR.* Cambridge: Cambridge University Press, 2011.

Merkel, Wolfgang. "Is Capitalism Compatible with Democracy?" *Zeitschrift für Vergleichende Politikwissenschaft* 8, no. 2 (October 2014): 109–128.

Neary, Rebecca Balmas. "Mothering Socialist Society: The Wife-Activists' Movement and the Soviet Culture of Daily Life, 1934–1941." *Russian Review* 58, no. 3 (July 1999): 396–412.

Oates-Indruchova, Libora, and Hana Havelková, eds. *The Politics of Gender Culture under State Socialism: An Expropriated Voice*. London: Routledge, 2014.

Peacock, Mark S. "The Desire to Understand and the Politics of Wissenschaft: An Analysis of the Historikerstreit." *History of the Human Sciences* 14, no. 4 (2001): 87–110.

Pence, Katherine, and Paul Betts. *Socialist Modern: East German Everyday Culture and Politics*. Ann Arbor: University of Michigan Press, 2008.

Piketty, Thomas. *Capital in the Twenty-First Century*. Cambridge, MA: Harvard University Press, 2014.

Pipes, Richard. *Communism: A History*. London: Modern Library, 2003.

Pomerantsev, Peter. *Nothing Is True and Everything Is Possible: The Surreal Heart of the New Russia*. New York: Public Affairs, 2014.

Port, Andrew I. "Love, Lust, and Lies under Communism: Family Values and Adulterous Liaisons in Early East Germany." *Central European History* 44, no. 3 (2011): 478–505.

Pribic, Rado. *The Trouble with German Unification: Essay on Daniela Dahn*. Berlin: NORA, 2008.

Priestland, David. *Red Flag: A History of Communism*. New York: Grove, 2009.

Pritchard, Gareth, *The Making of the GDR 1945–53: From Antifascism to Stalinism*. Manchester: Manchester University Press, 2000.

Raza, Maple. *Bastards of Utopia: Living Radical Politics after Socialism*. Bloomington: Indiana University Press, 2015.

Sarotte, Mary Elise. *1989: The Struggle to Create Post-Cold War Europe*, 2nd ed. Princeton, NJ: Princeton University Press, 2014.

Sarotte, Mary Elise. *Collapse: The Accidental Opening of the Berlin Wall*. New York: Basic Books, 2014.

Schönpflug, Daniel. "Histoires croisées: François Furet, Ernst Nolte and a Comparative History of Totalitarian Movements." *European History Quarterly* 37, no. 2 (2007): 265–290.

Scott, David. "Norms of Self-Determination: Thinking Sovereignty Through." *Middle East Law and Government* 4 (2012): 195–224.

Service, Robert. *Comrades! A History of World Communism*. Cambridge, MA: Harvard University Press, 2010.

Sewell, Sara Ann. "Mourning Comrades: Communist Funerary Rituals in Cologne during the Weimar Republic." *German Studies Review* 32, no. 3 (2009): 527–548.

Spilker, Dirk. *The East German Leadership and the Division of Germany: Patriotism and Propaganda, 1945–1953*. Oxford: Oxford University Press, 2006.

Stack, Heather M. "The 'Colonization' of East Germany? A Comparative Analysis of German Privatization." *Duke Law Journal* 46, no. 5 (March 1997): 1211–1253.

Steiner, André. *The Plans That Failed: An Economic History of East Germany, 1945–1989*. New York: Berghahn, 2010.

Stites, Richard. *The Women's Liberation Movement in Russia: Feminism, Nihilism, and Bolshevism, 1860–1930*. Princeton, NJ: Princeton University Press, 1978.

Stokes, Raymond G. *Constructing Socialism: Technology and Change in East Germany, 1945–1990*. Baltimore, MD: Johns Hopkins University Press, 2000.

Taubman, William. *Krushchev: The Man and His Era*. New York: Norton, 2004.

Thieme, Teressa, ed. *Freundschaft! Mythos und Realität im Alltag der DDR*. Jena: Stadtmuseum/Städische Museen Jena, 2015.

Todorova, Maria. *Remembering Communism: Genres of Representation*. New York: Social Science Research Council, 2010.

Todorova, Maria, Augusta Dimou, and Stephen Troebst. *Remembering Communism: Private and Public Recollections of Lived Experiences in Southeast Europe*. Budapest: Central European University Press, 2014.

Todorova, Maria, and Zsuzsa Gille. *Post-Communist Nostalgia*. New York and Oxford: Berghahn Books, 2012.

Vaizey, Hester. *Born in the GDR: Life in the Shadow of the Wall*. Oxford: Oxford University Press, 2015.

Verdery, Katherine. *What Was Socialism and What Comes Next?* Princeton, NJ: Princeton University Press, 1996.

Weitz, Eric D. *Creating German Communism, 1890–1990: From Popular Protests to Socialist State*. Princeton, NJ: Princeton University Press, 1997.

Weitz, Eric D. "'Rosa Luxemburg Belongs to Us!' German Communism and the Luxemburg Legacy." *Central European History* 27, no. 1 (1994): 27–64.

Wood, Elizabeth. *The Baba and the Comrade: Gender and Politics in Revolutionary Russia*. Bloomington: Indiana University Press, 1997.

Zatlin, Jonathan R. *The Currency of Socialism: Money and Political Culture in East Germany*. Cambridge: Cambridge University Press, 2008.

Žižek, Slavoj, ed. *The Idea of Communism 2: The New York Conference*. New York: Verso, 2013.

Žižek, Slavoj. *Revolution at the Gates: Selected Writing of Lenin from 1917*. New York: Verso, 2002.

Žižek, Slavoj. *The Year of Dreaming Dangerously*. New York: Verso, 2012.